THE NEW URBAN AGENDA

BILL FREEMAN

THE NEW URBAN AGENDA

The Greater Toronto
and Hamilton Area

Foreword by
Christopher Hume

DUNDURN
TORONTO

Editor: Michael Melgaard
Design: Courtney Horner
Cover Design: Laura Boyle
Printer: Webcom

Library and Archives Canada Cataloguing in Publication

Freeman, Bill, 1938-, author
The new urban agenda : the greater Toronto and Hamilton area / Bill Freeman ; foreword by Christopher Hume.

Includes index.
Issued in print and electronic formats.
ISBN 978-1-4597-3109-7

1. City planning--Political aspects--Ontario--Toronto Region. 2. City planning--Ontario--Toronto Region--Citizen participation. 3. Toronto (Ont.)--Politics and government--21st century--Citizen participation. 4. Hamilton (Ont.)--Politics and government--21st century--Citizen participation. 5. Toronto (Ont.)--Social conditions--21st century. 6. Hamilton (Ont.)--Social conditions--21st century. I. Hume, Christopher, 1951-, writer of supplementary textual content II. Title.

HT169.C22T581875 2015   307.1'21609713541   C2015-901262-7
C2015-901263-5

1   2   3   4   5   19   18   17   16   15

We acknowledge the support of the **Canada Council for the Arts** and the **Ontario Arts Council** for our publishing program. We also acknowledge the financial support of the **Government of Canada** through the Canada Book Fund and **Livres Canada Books**, and the **Government of Ontario** through the **Ontario Book Publishing Tax Credit** and the **Ontario Media Development Corporation.**

Printed and bound in Canada.

VISIT US AT
Dundurn.com | @dundurnpress | Facebook.com/dundurnpress | Pinterest.com/Dundurnpress

Dundurn
3 Church Street, Suite 500
Toronto, Ontario, Canada
M5E 1M2

To the people of the Greater Toronto and Hamilton Area
and the hope for progressive change

CONTENTS

FOREWORD

If Bill Freeman's *The New Urban Agenda* tells us anything, it is that Toronto can no longer take its success for granted. For a number of reasons, which Freeman outlines in clear, concise but conversational prose, the future of Canada's largest city and the vast region that surrounds it is threatened. The problem, of course, is us. But, as he points out, we can also be the solution.

Underlying the situation are the growing urban/suburban solitudes that divide the Greater Toronto and Hamilton Area (GTHA). In the aftermath of the so-called Megacity — created in 1998 when Conservative premier Mike Harris forcibly amalgamated towns and cities across Ontario — those divisions took on new significance. Politicians from the city and the suburbs found themselves sitting side by side in newly formed councils. Not surprisingly, these shotgun political marriages only made things worse. The most dramatic example of the new tensions was the four years that followed the election of Rob Ford as mayor of Toronto in 2010.

Though Freeman takes heart from Ford's departure, he is quick to point out how the governance structure throughout the GTHA — and Canada for that matter — leaves our cities creatures of the province, largely impotent and certainly underfunded.

But it is local communities that know what's in their own best interests. "They need help and organizational support," Freeman writes, "but they can do it themselves, and in doing this their connection to their community deepens and becomes more meaningful."

Though transit is close to the top of Freeman's New Urban Agenda, he also insists we need to "empower communities and deepen democratic practices."

At the same time, he doesn't shy away from proposing measures that would surely be met with outrage. "Disincentives to driving will be politically difficult," he asserts, "but it must be done or the enormous investments in transit could be wasted."

This book is exactly the sort of commonsensical discussion the GTHA so badly needs. Stripped of jargon and political non-speak, Freeman's observations and arguments remind us that before we can solve our problems, we must be able to talk about them. *The New Urban Agenda* is a valuable next step in that direction.

Christopher Hume
Toronto, 2015

THE TORONTO-CENTRED REGION

Much of Toronto heaved a sigh of relief with the election of John Tory as mayor in November of 2014. Former mayor Rob Ford had brought division and intimidation to city council, along with ideas more appropriate for the 1950s and an out-of-control lifestyle. But politics are more than politicians getting along happily together.

Can John Tory be a progressive force? Will he champion innovative programs that create a sustainable, affordable city? That is what we need, but I'm not optimistic Tory will be the man to do it. He is a lawyer and a businessman who believes the market will sort things out. His SmartTrack plan ignores the pressing transit problems of the suburbs. His first policy announcements as mayor emphasized making the city more navigable for cars. In the election he rarely spoke about cycling, creating a safe city for pedestrians, the growing problem of poverty, or new initiatives in planning.

And what about the other politicians in this sprawling city of ours? During the 2014 election there was a lot of talk about traffic gridlock, but nothing about how cars are a major contributor to climate change. There were dozens — possibly hundreds — of politicians making promises that taxes would not be raised, but little discussion of how we can create an affordable city where the quality of life in our neighbourhoods is the prime objective.

We have to think differently about our city and its problems. We have to begin by recognizing that a new city has emerged that is quite different from the old. Without most of us recognizing it, the Greater Toronto and Hamilton Area (GTHA) has emerged as the fourth largest urban centre in

North America. With a population of 7.3 million people, only New York (18.9 million), Los Angeles (17.8 million), and Chicago (9.8 million) are larger.

Toronto is the financial capital of Canada. All five of the country's largest banks have their head offices along Bay Street. The Toronto Stock Exchange (TSE) is the third largest in North America and seventh largest in the world. The tall, glittering towers in the city's financial core are symbols of the wealth and power of the city. Toronto is Canada's centre of media, publishing, telecommunications, medical research, education, and software development, as well as a leader in a host of other industries.

Outside Toronto, cities like Mississauga, Hamilton, Vaughan, Markham, and Pickering bring other assets and make major contributions to the wealth of the region. But size and the economic prosperity of a few does not mean that the whole city is prosperous. In fact, we are facing an array of urban problems.

Ontario at one time was the economic leader of the country, and Toronto and the GTHA the economic leader of Ontario, but this changed over the last decade. Today unemployment in Toronto remains above the rest of the GTHA, and is higher than the Canadian average — much higher than western Canada. The incomes of people in Toronto, on average, are lower. Our standard of living has been slipping for three decades according to the Conference Board of Canada.[1] This may change again with the drop in the price of oil and the fall of the Canadian dollar. Perhaps Ontario's manufacturing sector, with its high wages, will make a dramatic comeback, but that remains to be seen.

Economics is only one of the problems we are facing. The environmental crisis is mounting. The most recent warning comes from the Intergovernmental Panel on Climate Change.[2] These leading scientists from around the world have concluded that climate change will lead to the rise of ocean levels that will threaten coastal cities and it will reduce our freshwater supplies and bring destructive weather.

It is estimated that cities are responsible for 70 to 75 percent of all greenhouse gas emissions; the GTHA contributes its share. Suburbanization has created a sprawling city along the northwest shore of Lake Ontario, and suburbs mean car dependency that results in the burning of fossil fuel and greenhouse gas production. The heating of our buildings is another cause of greenhouse gases. Energy costs, the reduction of farmland, less food production — all of these things are turning the GTHA into an unsustainable, unaffordable city with slowing economic growth. We have to start doing things differently or suffer the consequences. The province, to its credit, has created and funded a program to improve transit for the GTHA. The hope is that it will relieve the traffic gridlock problem, and so reduce our environmental impact, but municipal leaders are reluctant to introduce measures to slow or restrict traffic or encourage people to commute by bicycle.

We do little about our energy inefficient buildings. A recent study found that Canada was dead last in a ranking of twenty-seven developed countries on environmental protection. Our federal government continues to say that we will meet our 2020 target for reducing greenhouse gas emissions, but is well behind schedule and has no plan to make up the shortfall. As *NOW* magazine quipped, the feds have their heads in the oil sands.

Another set of predictions from a different group of social scientists show the income inequality in Canada and much of the rest of the world is getting worse. Here in the GTHA this has contributed to an affordable housing crisis and increased poverty for the most vulnerable: children, immigrants, and single-parent families.

So what is going so wrong? Politics is one problem, but not the only one. We have shown a great reluctance to change our way of life and adapt to the new reality. We lack boldness. We stubbornly refuse to look at what is wrong with our cities, how we can build a more efficient, productive economy, and a more affordable lifestyle.

THE SEARCH FOR COMMUNITY

Change is difficult, and lifestyle change is the most difficult of all. I know, because I have lived through it myself. I was trained as a sociologist and spent the early part of my career teaching in universities and community colleges in Hamilton and Montreal. Thirty years ago family circumstances led me to move to Toronto. Up until then I had lived a pretty conventional life, with a house, car, and all the rest. I was excited about the move, but the difference in house prices between the two cities panicked me. How could I afford to live in Toronto? Then, as luck would have it, I managed to buy an inexpensive house on Toronto Island. That house not only saved my skin financially, but it allowed me, in time, to become a full-time writer. More important, it radically changed my lifestyle, drew me into Toronto politics, and helped me understand cities in a different way.

What I have learned from living on Toronto Island is the importance of community. Toronto has some wonderful communities, of course. Riverdale, Bloor West Village, the Annex, Cabbagetown, and many more. Virtually all of them require residents to be high-income earners, but Toronto Island has always been unique. When I moved there, the Island was under threat of destruction by Metro Toronto, and that led to a middle- and even low-income community made up of people willing to endure the threat of eviction the situation demanded. Only after a protracted struggle was the community saved. It was one of the longest fights for community survival in the country, and I am proud to say I played a role in that struggle.

But it is not only shared politics that makes the Island different. The community is like a small town of seven hundred people, a short fifteen-minute ferry ride from the downtown heart of the city. There are no private cars allowed on the Island and so the narrow streets are safe. Children run free from an early age. Neighbours know each other because they participate in community events. There are no stores, so if you need something you borrow it from a neighbour and replace it the next time you shop in town. There are two community halls built and maintained by volunteer labour, and recently a small home for seniors was built with the same community spirit.

Because the Island was under threat for so many years, and because of the close nature of the community, city politics are a vital concern for everyone. It became a passion of mine, and it remains so. For a time in the early 1990s I was a policy advisor on municipal issues for the Bob Rae provincial government. That expanded my experience of the city, and the GTA, but for me it was Toronto's municipal politics that fascinated me. It is far more interesting than the dull and predictable debates along party lines in Ottawa or Queen's Park. Real problems are discussed at city hall and the final outcomes of contentious issues are never certain until the votes are counted.

Living on Toronto Island, I also became involved in the fight against the expansion of the Island Airport (now called the Billy Bishop Toronto City Airport). This issue drew me into the politics of the city in a different way, illustrating the power of business elites in Toronto. Community groups, such as the one involved in fighting the airport, have a very difficult time going head-to-head with entrenched, vested interests.

I tell these stories about myself and the Island not because I think people might be interested in my history, but because it informs the point of view of this book. I believe that if we are going to build a sustainable city, our approach must be rooted in communities. That is the lesson I have learned from living on Toronto Island. Fundamental change has to come from below, not from government, though governments still must play a role in bringing change.

To mobilize people for change, and bring our politicians to the table, we must first understand how the changes we propose will benefit or harm us. Coalitions have to be built and resources put together. Individuals acting alone become frustrated in politics because they soon learn the lone voice has little impact, but a mobilized community, with a clear set of objectives, is a political force that is hard to deny.

But though communities are important, our municipalities and the provincial government are vital if there is to be change. Governments hold the levers of power, and in a vast urban area like the GTHA, they can be an agent of change like no other.

THE NEED FOR A NEW URBAN AGENDA

I am not the only one to feel the need for change in our cities is urgent. Jane Jacobs, the great urban thinker, moved to Toronto in 1968 and lived here until her death in 2006. She influenced a whole generation of planners and those interested in cities with her ideas of how people relate to their cities. She emphasized the human scale — the shops, streets, and public domain. She wanted to put people, rather than buildings and cars, at the centre of our concern about cities.[3]

Today the leader of this type of humanitarian planning is Jan Gehl, a Danish planner and architect who is credited with leading the transformation of Copenhagen and many other cities. He takes a sensible approach by emphasizing that the urban environment can only change by making gradual, incremental improvements; it took forty years to transform Copenhagen, he points out. His aim is to create lively, healthy, livable, safe, sustainable cities.

Gehl focuses on the public realm — the space between the buildings, he calls it. He is best known for encouraging cycling, but he also promotes walking. The way we should see a city is at a walking speed, he argues, not the speed of a car. In a recent talk I attended in Toronto, he said, "Children are a sign of a healthy city." The title of his recent book is *Cities for People*, and that sums up his approach.[4]

As I researched for this book, and walked or rode my bike through the city's streets, I tried to think about what would really improve this giant metropolis of ours. I came to feel that not only should we build a city for people, we must also build a city that is economically viable, where the great disparities of income and opportunity are moderated. I felt frustrated because I came to see that we suffer from a lack of ingenuity; an inability to think outside the box.

A new set of green technologies has been developed that can help to make the city more economically viable, while at the same time increasing the quality of life. Our city, however, is ignoring the technologies because we don't know how to pay for them or how to organize their implementation. Our political leadership is failing us, but, as well, citizens don't know how to mobilize to bring the changes we need. We need to create a practical program for change, and develop the political support for that program by showing how all of us will benefit if it is implemented.

I became convinced that what we need is a New Urban Agenda that deals with fundamental issues like transportation, affordable housing, planning, and pollution; an agenda that will lead to an improvement in the quality of life in our neighbourhoods and downtowns and make our cities more efficient, economically viable, and affordable. Above all cities must be for people — everyone, regardless of their income, backgrounds, or beliefs.

So this book begins with a diagnosis of what is wrong with our city, and by projection what is wrong with all North American cities. It goes on to describe, in concrete ways, what we can do to create a more sustainable, economically prosperous place to live where the quality of life of our neighbourhoods is a priority.

It is an enormous task to transform something as huge and complicated as a city — it takes the arrogance of the naive, some might say — but if we don't begin talking about the problems of Toronto and the GTHA, and sketch out a plan to meet those problems, they will only multiply.

ONE

THE NEW CITY

Before we can begin to appreciate the problems we face in the GTHA and consider the possible solutions, we have to have an understanding of the forces that have shaped and continue to shape our city. If the source of the problems can be summed up in one word, it would be "growth."

The population of the region has been growing dramatically since the area was first settled in the late eighteenth and early nineteenth centuries. Today the GTHA is increasing by about one hundred thousand people every year. Virtually all of that growth comes from immigration — there are people who move here from other parts of Canada, but that is about balanced by those who move out of the GTHA to other parts of the country.

Growth, as any economist will tell you, is very important in the creation of an expanding economy, but growth brings with it a wide variety of problems.

THE EARLY PROBLEMS OF GROWTH

Before the Second World War, municipalities in the GTHA were separate towns and cities, each with its own local economy. Hamilton was an industrial city and steel was its most important industry. Oshawa had been an auto industry town since 1907. Brampton had some local industry, and there were scattered towns like Milton, Newmarket, and Uxbridge that served the local rural population. But Toronto was different. It was the largest city, and its workforce covered a broad range of occupations, with many working in government and finance, as well as manufacturing. With all the varied opportunities, the population of the city grew rapidly.

As early as the late nineteenth century there was not enough land within the City of Toronto to house all of the newcomers, and many found accommodation or built new houses in small towns like Yorkville, Brockton, and Riverdale, or on the farmland surrounding Toronto. The new residents needed services like water, schools, streets, sewers, and other basic infrastructure. The small towns had a limited tax base and could not afford to provide these services. Many residents of the outlying areas asked to amalgamate with the City of Toronto, which had a larger tax base and could afford to put in the services. By 1912 Toronto had absorbed thirty surrounding municipalities in this way, but the city was finding it difficult to pay for all of the additional services, and resistance to amalgamation by Toronto ratepayers increased. As government services grew, so did the costs, and that meant higher taxes.

The Great Depression brought some relief to the problem of growth. In 1933, 30 percent of Toronto's population was jobless and a quarter of Torontonians were on relief. There was virtually no immigration, population growth, or building of new houses.

The Second World War brought with it unprecedented boom times. Toronto's manufacturers could not get enough workers. People came from across the country eager to work, only to find that there was nowhere to live because there was a moratorium on building. All resources had to be devoted to the war effort. Cottages on the Island were winterized, workers slept on chesterfields and in damp basements, but with no building of residential housing the problems only got worse.

Before the Second World War, Toronto was an Anglo-Saxon city. As late as the 1931 census the population of the city claimed 81 percent British ancestry. The largest non-Anglo-Saxon groups were Jews, at 7 percent; Italians, 2 percent; and those from Poland, 3 percent. After the war Canada accepted hundreds of thousands of people, mainly from Central and Eastern Europe, who were displaced by the conflict. Many settled in Toronto and other cities in the GTHA. By the early 1950s immigrants from Italy, Portugal, and other southern European countries arrived in the thousands. Pent up demand from the years of depression and war, along with immigration, led to an unprecedented housing boom. The problems surrounding population growth would only get worse.

THE AGE OF THE SUBURBS: 1950—2000

The generation that came of age in the 1930s and 1940s had struggled through the Depression and then fought in the worst conflict of the modern era. It took time for them to get back on their feet after the war ended in 1945, but by 1950 they were ready for change, major changes, and our cities would never be the same again.

Urban sprawl in the GTHA was part of a broader movement of people who were moving from the downtowns of cities across North America into the semi-rural areas that surrounded them. The rise in wages due to the economic boom, unionization, and the scarcity of labour, combined with the amended financial regulations that allowed the entire value of houses to be used as an asset, gave financial institutions security and made mortgages on houses one of the most profitable and risk-free investments. By 1950 virtually anyone with a reasonably secure job and good wages could get a mortgage to buy a house.

The other important change that encouraged suburbanization was the proliferation of automobiles. Until the 1920s, cars were expensive luxury products that only the rich could afford. Henry Ford understood that more cars could be sold, and a lot more money could be made, if the cost of cars was reduced, and he and his company introduced mass production methods to make that happen. Other companies soon followed that lead. By the 1950s practically anyone who had a job could own a car.

The car gave the mobility that was necessary if people were to live in low-density suburbs. Cars meant that drivers could commute from home to work and back again without relying on public transit. It was convenient. The car could sit in the driveway steps away from the front door of the house and be parked free, in most cases, close to the work place. Above all, commuting by car was fast, not like the slow-moving buses that lumbered along, stopping at every corner to pick up or discharge passengers.

Cars provided increased mobility that people welcomed, but there were also many negatives. Cars are dangerous. Traffic accidents produced increased injuries and deaths, not only for the people in the cars but also those on the streets. The public realm of cities was degraded as streets became places dominated by automobile traffic rather than those on foot. Air pollution became much more serious as cars proliferated, and today we recognize that cars are a major contribution to climate change.

As time went on, cars became more expensive to buy and maintain, and the price of gas increased. Added to this was the increased public expense of building roads to the housing developments that sprawled across the countryside. Highways had to be built. Services to the low-density communities had to be delivered by governments. All of this added to the costs and again taxes had to be increased to cover these costs.

Cars were important but the house was the real pride and joy of the suburban family. For the growing middle class, houses were substantial, detached structures with three or four bedrooms, built on large suburban lots. Birth rates were high in that baby boom era, and an ideal suburban home would have a large backyard for the kids and be within walking distance to a new school. Houses needed lots of land, and that meant low-density suburban communities, in contrast to the higher densities of the older city.

The move to the suburbs was an attempt to find open spaces, fresh air, and new schools with good recreation for the kids, but it was also a cultural shift that changed the lifestyle of people. In the United States, suburbanization is linked to white flight to get away from the blacks who were moving into the inner-city neighbourhoods. Neil Smith, an American expert on cities, writes that the inner cities in the U.S. were seen as "an urban wilderness … [with] the habit of disease and disorder, crime and corruption, drugs and danger."[1] People fled to the suburbs to get away from the problems of urban decay.

In Canada, the city was not seen in such stark terms. The problems of racism were not as apparent in this country, but many wanted to get away from congestion of the inner city. Suburbs sprang up almost everywhere that there was vacant land close to the city. The automobile industry and home construction became the heart of the North American economy.

Don Mills, a community of single-family houses on suburban-sized lots built in the 1950s, is considered the first suburb of Toronto. Soon after it was built there was suburban growth in Scarborough, North York, and Etobicoke. Suburban sprawl leapt over municipal boundaries into Peel, York, and Durham. Satellite cities like Mississauga, Brampton, Oakville, Vaughan, Markham, and Pickering grew rapidly. Sprawl on a massive scale had arrived.

John Sewell, the former Toronto mayor (1978–80), points out in his book *The Shape of the Suburbs*[2] that after the Second World War, the Ontario government subsidized the building of suburbs with highway construction and financing for infrastructure projects like sewers and water. The federal government provided funds through its agency Canada Mortgage and Housing Corporation (CMHC).

The most important way that the province contributed to urban sprawl was in highway construction to service the ever growing number of vehicles on the road. The expressway movement took hold in Ontario; the Queen Elizabeth Way (QEW) had been built as a showcase in the 1930s, and in the 1950s the 400-series of expressways began to be constructed.

The expressways were important to commuters, but they also led to a reorganization of industry. Until the 1950s most factories were located along rail lines in the centre of cities like Toronto and Hamilton. Companies would receive raw materials and ship finished goods using the railways, and the factories or warehouses remained in the downtown of cities because they needed to be close to where their workers lived.

With the coming of suburbanization and expressways, many companies found it more convenient, faster, and more reliable to ship goods by transport truck rather than rail. The almost universal ownership of cars meant that workers could commute from their homes to the new factories and offices. As a result, much of the manufacturing of Toronto and other cities left the downtown and relocated along the expressways. That reorganization did not happen overnight, but today there are very few large industrial concerns in Toronto. New factories, like automobile plants, are being built even further away from the downtown of cities and are all located along expressways.

Hamilton, the other major industrial centre in the GTHA, went through a different type of development. The huge steel companies located on the harbour and reliant on shipping could not be relocated so easily. They remain there to this day and many of the steel fabricating companies that use Hamilton steel have remained close by as well.

Still, suburbanization affected Hamilton. Towns like Stoney Creek, Dundas, Ancaster, and even Burlington experienced growth, but it was Hamilton Mountain, south of the city, that grew into a huge suburb after 1950. There had long been a small settlement on the Mountain, which was served by two incline railways that came up the very steep climb of the Escarpment. The inclines were closed in the 1930s. By then the new vehicles could travel new access roads like the Jolley Cut with ease, and so the Mountain suburbs, just like those in the rest of the GTHA, quickly expanded.

Table 1 illustrates the rapid suburbanization of Toronto. The column "Rest of GTA" includes the regions of Peel, York, Durham, and Halton. Hamilton is left out of this calculation because it is only recently that that city has become integrated into the GTHA.

Table 1: Population of Toronto and the rest of the GTA 1951–2011

Year	Toronto	Rest of GTA	GTA as a % of Toronto
1951	1,117,470	261,903	23.4%
1961	1,618,787	487,005	30.19%
1971	2,086,017	836,927	40.1%
1981	2,137,395	1,280,306	59.9%
1991	2,275,771	1,959,985	86.1%
2001	2,481,494	2,600,332	104.7%
2011	2,615,060	3,439,131	131.5%

Toronto's population increased by a little more than 2.5 times in the sixty years between 1951 and 2011, but population of the GTA outside of Toronto increased almost 13 times. Most of that increase has gone to Peel and York Regions.

CHANGES IN LOCAL GOVERNMENT

Up until the early 1950s municipal governments across Ontario remained pretty much as they had been since they were created in the early nineteenth century. Each council had its own geographic area and the local councillors governed the municipality as they saw fit. The provincial government kept an eye on the debt of local municipalities, but by and large they stayed out of local politics and local issues.

As development sped up in the 1950s and the pressures of growth increased, the old way of doing things caused increasing problems. Members of the provincial Conservative government in power after the war felt that the local municipal governments around Toronto were not doing enough to facilitate growth; many councils opposed development and building new infrastructure because it would lead to higher property taxes. The Conservatives were a party of business, and they believed that the growth needed to be managed with business principles. There were discussions and consultations about what to do, and finally, in 1953, the Ontario government imposed a new level of government on the city, called Metropolitan Toronto, which became known as Metro.

What the legislation did was leave the local municipalities of Toronto in place, but created a second tier of municipal government. Power was given to Metro to build infrastructure and manage growth, but planning approvals still remained with the local municipality. The premier, Leslie Frost, appointed Frederick Gardiner to be Metro's first chairman.

Gardiner has been credited with making Metro work. He was a lawyer, a Conservative in his politics, and a progressive by ideology. He had been a municipal councillor for about twenty years before his appointment, and that gave him extensive political connections at all levels of government. Gardiner knew how government worked, but his success came from more than that. As his biographer wrote, he was, "big in size, big in ambition, big in appetites, and big in rhetoric."[3] Soon he came to be called "Big Daddy."

Gardiner was the dominant political force while he was the chairman of Metro. Big Daddy was a politician who wanted to get things done and knew how to make them happen. He could win votes on a Metro Council made up of politicians with no allegiance to political parties, and whose chief loyalty was to their ward. Gardiner believed that government should be run like a business by incorruptible administrators; he had nothing but disdain for those who tried to protect their turf and their friends. He disliked academics, theorists, advisors, and consultants. He was the strong man, the boss. Once, when a senior administrator used the phrase, "I think," Gardiner stopped him in mid-sentence to say, "I'll do the thinking; you just give me the facts."[4]

The chairman was intent on building the infrastructure required by a big city. Hundreds of miles of sewer pipe were laid across Metro while he was in office. He oversaw the approval of expressways, including the one that carries his name. The Yonge Street subway from Union to Eglinton was completed, and before he retired he won approval to build the Bloor–Danforth line.

Over time, however, political opposition to Gardiner and Metro government increased. Two of his favourite projects — the demolition of houses on Toronto Island for the expansion of the Island Park and the Spadina Expressway that was to cut through established neighbourhoods in the centre of the city — met fierce opposition from citizen groups. In time local governments within Metro, particularly the City of Toronto, grew in strength and became the centre of opposition.

A split on Metro Council, between councillors from the downtown and those from the suburbs, eventually formed. Most suburban councillors supported Metro's agenda of roads, sewers, and other infrastructure spending, while those from the downtown tended to support neighbourhoods, services for low-income residents, and attempts to adapt new development to fit into existing communities. This split between the suburbs and the downtown remains the fundamental fault line of Toronto politics, only today it is played out in the council of the amalgamated city, rather than Metro Council.

The move to create Metro by the provincial government was done to facilitate development and growth by providing the necessary infrastructure. The builders, construction companies, and developers had emerged as a powerful political force in the province, allied, at that time, to the Conservative Party. For the province, development meant economic growth that they felt was essential for the prosperity of Ontario. For the developers, it meant profits.

Over time, those with influence in the Ontario government deemed the Metro experiment of two-tiered municipal government a great success. Regional councils were established in the rapidly expanding suburbs outside Toronto. York Region was formed in 1971, Halton in 1973, and Peel and Durham in 1974. Again, the reason was to facilitate growth.

In 1998 the provincial government, led by Mike Harris, changed the governing structure of Toronto yet again by integrating Metro and all of the lower-tier municipalities into the City of Toronto. As we will see, that has created yet another set of problems. The regional governments in York, Halton, Peel, and Durham remain in place. Hamilton and Wentworth Country became an amalgamated city in 2001.

REBIRTH OF THE DOWNTOWN

If the rise of the suburbs after the Second World War created a new type of city, then what is changing our city today is the rebirth of the downtown. Toronto's core is being transformed into a high-density, high-rise residential community and the largest centre of employment in the GTHA.[5]

There are a number of reasons for this growth. New suburbs are expensive to build because municipalities are insisting the necessary infrastructure, like roads, water, sewers, and storm sewers, be installed by developers, rather than the government. That is increasing the costs of the houses so that they are now out of reach of many people, even those with middle-class jobs. Property taxes in all of the suburbs are going up because it is expensive for municipalities to service low-density communities. But housing costs are only part of the problem.

Traffic congestion has become extremely bad and public transit totally inadequate for life in the suburbs. The rising costs of transportation are making long commutes unaffordable, and many young people have lost the sense of romance of owning a car. They simply do not want the lifestyle of their parents that locks them into their cars for long periods every day.

Demographic changes have led to smaller families and an increasing number of singles. Many don't find the suburbs, with its emphasis on children, an attractive place to live. Young people are staying in school longer and finding it more difficult to get established in jobs that give them the income to buy a home. The condo, on the other hand, provides ownership and a chance to build assets. At the same time, they are designed for singles or couples. They provide safety and security, and proximity to jobs and communities of people much like themselves.

Today, condo living in the GTHA is spreading well beyond the downtown core of Toronto. Towers are springing up all over the region, but they are all being built close to densely populated urban complexes like Mel Lastman Square, the Mississauga City Centre, or Vaughan Civic Centre. These condos are providing the density that supports shops, restaurants, bars, entertainment, and good public transit. That commercial activity is creating a new type of urban mix.

Unlike many North American cities, Toronto's downtown business district did not decline after the Second World War. The primary reason is that, like Manhattan, Toronto has thousands of people who come into the downtown core every day to work in the financial industry, corporate head offices, government buildings, universities, and any number of profit or non-profit organizations. They support the retail outlets, restaurants, theatres, and other establishments that give life to the city.

By contrast, Hamilton does not have that critical number of people working downtown, so the central core of the city has suffered decline and stagnation as a result. In the late 1960s John Munro, a powerful federal cabinet minister from Hamilton, and Mayor Vic Copps used the Urban Renewal Program funded by the federal and provincial governments to knock down forty-four acres in the heart of the business district in order to build cultural facilities and a shopping mall. It was a disaster. Much of the land sat vacant for years and when the city finally did find a developer to build the mall it turned out to be a dreary, inward looking complex with retail outlets that had difficulty staying in business.[6]

Toronto's downtown core began to change in the 1960s without government help. In the early 1960s the Toronto-Dominion Centre was opened. In time, all five of the major banks built new corporate headquarters along Bay Street. In the process, the PATH, a series of interconnected underground walkways, retail complexes, and food courts, was constructed. The Eaton Centre opened in 1977 and still receives a million visitors a week. In time, much of the rest of the downtown was refurbished and new buildings were added, a process that is continuing. Visitors, particularly Americans who were seeing the centres of their cities fall into decay, were astounded at the vitality of Toronto's downtown.

Gentrification of old neighbourhoods in Toronto close to the downtown also contributed to the revitalization. There were always well-maintained neighbourhoods like Rosedale and Forest Hill where the wealthy lived. Then, beginning in the 1960s, houses in the inner-city neighbourhoods were bought and refurbished by people who preferred to live in the downtown. These tended to be middle- or upper-income families who, over time, displaced the poor who had long clustered in inexpensive housing near the inner core of the city.

An architect cousin of mine and his wife bought a house just off Yonge Street north of Bloor in 1964. Our parent's generation disapproved, they thought the only place to bring up children was in the suburbs. But soon my sister and her family moved downtown and another cousin followed. All three families had young children. They were not atypical. They wanted to live in the city close to work and the rich cultural life that was available to the family. They were the new urbanites who, rather than rejecting the city, welcomed the diversity and riches of city life.

A young John Sewell, the future mayor of Toronto, earned his political stripes by working with others to stop the urban renewal wrecking ball from destroying Trefann Court, a part of Cabbagetown, in the late 1960s. In time, this neighbourhood developed into one of the trendiest parts of Toronto. Other neighbourhoods followed: Riverdale, the Beaches, the Danforth, High Park, the Annex, North Toronto, Bloor West Village — the pace of gentrification was remarkable and it continues to this day.

The gentrification of the downtown as well as the strength of the financial and the retail districts contributed to the boom in condo development in the central core after 2000. New high-rise residential buildings had gone up prior to this, but early in the new millennium construction in the downtown began in earnest. First it was individual buildings on vacant properties and parking lots. Then some very stylish and pricy buildings went up on the waterfront, west of Spadina. The lands around the Rogers Centre and the Railway Lands were under redevelopment. Suddenly it seemed high-rise condominiums were being built everywhere in the downtown and the units were being sold in record numbers.

These are some figures from a recent City of Toronto study that capture the scale of this growth.[7] The core of the city — defined as lying between Bathurst Street in the west, Dupont and Rosedale Valley Roads in the north, the Don Valley Parkway in the east, and Lake Ontario in the south — has grown from a population of 102,289 in 1976 to 188,485 in 2012, a 95 percent increase. Today the population is estimated to be well over 200,000. This area produces 51 percent of the GDP of Toronto, 33 percent of the jobs, has 25 percent of the city's tax base, but covers only 3 percent of the land area.

It is young people, the so called "millennials," that make up the largest group that live in the core, but the population of all age groups has been growing. (The exception is children from 0 to 19.) From 2003 to 2013 there were 11,686 new floors of residential units that came onto the market. The study found that 65 percent of the units in the core were rental accommodation and only 35 percent owner occupied. Many of the condo units have been bought by speculators and are rented. Most of the people living in the core are highly educated, and are singles or childless couples. Many do not own cars. Forty-one percent either walk or cycle to work and most of the rest take transit.

A recent study by the TD Bank described "an explosion in density in the heart of Toronto." The population of the downtown core more than tripled in the five years between 2006 and 2011[8] and the growth continues unabated. Another report found that Toronto had 132 high-rises under construction. This was more than any other city in North America.[9] Some predicted that condo sales would peak in 2012 and there would be a slump, but sales have continued to be strong.[10]

Statistics on housing sales show the dramatic shift. In 2001, 75 percent of the new homes sold in the GTA were low-rise and 25 percent high-rise. Ten years later, in 2011, 65 percent were high-rise and 35 percent low-rise.[11] This is bringing more people downtown, where condo development is strongest, but high-rise condominiums are being built all over the GTA. There is no indication that this shift to high-rise living is changing. In the first quarter of 2014, there were 2,496 high-rise condos sold in the GTA and only 1,631 low-rise.[12]

As well as condo development, Toronto's downtown is going through a boom in office buildings. The TD reported that between 2009 and 2012, 4.7 million square feet of office space were built. This, in part, was being driven because companies want to be located in the downtown where their employees live.[13] Corporate leaders know that if they can't recruit young, well-educated employees their company will not have much of a future. Today, Toronto's downtown core is the employment hub of 500,000 people.

I talked to Ken Greenberg, Canada's best known urban critic and city planner, about the return to the Toronto's downtown. Greenberg was trained as an architect, but rather than designing buildings his practice evolved into the design of public spaces in cities. Influenced by Jane Jacobs and other planners like Jan Gehl, he has developed an international reputation. Greenberg has worked in cities all over the world, but particularly in Canada, Holland, and the United States. He is a serious, sober man by nature, but he was moved to eloquence and enthusiasm as he described to me what was happening in the downtown:

> It is a time that is perilous; it is thrilling; it is anxious making; it is all of the above. It is almost as if I look out my window, and I am right in the thick of it, I see a city giving birth to itself in a new form…. It is not an even or orderly or well understood process so it is fraught with strange political upheavals and struggles.
>
> People want to live in the hearts of cities and want to be in walkable places or places that have access to transit. This is playing itself out especially with young people but not only — people like us. [Greenberg and I are about the same age.]
>
> [This] is really happening across North America, in cities large and small. But this is the epicentre. Toronto is experiencing the most powerful version of this. There is no other city to compare. We don't even have a close second. This is quite incredible.

And that is perhaps the most interesting element about this movement. Toronto is ahead of other North American cities in the return to downtown.

We are witnessing a cultural change in the GTHA driven by the desire for a new lifestyle shaped by high-density living that is close to work and cultural amenities.

Suburbanization was the rejection of the city and the acceptance of a middle-class, homogenous lifestyle. By contrast, those coming to live downtown today welcome the urban experience and enjoy the buzz of the city. They hang out in the restaurants and bars, go to theatres, films, dance clubs, sporting events, and any number of other mainstream or offbeat things that are available. There is no end to the variety of events in downtown Toronto.

Toronto and the GTHA is no longer a predominantly white, Anglo-Saxon enclave. Anyone under thirty-five who grew up here has close friends, or at least acquaintances, with people of diverse backgrounds. Alternative lifestyles are accepted. There is still prejudice and discrimination, but for the young living in the downtown, diversity is the norm.

It is these social and cultural changes that are leading to a much different city than we have known before. The entire GTHA is becoming incredibly multicultural and diverse. Without knowing it, or planning for it, we have become the leader of a new type of city, one with endless possibilities of creative expressions. Toronto has become the new urban vanguard of North America.

Again, these are Ken Greenberg's words:

> I'm pretty convinced we're in a transformation which is probably as profound as what happened immediately after the Second World War, when we all got excited about automobiles and in a sense turned our backs on cities.[14]
>
> For better or worse, it's happening. Like it or not, Toronto is becoming a different city. It's now clear that we're transitioning to a city with a vastly different level of intensity."[15]

THE FOUR CITIES OF THE GTHA

The GTHA is changing rapidly, but we still think of our city in terms of its original boundaries: Hamilton, Pickering, Newmarket, Toronto, and so on. These are the old political units that have gone through change, but they were first defined in the early nineteenth century. It makes sense to use these names because it is how the region is governed and administrated, but today growth has created one vast city where it is difficult to see where one municipality stops and another begins.

In the 1980s the provincial government began to talk about the Greater Toronto Area, the GTA, to denote the broader urban complex. They did this because they could see that the entire area needed to be thought of as one city that faced problems that demanded coordinated planning and investments in infrastructure. More recently the province decided Hamilton should be included because they understood the whole complex was one integrated economic region, and so now we call it the GTHA.

Then there are the regions. Once there were six in the GTHA — Toronto, Hamilton, Peel, York, Durham, and Halton — but today Toronto and Hamilton are amalgamated cities with one-tier governments. Confusing? I think so. We need a new way to understand the city that is emerging.

I believe there are four different types of cities within the GTHA and a number of small towns and villages. They are: downtown Toronto, the inner suburbs, the outer suburbs, and Hamilton. Each of these cities has different types of urban forms (that is buildings, streets, and so on) and different types of social characteristics. Each of them has different needs and even different types of politics. There are also a number of small towns and villages in the GTHA that are worth looking at as well.

Let's look at each in turn and ferret out how they are similar and different from each other.

DOWNTOWN TORONTO

Toronto's high-density core of condominiums, office towers, and rental units, along with the pre-Second World War communities that surround it, constitute downtown Toronto. In a general sense, this city follows the boundaries of the old City of Toronto before amalgamation. The high densities and compact natures of these communities, along with the lifestyle of the people who live there, their politics, and social demands, have created communities that are much different than any other part of the GTHA.

It is expensive to live in the downtown and people tend to have higher incomes and are better educated than those in the suburbs. The contrast in lifestyle is also striking. Many in the condos are singles or couples without children, while families and older couples live in the gentrified neighbourhoods.

There are a number of problems facing the downtown community. Air pollution is one, the cost of housing is another, and the lack of affordable housing for families is yet another. Rents and condo prices are high not only because of demand, but because speculators have moved into the market and have driven up prices.

But by far the most serious problem is traffic congestion. That is not unusual. People everywhere are complaining about traffic in cities, but while those living in the suburbs complain about gridlock and their long commutes, the downtowners complain about too many cars on the streets that bring pollution and dominate the streets to the point where they make it uncomfortable and unsafe for pedestrians and cyclists. There are also increasing complaints about the congestion on the TTC streetcars, buses, and subway trains.

THE INNER SUBURBS

Some time ago journalists began to make a distinction between the inner and outer suburbs. The inner suburbs are those within the City of Toronto, and the outer suburbs are outside the city, in Peel, York, Durham, and Halton Regions. It is a useful distinction because they are quite different types of cities.

I believe that the one area of the GTHA that we should be most concerned about is the inner suburbs. The downtown is the focus of interest of business and the media. People living there have higher incomes and can afford the housing. Meanwhile, people living in the inner suburban communities languish with low incomes and poor services. These are the forgotten people and communities of Toronto.

There are essentially two types of people living in the inner suburbs. Homeowners live in the small bungalows that were built in the suburban boom after the Second World War. Many of them are the original occupants. A large number worked in manufacturing or other well-paid, blue-collar jobs, but many of the companies have either gone out of business or moved. Many of the homeowners are now older residents on fixed incomes and are finding it very difficult to maintain their homes and lifestyles. There are exceptions to this rule. Some communities in the inner suburbs are high-income neighbourhoods, but incomes, on average, are considerably lower in the inner suburbs than either the downtown or the outer suburbs.

The other group in the inner suburbs are apartment dwellers. They live in high-rise buildings constructed between the 1950s and 1980s. These buildings are a unique feature of Toronto not found in these numbers anywhere else in North America. Originally, they were built for middle class, singles, or small families, but today they house mainly low-income, immigrant families. Some are large extended families with multiple generations.

There are roughly two thousand high-rise towers like this across the GTHA, most of them in the inner suburbs of Toronto. They house about one million people. This represents the largest pool of rental housing in the region. Originally they were built with federal funding from CMHC to avoid the slum conditions in the inner city, but many of the buildings have deteriorated, creating serious problems.

It is in the high-rise towers of the inner suburbs where people with low incomes live, and it is often the housing for new immigrants. I wanted to talk someone who had first-hand information about the inner suburbs, so I met with Glenn De Baeremaeker, the councillor for Scarborough Centre, Ward 38. De Baeremaeker's ward is about evenly divided — 51.5 percent live in high-rise over five storeys and 42.9 percent live in houses. This is what he told me about the nature of the community:

> People bought the houses in the 1950s and 1960s and had lots and lots of babies and children. That's what you did in the suburbs. And the schools were full. Now the kids have moved away, but the parents have stayed there, and many are eighty years old now. In Scarborough, in fact, we are at the stage where some of our schools are being closed and sold off because there aren't enough kids.

It is mainly immigrants who live in the high-rises in his ward:

> We have, in Scarborough, the United Nations living on every street. I look out my window and I say to my partner, "We could be living in India right now." This picture of our street with the kids running down the street and the grandma with the saris on and the kids are going to the baseball diamond to play cricket. It's really diverse and amazing.

The homeowners dominate the electoral politics of these communities, and it is their views that are reflected in their councillors at city hall, not the views of the immigrant tenants who live in the crowded high-rises. There are a number of reasons for this. Homeowners across Canada vote in higher numbers than renters, older people go to the polls more frequently than the young, and immigrants can only vote when they become citizens.

Social problems, as we will see, are multiplying across the inner suburbs and the lack of affordable housing is the source of many of those problems.

THE OUTER SUBURBS

Travelling along the major streets of the outer suburbs is a strange experience for those of us who live in the downtown. Dundas and Hurontario Streets in Mississauga or Highway 7 from Brampton in the west, through Vaughan to Markham in the east — all these streets seem barren of life. No one can be seen walking or riding bikes. The suburban houses face inward towards the others and present their backyards or board fences to the major roads.

The shopping malls, and there are dozens of them, are well back from the roads and out in front are the parking lots. The stores are almost invariably chains found in all of the malls across Ontario, and some in malls across North America. In the case of Walmart, its stores are found around the world. The high-rise office and apartment buildings, like the malls, are well back from the road surrounded by parking lots and grass.

The houses, the heart of these communities, hide from the major roads as if they too are trying to avoid the traffic. They line the crescent-shaped streets, presenting prominent two- and three-car garages to the street. Many are big houses of two thousand square feet or more, that orient life toward the backyards where the kids can play and the adults sit on large decks with their lawn chairs, picnic tables, and barbeques. These are nice homes but most of the adults don't have much time to enjoy them. It takes two good salaries to buy and maintain houses of this size and every adult needs a car.

To say that these suburbs have no sense of community would be wrong. Neighbours socialize and the schools, particularly the elementary schools, give the communities a sense of identity. But because most of the adults are away for long periods during the day and evening there is little time to develop a sense of neighbourhood. Shopping is reserved for the weekends and that means a trip to the mall. Except for the kids, walking is almost unheard of. Outside the malls, there are almost no places, like coffee houses or restaurants, where people can meet and socialize, get to know their neighbours, and discuss the issues of the community. There is a low level of involvement in local politics.

Immigration is having an impact in the outer suburbs, like everywhere else in the GTHA. For example, until the 1980s Brampton was a white, Anglo-Saxon city. Today it is over 50 percent South Asian; 47 percent of the 700,000 residents of Mississauga have a mother tongue that is neither English or French, and Markham has a large population of people of Chinese origin.

Studies show that incomes, on average, are higher in the outer suburbs than in the City of Toronto, but like in the city, there is an increasing polarization of income. Even poverty is increasing. This has particularly affected Mississauga and Brampton. Vaughan and Markham tend to be more affluent. If there is a serious economic downturn many families will face economic eviction.[16] A drop in the price of houses might be good for people who want to buy, but it would be a disaster for owners. Many would lose their homes because they are mortgaged to the hilt and a drop in price would mean a loss of their equity.

These are car-dependent communities where, as the saying goes, "You have to burn a litre of gas to buy a litre of milk." Most activities, whether that means getting to work or taking the kids to soccer games, can only be reached by car. Even today only 6 percent of rush-hour trips in Mississauga are by public transit. No thought has been given to transit until recently because the low-density communities and the near universal ownership of cars makes the demand for transit low and the expense of providing it by the local municipality prohibitive.

That is beginning to change. Architects and planners are hard at work designing high-density developments in the suburbs that will give a new focus to these low-density cities. The great irony is that the same leaders of these suburban municipalities that once promoted low-density suburban sprawl, like the former mayor of Mississauga Hazel McCallion, are now seeking to reinvent their communities with plans of high-density urban development like they once rejected.

The main reason for this is the market is changing and the demand for high-rise condos is increasing, but there is another reason. It has finally sunk in with the politicians and planners that low-density suburban development is unsustainable. These communities are very expensive to service, and that means high taxation, something that people in the outer suburbs oppose as vehemently as the homeowners in the inner suburbs.

Suburban problems are mounting. Young people are rejecting the suburbs; car culture is on the wane; it is expensive for municipalities to service low-density communities; property taxes are climbing; the lifestyle of the suburbs is environmentally unsustainable and contributes to climate change. House prices remain high in the outer suburbs, but these mounting problems raise the threat of a price crash. All of these elements have led to some predicting, "The End of the Suburbs."[17] I don't think we are anywhere close to seeing the end of the suburbs in the region, but the storm clouds are gathering.

HAMILTON: THE INDUSTRIAL CITY

Hamilton is an industrial city and that is both its strength and weakness. "The age of the industrial city is over ... and it will never return." So predicts Edward Glaeser, an American expert on cities.[18] Across the rust belt of the American northeast, industrial cities are languishing, with high levels of unemployment, vacant factories, and a loss of population. But this is not happening in Hamilton. Although the city has shed 33,000 manufacturing jobs in recent years, the economy of the city remains strong. Recently, Hamilton's reported unemployment was 5.9 percent, compared with 8 percent across the province at the same time.

Hamilton still has a strong industrial base. U.S. Steel Canada, the once-giant steel producer, has 4,500 employees, and ArcelorMittal Dofasco, the other steel maker, has about the same. The factories along Burlington Street are prosperous. Steel remains the heart of the city's heavy industry, and there are a number of other companies, such as National Steel Car, that are dependent on the steel producers. There are many other diverse industries, like grain handling companies and soy bean processors. On Hamilton Mountain, Canada Bread has built the largest bakery in the country. Even though the recession lingers on, the city's industrial workforce is well paid.

But the key to Hamilton's continuing prosperity, and why it has not followed the decline of industrial cities in the United States, is the economic transformation that has been going on in the city for some decades now. The largest employer of the city today is Hamilton Health Sciences Corporation, followed by the City of Hamilton. McMaster University is the fifth-largest employer and the number of employees around the university complex totals almost seventeen thousand. Hamilton is in the process of transforming from an industrial city to one based on a mixed economy of education, health sciences, the public sector, and manufacturing.

The other great strength of Hamilton is that housing is much more afford-able than in much of the rest of the region. It would be wrong to say that this has lessened poverty in the city, but middle income people can still afford to buy their own home because the prices are within reach. This has lessened the cost of living in the city.

The other factor that has changed the city is it has become integrated into the broader region. Today more than one-third of Hamilton's workforce commutes outside the city, 82.5 percent of them travelling into the GTA for work. Like those in the suburbs, most travel by car. Only 7 percent of commuters use local transit and 1 percent the GO Transit system.[19] It is the integration of the city into the region that has led the province to include Hamilton in its transit planning.

Like many North American cities, the downtown core of Hamilton has shown signs of deterioration for years, with vacant stores and empty parking lots, but there are signs that even this is changing. The redevelopment of the Royal Connaught Hotel, which sat vacant for decades, promises to revitalize the central core and bring new life into the downtown. People are moving into the city to take advantage of low house prices. Perhaps in time Hamilton will see a rebirth of the downtown like Toronto and other large Canadian cities.

SMALL TOWNS AND VILLAGES

Within the GTHA there are not only cities; many small towns and villages exist in the northern, rural parts of the region, such as Georgina in York Region and the sprawling Township of Brock in Durham Region. The big cities domi-nate the GTHA but the smaller centres are an interesting contrast.

I have a pretty good grasp on what is happening in the larger centres, but I have never lived in a small town, and it would be presumptuous of me to try and describe what is going on. Robert MacDermid, a political science professor at York University, is an expert on Ontario municipal politics. He lives in two worlds. He comes into the university and is involved in issues in Toronto, but he also lives in a small town in the northern reaches of Durham Region. Bob is a careful observer, and I met with him to try and understand what is going on in these small towns. The discussion was fascinating.

The politicians in small centres across Ontario, he explained, are in trouble.[20] They are under pressure to provide services for their constituents and the only way that they can get the income to do that is with increases of the assessment.

> Costs are going up. They don't want to raise taxes. They hate raising taxes. They get elected promising that they won't raise taxes ... and then they say 'Oh my God, how are we going to meet these rising costs?' The only way they can do that is by bringing in more development to broaden the tax base. But that leads to a different set of problems. Developers take advantage of them.
> "More development? We'll help you. Step right this way." Some councillors get gulled into some of the most improbable, most stupid proposals.

He went on to describe a number of other problems that are characteristic of small towns across the GTHA — and across much of Ontario, I suspect: There are very few jobs. Young people don't see a future and many move into the city. Other people stay in the town because of family or low house prices but they commute into the city every day by car.

One special problem, MacDermid told me, was the lack of news coverage. "The major papers don't cover GTA politics. There is one reporter in the *Star* who occasionally writes about [small towns in the] GTA, but that's all. This is hugely important. People don't know what's going on. I think a lot of people do not even understand the division between the local municipalities and the region."

Very few people are interested in politics in the small town, he told me, and this has led to what he calls a "democratic deficit."

> What you have, in Ontario, is the loss of democratic control at the municipal level. In the 1950s the terms for councils were one year. Then it went to two years, then three, and now it is four years. There were also many referendums. They were very frequent at the

municipal level. Most capital expenditures could not go forward without approval by the electorate in a referendum. Much of that is gone.

There were organizations like the Public Utilities Commission where the board was elected by the citizens. Every town had a local hydro distribution system and there was a public board that administered them. Now they have been converted into stand-alone companies with corporate boards and token municipal councillors sitting on those boards.

Citizens do not have democratic control over the local issues that shape their communities and their lives. This was done on purpose to erode citizen control and to erode democracy. There has been a loss of community control, and I am convinced that this has led to the loss of democratic involvement on the part of the citizenry in civic issues. It's tragic.

MacDermid was bringing up a very fundamental question. Is the reason for low participation rates in political affairs because people have lost interest in politics, or have our political structures been redesigned on purpose to cut people out of the political process? And what are the consequences for people who have lost control over their communities?

These are not just problems for small towns. They are problems across the GTHA and Ontario, in big cities as well as small. In fact, the lack of political engagement has become a problem across the developed world.

DIFFERENT COMMUNITIES, DIFFERENT LIFESTYLES, DIFFERENT PROBLEMS

Everywhere you look in the GTHA there are problems, but the problems differ in the different types of communities. It is not possible to have one solution for all. There are some common problems — transportation is one — but the solution is quite different for those living in the inner or outer suburbs than it is for those living downtown.

The way that we are supposed to solve local problems is through our local governments. Each municipal council, supposedly, can create solutions tailored

to the needs of local people, but as the city has grown into a massive conglom-
eration local solutions don't work anymore. People are confused about the
responsibilities of local government, or even what municipality they belong
to, or who picks up their garbage.

Today the council of the City of Toronto is bedeviled by all of these conflicts.
Councillors from the low-density inner suburbs, representing modest homeowners, have a much different set of priorities for the city than the councillors
who represent the people who live in high-density communities of condos in the
downtown. This has turned Toronto City Council into a bizarre political fighting
pit where consensus is always difficult and reasonable solutions are often ignored
because the councillors want to make political points in a polarized council.

But the inability of communities to resolve conflicts and set an agenda that
benefits everyone is only one of the problems that we face. There are serious social
problems that are being ignored. That's what we examine in the next chapter.

TWO

THE SOCIAL AND ECONOMIC COSTS OF INEQUALITY

Toronto is one of the wealthiest cities in the world, and yet economic and social indicators show that many people who live here are in serious trouble, and it is getting worse.

The city is polarizing into the haves and the have-nots, and that has led to a level of inequality not experienced in Canada since the 1920s. If a New Urban Agenda is to be developed, the goals of social equity and a sustainable economy have to be fundamental parts of it. The difficulty is that, short of a radical restructuring of the way income is distributed in this country, it will be hard to solve this fundamental problem. That means tough political choices will have to be made.

What follows is a review of what we know about issues like the impact of changes in the economy, income inequality, poverty, affordable housing, and related issues. It is a disturbing picture.

ECONOMIC TRENDS

Economic and social indicators are not the only, or even best, way to understand what is happening in a city, but they can point out certain long-term trends and give a type of snapshot of the changes that are emerging today, and the problems that we will have to struggle with in the future.

One economic trend that is having a huge impact on our lifestyle and quality of life is the change in work. Jobs in manufacturing have been in decline in Canada for thirty-five years. "In Ontario, manufacturing jobs as a share of total industrial employment has fallen from 23 percent in 1976 to 12 percent in 2011."[1] One estimate is that 500,000 manufacturing jobs have been lost in Ontario since the onset of the 2008–09 recession.[2] The Toronto Region Board of Trade recently estimated that from 2000 to 2010 the region's productivity declined 6 percent. As manufacturing jobs declined, employment in the service sector increased so that today service jobs account for about 40 percent of the workforce — more people work in retail than any other industry.

Economists debate the reasons for the decline in manufacturing, and clearly there are a number of contributing factors, but there are two very important reasons for the decline in Ontario. The rise in the Canadian dollar, in the past, has made goods manufactured in this country uncompetitive in the United States, our chief foreign market. Globalization has also led to much more free-trade and the importation of many products manufactured in low-wage countries. Canadian-made products cannot match these prices.

This trend, in turn, has led to declining wages in Ontario, and that has broad impact on our level of wealth. In the past, both production and clerical jobs in manufacturing companies have been well paid. Typically, the blue-collar jobs in these industries were unionized and came with high wages and good benefits. By contrast, service-sector jobs are low paid, often part-time, and come without other benefits like pensions. As a result, the standard of living for hundreds of thousands of workers across the region and province has been eroded. It has also led to a loss of government revenue because the most lucrative tax in this country is based on income.

This economic restructuring has had a much more important impact on the GTHA than other parts of this country because the region remains the manufacturing heartland of Canada. Ontario is still responsible for over half of Canada's manufacturing output, and well over 50 percent of that is in the GTHA. The decline of manufacturing is the most serious economic issue facing people in the GTHA and Ontario.[3] Some believe the recent drop in the price of oil and fall of the Canadian dollar will improve Ontario's economic outlook because it will make manufacturing more competitive, but only time will tell if this is true.

Ontario, in the past, has been the cash cow of Canada, and Toronto the richest city. No longer is this true. The City of Toronto has been doing considerably worse economically than the municipalities in the outer suburbs or Hamilton. Unemployment in Ontario was 7.9 percent in July of 2013. In the outer suburbs, it was 8.2 percent, in Hamilton 6.0 percent. But in Toronto it was 8.8 percent. The City of Toronto is becoming the hole in the middle of the doughnut surrounded by wealthier suburbs, the province, and much of the rest of the country.

These economic changes have led to the growth of part-time work. In August 2014 it was estimated that 19.3 percent of workers were only working part time. Another study of workers in the GTHA found that nearly half of the jobs had "some degree of instability — from short-term contracts to self-employed, working with temp agencies or without benefits."[4]

Most part-time workers have virtually no job security. The decline in unionization of those employed in the private sector has meant that virtually all part-time workers are without protection or representation. The hours that part-timers work can vary from week to week. This makes it very difficult to plan or put away money for the future. It is especially hard for families with school-aged children or single-parent families.

The incomes of these types of low-wage workers has stagnated or declined while wages for upper management have increased.[5] This is one of the reasons that incomes have been polarizing. But it is not only low-skilled workers that now are doing part-time work. Many university teachers are sessional workers and have no job security. Other professionals and semi-professionals find themselves forced into part-time work. Immigrants often find the only work available is in low-wage, part-time jobs.

The job crisis for young people in Toronto is particularly bad. A recent study by the Canadian Centre for Policy Alternatives found the unemployment rate among people 15 to 24 in Canada was 14.3 percent in 2011. In Ontario it was 16.9 percent, but in Toronto it was 18.1 percent, well over the provincial and national averages.[6] A recent publication of the Toronto Board of Trade puts the regional youth unemployment rate at 17.4 percent. Hamilton, on the other hand, had a youth jobless rate well below average at 13.2 percent.

Within the GTHA there are major differences. People in Toronto now have significantly lower incomes than those who live in the outer suburbs, as this table illustrates.[7]

Table 2: Income in Toronto and the Outer Suburbs

	Toronto	Outer Suburbs
Per-Capita Income (2011)	$40,156	$41,000
Average Household Income (2011)	$100,212	$126,368
Median Hourly Wage	$20.03	$21.12

People living in cities, in the past, have had greater economic advantages and higher incomes than those living in smaller centres, but this may be changing. Certainly upper-income individuals in the GTHA have found great economic opportunities, but for lower-income workers economic prospects have worsened and that trend is continuing.

INCOME INEQUALITY AND NEIGHBOURHOODS

There has long been increasing concern about social inequality, but it was the Occupy Wall Street movement that turned it into a political issue. In the fall of 2011 a group of protesters occupied Zuccotti Park near New York's financial centre. Quickly the movement spread to Europe and Canadian cities such as Montreal, Toronto, and Vancouver. For a month the protests continued, until the police evicted the protesters from the park in New York.

Occupy Wall Street emphasized the increasing social and economic inequality of American societies. "We are the 99 percent," was their most popular and effective slogan. It dramatized that the top 1 percent earners had used their power to monopolize wealth and economic power while income for the rest of the population shrank relative to them. In time the movement faded, but not before inequality became a major political issue with demands for higher taxes for the rich and a fairer form of income distribution.

As it happens, one of the best-known researchers of income inequality is the Canadian J. David Hulchanski. He is a member of the Cities Centre and Faculty of Social Work at the University of Toronto. His research details income inequality, but it also shows how that inequality is changing the neighbourhoods of this city. I knew that if I was to understand the new Toronto, I would have to talk to him.

I met Hulchanski in his office at the School of Social Work and he took the time to review his research and draw the implications of his studies. He is a big, good natured, talkative man and we spent a pleasant afternoon discussing one of the most disturbing social trends reshaping Toronto and the rest of the GTHA.

He pointed out that income inequality has been increasing in this country at least since the 1970s. Since that time the very rich have gained more and more of Canada's income. The top 1 percent took home 11 percent of the income in 2009 compared to 7.4 percent in 1982.

One thing that is interesting about Hulchanski's research is that he relates income to where people live. His research shows that those with high incomes live in the central city along the north-south and east-west subway lines, while the low-income areas of the city today are found in the inner suburbs outside the core of the city. The shrinking middle-income group live in neighbourhoods located between these two groups. This is his summary:

> Poverty has moved from the centre to the edges of the city. In the 1970s most of the city's low-income neighbourhoods were in the inner city. This meant that low-income households had good access to transit and services. Some of these neighbourhoods have gentrified and are now home to affluent households, while low-income households are concentrated in the northeastern and northwestern parts of the city [the inner suburbs] with relatively poor access to transit and services.[8]

An article in the *Globe and Mail* supports this finding. "The majority of the city's richest neighbourhoods are on or very near subway lines. Only 19 of the city's 68 subway stations are within or near low-income neighbourhoods."[9] These high-income neighbourhoods are 82 percent white and 61 percent university educated. The low-income neighbourhoods have a disproportionate number of visible minorities, and they tend to be renters rather than owners and have less education.

The changes in the income distribution in the City of Toronto are most striking. "It is redistribution, but redistribution upwards to a tiny minority at the top," Hulchanski told me. This is shown in the changes in the thirty-five years from 1970 to 2005. The study projected these numbers to see what the income levels would be like in 2025. The data tells the story.

Table 3: Changing Income Groups in Toronto

	Very High and High	Middle-Income	Low and Very Low
1970	15%	66%	19%
2005	19%	29%	53%
2025 (projected)	21%	20%	59%

Our perception is that Canada is a country where the middle class dominates, but Toronto is becoming a city of extremes and most middle-income individuals and families are being forced into the low-income group.

Hulchanski also went on to study the outer suburbs — the "905" area — using the same research methods, and found similar trends, although the middle-income group in these suburbs remains stronger than in the City of Toronto.

Table 4: Changing Income Groups in Toronto's Outer Suburbs

	Very High and High	Middle-Income	Low and Very Low
1970	13%	86%	0%
2005	18%	61%	21%
2025 (projected)	19%	47%	24%

Clearly there has been a shift in income in Toronto and GTA, and unless there is political intervention to correct this trend, it is going to get worse.

It is the price of housing that is the key determinant of where people live. This has always been true, but in smaller towns neighbourhoods are more mixed. In a large city like Toronto, expensive houses result in exclusive neighbourhoods where wealthy people have access to good transit, schools, and other public services. Neighbourhoods where low-income people live suffer from poor transit, poor schools, and inadequate services. Some even lack supermarkets where nutritious food at reasonable prices can be bought.

Hulchanski went on to explain the most important causes of this polarization of income. After the Second World War the economy expanded rapidly. That led to more economic opportunities, low unemployment, and greater social mobility. In recent decades, economic growth has slowed. Social mobility is much less. The efforts to fight the deficit have slowed economic growth even more, and that has hurt those with low incomes. Added to all of this, increased economic competition from globalization and the decline of manufacturing have created a serious crisis for those with low incomes.

All of these changes are having a huge impact on our cities. Mixed neighbourhoods of different ages and varied ethnic and income groups is the ideal, Ken Greenburg told me. The trends in the GTHA, and Toronto in particular, are going in the opposite direction.

IMMIGRATION

One factor that is changing the nature of the region is immigration. At the end of the Second World War the people of Toronto and the rest of the GTHA were overwhelmingly white and Anglo-Saxon. It has been immigration that has changed the face of the city. Today 47 percent of Torontonians describe themselves as visible minorities. Further away from Toronto, that proportion gets lower: Peel, 42.8 percent; York, 37.2 percent; Durham, 35 percent; Halton, 29 percent (estimated); Hamilton, 13 percent (All of these figures are based on the 2006 census). [10]

The majority of new immigrants are in low or very low-income groups. This is not surprising. It takes time and considerable sacrifice to adapt to a new country. Canadians have become remarkable in welcoming of new settlers because we know we will depend on them for our future prosperity. But that does not mean that immigration does not present special problems. Hulchanski gave me a historical perspective:

> When the Italians and Portuguese came to Canada in the 1950s and 1960s there was an active job market in things like construction. They were well paid. But now, with the new wave of immigrants since the 1990s, good jobs have not been available. They end up working in fast food restaurants, cleaning, or driving a taxi. Those with professional qualifications in their home countries have been denied Canadian qualifications in many cases. A lack of Canadian experience is often the reason given for refusal to hire but that is often an excuse.

Women are particularly impacted. In 1980 immigrant women earned 85 cents for each dollar earned by Canadian-born women. By 2005 this had fallen to 56 cents, even though the education of immigrant women has been rising faster than the Canadian born.[11]

Across the GTHA new immigrants are settling into inexpensive housing. In Toronto this often means that they live in high-rise apartment buildings in the inner suburbs, because this is the only rental accommodation available to them that they can afford. This question has to be asked: Are these buildings the new ethnic and racial ghettos in Toronto, not unlike the black ghettos in American cities?

When I talked to Glenn De Baeremaeker, the city councillor for Scarborough, Ward 38, he gave me an optimistic view of the issue:

> I can go to some buildings with 100 percent Pilipino and 100 percent Tamil, not one white person in those buildings. I don't want to call it a ghetto, but it is ethnic concentration. But you see the kids running around and playing on the monkey bars. They are laughing, happy. How many movies will they go to compared to the kid who lives in the Beach? Not as many. They are not going to go to the IMAX theatre. But they are healthy. They are happy. Their parents love them and they are all going to go to university.

But this isn't the full story. New immigrants are getting caught in low-income jobs and living in housing that is not appropriate for their families. However, they remain optimistic. The families are making sacrifices for their children, and education is seen as the vehicle that will lead to greater prosperity. But is it true? Will the shrinking job market lead to a lack of opportunities and increasing frustrations? In the past it has been minorities who have suffered the most when job opportunities disappear.

Toward the end of my conversation with David Hulchanski, we came to discuss the 2005 riots in the suburbs of Paris and other European centres. All of these riots were similar. It was young people from minorities who were involved, and they lived in low-cost housing projects outside the central areas of the city. Their chief grievance was the frustration from lack of opportunity, particularly a lack of jobs that would afford a decent life. These social conditions have an uncanny similarity to the conditions of immigrants in Toronto.

This is not a prediction that riots like this is going to happen in the GTHA, but it is a warning. If we do not do something about jobs for young people, income inequality, and the living conditions of immigrants, the mounting problems could lead to disturbing consequences.

We don't like to think that the problems immigrants face are as a result of discrimination. We tell ourselves that we are a tolerant society — and we are in comparison to others — but discrimination and prejudice does play a role. Young black men and aboriginals pay the highest costs. They are over-represented in criminal convictions and jail populations and under-represented in high-school graduates and post-secondary school enrollments.

Another place to find discrimination is in the professions. Anyone who takes taxis regularly in Toronto has met a driver with a Ph.D. who cannot get work in his field. Not long ago I was given a ride by a driver in his mid-thirties and we got talking. He told me his family was from Afghanistan, and they ended up in India as refugees. There he was trained as a civil engineer. He married, and because of his good education, he qualified as an immigrant.

In Canada he began work as a taxi driver to earn a living while he looked for a job as an engineer. For months he applied for work all over the country without success. "You need Canadian experience," he was told. So he took a retraining course and then worked as an unpaid intern in an engineering company in Barrie, but at the end he still couldn't get work. Now he has given up and drives a taxi. "I have two young children," he told me. "I need to think of their future."

This is not an unusual story. Those with professional qualifications receive priority under our immigration system, but when they arrive they often are discriminated against by the professional associations that examine their qualifications. Even those who qualify, like the Afghan engineer I met, still cannot get work. Is this discrimination? The excuse of a lack of Canadian experience smacks of discrimination to me. Every engineering company expects to invest months, if not years, training a recently graduated engineer before they begin to pay dividends for the company. It is the nature of the work. But my taxi driver was not given the chance.

Our immigration system creates injustices at every turn. We give priority to people with special skills, but then we deny them jobs in their field once they get here. By luring people like this to Canada we are denying the developing country they come from of the trained people that they need. And then it is tremendously disappointing to the immigrant who has to work at low paying, unskilled jobs.

POVERTY

Poverty remains one of the most controversial areas of public policy. Today we cannot even agree on a poverty line that would determine who is poor and who is not poor. Statistics Canada refuses to endorse any measure of poverty because they do not have a mandate from the government.[12] That is bureaucratic code saying that poverty is so sensitive that the politicians have told the agency not to establish a poverty line in order to avoid trouble.

There hasn't always been a political attempt to control our perception of poverty. In 2005 a Statistics Canada study put the rate of poverty at 10.8 percent. A study in Hamilton put the rate of poverty in that city at 18.1 percent, the right-wing Fraser Institute put poverty at 4.9 percent in 2004, and the Toronto Region Board of Trade gives an estimate of 10.7 percent living in poverty.

If groups such as these, with all of the resources that they can command, cannot agree on a useful measure of poverty, then a lone researcher like myself is not going to try, but the problem that results from this political meddling is that we do not have a base measurement of poverty in Canada. That makes it difficult to understand what is happening in a vital area affecting millions of people.

But even if there is no agreement, there are some well-established facts. Those living in poverty include the so-called working poor as well as those on social assistance. Low income is the most important determinant of poverty, but the cost of living is also very important in deciding who is poor and who is not poor, and that can vary from community to community. For example, housing is much more expensive in Toronto than in smaller communities in Ontario, but that is offset by good transit — in Toronto it is not essential to own a car.

Economic conditions can make a big difference in poverty. The recession that began in 2008–09 led to rising unemployment and that, in turn, led to an increase in the level of poverty. On the other hand, government programs can help to reduce poverty. For example, universal, affordable child-care programs, such as the one that exists in Quebec, reduces poverty because it helps members of families to return to work and that raises their income.[13]

The change in family composition in recent years has also affected poverty. The 2011 Canadian census found that 16.3 percent of all families with children were headed by a single parent, mostly women. This often results in the dramatic drop of income of these families and an increased risk of poverty. These factors combine to increase child poverty. In 2012, 29 percent of Toronto children under seventeen were living in poverty.[14]

There is an assumption that poverty is the result of personal attributes — people are lazy or they don't work hard enough — but there is a political component to poverty. Until the 1960s seniors represented the most serious poverty problem in this country. Today, the expansion of Old Age Security, Canada Pension, and income supplement programs has virtually eliminated the poverty of seniors. Somehow we have found ways to politically justify income support for seniors, but not single parents and children. Social policies make a difference.

The operation of food banks is one indication of poverty. In 1981, a little more than thirty years ago, the first food bank was founded in Canada. Today there are over eight hundred in the country. Since the 2008 economic downturn, food bank use has increased 25 percent. The most dramatic growth has been single people. They now make up 43 percent of the total food bank clients. In large cities, 20 percent are immigrants or refugees. There were 946,000 visits to Toronto food banks last year. One in six of the food bank clients are employed.[15]

High-income earners have various ways to shelter their earnings that middle- and lower-income individuals and families do not have. Those in the lowest income brackets in this country do not pay income taxes, but they still pay a range of taxes like HST, property taxes, and various service taxes. In Canada the effective tax rate of the poor is about the same as the wealthy. In fact, our tax system is not very progressive.

All this is quite technical, but there is nothing technical about the impact of poverty. These are some facts:

- Because it is usually women who are the single parent of families, poverty impacts women more than men.

- On average women earn 76 percent of the wages of men in Canada.[16]

- Almost 30 percent of immigrant renter households spend 50 percent of their income on shelter compared to 22 percent of non-immigrants.[17]

- A Hamilton study in 2006 found 18.1 percent of the city's population live in poverty. The rate for children under twelve was 25 percent, and 52 percent of recent immigrants were living in poverty.[18]

- A Peel Region report based on the 2006 census found 15 percent of the population was living in poverty, an increase from 11.5 percent in 2001. Twenty percent of children under five live in poverty.[19] A more recent study found one-third of recent immigrants in Peel are living in poverty. This is a comment by Alan Walks, an associate professor at the University of Toronto, who studied poverty in Peel: "The effects of poverty are often compounded by the fact that ... subdivisions were planned for homeowners with cars.... These places are more isolated."[20]

- A study of poverty in York Region published in 2012 found 12.7 percent of all residents lived in poverty and 14.8 percent of youth.[21]

- The United Way Report "Vertical Poverty" found nearly 40 percent of the families in high-rise buildings in the inner suburbs were poor, up from 25 percent in 1981.[22]

- A recent study found that 145,000, or nearly one-third of children in Toronto, live in poverty.[23]

- A study by Toronto's Wellesley Institute found that "between 1996 and 2009, the percentage of working poor Ontarians who reported their health was 'excellent or very good' dropped from 68% to just under 49%."[24]

- For the poor the lack of income leads to a raft of social problems, such as poor physical health, lower life expectancy, lower levels of social mobility, lack of opportunity, and higher crime rates. For all of us it can result in a lower quality of life, particularly in our cities.

- A recent study found that poverty in Canada is worse today than it was in 1989.[25]

Toronto has seen a series of reports on poverty over the years. Perhaps the one that had the greatest political impact was the United Way of Greater Toronto report called, "Poverty by Postal Code,"[26] published in 2004. It dramatically illustrated how poverty had migrated out of the downtown and was now primarily located in the inner suburbs. This has been confirmed by the research of Hulchanski and others.

David Miller was first elected mayor in 2003, and he acted on the United Way report to establish the Toronto Priority Neighbourhood Strategy. Thirteen neighbourhoods were targeted by the city for special attention and additional social services. Youth programs were an important element of this program. That program has altered and changed over time but it is still in effect.

No doubt this strategy has helped some people, but poverty in the City of Toronto has been increasing. A 2014 study by the Social Planning Council called child poverty at "epidemic levels" in the city.[27] This study shows that child poverty has been on the rise since 2010, and that means all poverty is rising in the city. Of the thirteen largest municipalities in Canada, Toronto is now tied with Saint John, New Brunswick, for having the highest child poverty rates.

Again, this study shows that the highest concentrations of child poverty are in the inner suburbs. There are pockets in the downtown, but it is in neighbourhoods with a high concentration of immigrants that suffer the most. The study found that residents of African, Asian, Middle Eastern, Caribbean, and Latin American heritage are the most likely to be poor. This suggests that it is our recent immigrants who suffer the most from poverty — because of a variety of factors: the sagging economy; lack of low-skilled jobs that pay decent wages; discrimination; and the inadequacy of the social welfare system.

One thing is clear: there is little that a municipal government can do about poverty, even one as large as the City of Toronto. Municipalities can help people in crisis, but only the federal government and the province have the fiscal resources to make a difference. Those levels of government can create income supplement programs or affordable housing, but, in fact, the federal government and Ontario have done very little. Ontario now leads all Canadian provinces in rates of poverty, but the province spends less than other provinces on social programs.[28] This is yet another clear indication of the decline of the province that was once the economic powerhouse of Canada.

Income support benefits have become politicized. When the Mike Harris Conservative government gained power in 1995 they immediately reduced all welfare benefits by 20 percent, and rates still have not returned to previous levels. With the election of the McGuinty government there were promises to increase welfare levels, but little was done. Finally, the Liberals appointed a commission to study the issue. In October 2012 Frances Lankin and Munir A.

Sheikh tabled their report called "Brighter Prospects: Transforming Social Assistance in Ontario."[29]

Like all reports of its kind, it is written in polite language and does not attack anyone, but it is a condemnation of the way that social assistance is practised in Ontario. The report makes 108 recommendations that focus on helping people return to work whenever possible. It argues for a much more open, transparent system where the rules are streamlined. It also argues that recipients should be allowed to keep more of their earnings, if they can get work.

The biggest failing is that the report does not recommend that income support levels be raised so the people can improve their standard of living. Presumably, this was not part of their terms of reference. As Carol Goar of the *Toronto Star* comments, social assistance as it is practised in Ontario is "essentially a poverty maintenance system,"[30] and the attempt to change this bureaucratic monolith into a system to actually help people move out of poverty will be very difficult.

It appears that the Liberal government led by Premier Katherine Wynne will implement some of the recommendations, but it will be a long time before there is the political will to eliminate poverty in this province and the Greater Toronto and Hamilton Area.

AFFORDABLE HOUSING

I believe we don't just have a poverty problem in GTHA; we have an affordable housing and poverty problem. The two issues are linked. If we could provide decent, affordable housing, many of the problems faced by low-income people would disappear, but there is little attempt to solve this problem or even discuss it in political forums in Toronto today.

The ideal of home ownership remains very strong in Canada, but 46 percent of the people in the City of Toronto live in rental accommodation. The proportion of renters is less in the outer suburbs of the GTHA. The Region of Peel has 22 percent renters while Durham, Halton, and York have 15 percent.[31] In Hamilton renters make up 31.8 percent.[32] In this, like many other respects, Hamilton is similar to the City of Toronto.

The main reason for the growth of renters is cost. In May of 2014 the average cost of a single-family home in Toronto was $965,670, a jump of 13 percent over the previous year. In the 905 region it was $648,439, while in the Hamilton–Burlington area it was $402,500. The condo market continues to be hot. In Toronto the average cost was $390,569, and in the 905 region it was $309,719. All but the affluent are finding it impossible to buy a single-family home and even condos are out of reach of many. Increasingly, the GTHA will become a city of tenants living in multi-unit buildings.

Rental costs are another problem. Hundreds of thousands of people spend 50 percent of their income on housing. Immigrants particularly face hardships. A study found most newcomers spend 50 percent of their income on housing with 15 percent spending 75 percent or more. That leaves them with little money to pay for other necessities like food and transport.[33] In Toronto, a combination of low vacancy rates, high housing costs, and the lack of an adequate affordable housing program has made housing a crisis for hundreds of thousands of people

We are not producing housing at a price that people can afford and the housing that is produced is not the type people need. This has become the greatest contributor of the growth of poverty and hardships for people in the GTHA.

Because it is so important in our effort to develop a new agenda for cities, Chapter 7, later in the book, is devoted to affordable housing.

HOMELESSNESS

The most extreme form of poverty is homelessness. A study completed in 2013 found that on any given night, 30,000 people are homeless in Canada, and 200,000 experience homelessness in a given year. The "chronic homeless" make up between 4,000 and 8,000 people, those that experience "episodic homelessness" numbers between 6,000 and 22,000, and the "transitionally homeless" between 176,000 and 188,000 — these are the so called "couch surfers" who do not have a home and rely on family and friends. This same study estimated that homelessness in Canada costs $7 billion yearly for such services as shelters, social services, health care and corrections.[34]

But there is some good news in the area of homelessness. In Toronto there was a decrease of 51 percent between 2006 and 2011.[35] It was David Miller who took on the issue of homelessness and made a real difference. It was a hotly contested debate at the time. Mental illness, alcoholism, and drug addiction are common among those who live on the street. Some argued that these basic problems have to be solved before the problem of the homeless can be dealt with. Miller disagreed. He argued that the housing problems have to be solved for the homeless before any of the other related problems can be tackled.

Miller prevailed in the debate and the Streets to Homes project was established. The project sent social workers into the street to contact the homeless and refer them to housing, usually existing rooming houses across the city, and then arranged income support for them. The success of the program was not only in moving the homeless off the street; the quality of life of many of these people has been improved.

A recent study, called "At Home/Chez Soi," found that not only did a housing first policy improve the living conditions of homeless people, but it resulted in considerable savings. A 2008 study in Vancouver found that it was costing at least $55,000 a year per homeless person for things like police, ambulance, hospital care, and other services. A Calgary study concluded it was costing $135,000 a year.[36] The "At Home/Chez Soi" study found that every dollar invested in housing for the homeless resulted in $2.17 savings for government because they spent less time in hospitals, jails, and shelters.[37] The federal government has provided new money to municipalities to deal with the homelessness crisis but the problem continues.

SOCIAL PROBLEMS AND THE LACK OF POLITICAL WILL TO SOLVE THEM

A New Urban Agenda has to include a way to find solutions to social problems in our cities. I have touched on some of the most obvious — income inequality, affordable housing, unemployment, homelessness, poverty — but there are many more related problems. Youth unemployment, discrimination against minority groups, unequal economic opportunities, addictions — the list is long.

Traditionally, we have looked to government to provide a strategy, and the funds to deal with these types of problems, but today the attention of government is elsewhere. Recent tax cuts have led to a reduction of almost $30 billion a year in income taxes and GST/HST by the federal government. The tax cuts have resulted in an increase in income of almost $1,000 per Canadian, except this is not the full story. The top 20 percent of income earners got $10.9 billion, or 36 percent of this money, and the bottom 20 percent only got $1.9 billion, or 6 percent.

Even this does not include all of the cuts. In 2000, the Paul Martin government made income tax cuts larger than the Conservatives, and there have been massive cuts to corporate taxes. If all of these cuts are added up, it comes to close to $80 billion a year.[38] Most of that money has gone to those who already have high incomes.

Those who believe that taxation and economic policies of government are unimportant should simply look around at what is happening in the GTHA. Our communities are increasingly becoming polarized along income lines. The wealthy live in their downtown enclaves of exclusive neighbourhoods. Immigrants struggle in the deteriorating high-rise apartment buildings in the inner suburbs, and the middle class search for neighbourhoods and housing that they can afford. Home ownership is becoming increasingly difficult for all but a few. Meanwhile, our municipal governments have no money to provide the needed social programs.

As I moved around the GTHA talking to people about the region and its problems, the one idea that came back again and again in different forms was that we should be building integrated, diverse communities. We need neighbourhoods with a balanced mix of incomes, young and old, families and singles, and ethnic and racial groups. Our economic and social policies are leading us in the opposite direction.

But it is not too late. We can build healthy, integrated cities, but it needs political will both on the part of the public and government. If we can do it, the benefits will be enormous. Our housing stock will improve, the city will become more affordable, and in the process we will build a more integrated city.

THREE

THE ENVIRONMENTAL REPORT CARD

Canada has become the "bad boy" of the worldwide effort to reduce the threat of climate change. Our federal government is so committed to developing and promoting the Alberta oil sands that it will be very difficult to reduce the level of the country's air pollution unless there is a radical change in the technology used to extract the oil, and that seems unlikely. Other countries predict their greenhouse gas emissions will decrease, but ours are expected to increase.

The federal government's own commissioner of the environment and sustainable development released a report in October 2014 saying the government has no specific plan to meet its greenhouse gas emissions reduction target and will fall well short of its goal.[1]

The target for the reduction of Canada's greenhouse gas emissions set by the Kyoto Accord was to reduce emissions, from the base year of 1990, 6 percent by 2012, 30 percent by 2020, and 80 percent by 2050. Our government's reaction was simply to withdraw support for the accord. Five years ago Canada and the U.S. signed the Copenhagen Accord, which set new targets. Canada pledged to reduce greenhouse gas emissions by 17 percent from 2005 by 2020, but although this is a considerably lower target than that set by the Kyoto Accord, the country will still fall short.

Ontario and the GTHA, on the other hand, have done considerably better than Canada. In fact, the province reached the 2012 Kyoto target. The City of Toronto reduced greenhouse gas emissions 15 percent by 2012 and much of the rest of the province has achieved similar reductions. The single most important reason has been that Ontario has shut down all coal-fired electric power plants. This is an accomplishment, but it will be much harder to meet targets in the future.

The GTHA must do more to reduce greenhouse gas emissions. It is the largest urban centre in the country, and the policies that are set here are followed across the country. If we can reduce our emissions, then the country has the possibility of reaching its targets. That is an essential step to reducing the threat of climate change and avoiding the disastrous consequences of climate change.

POLLUTION THEN AND NOW

In the late 1960s, when I lived in Hamilton, pollution was a polarizing issue in the city. I lived in the East End, downwind from the steel mills, and often I would come out in the morning and find black soot all over my car. I became pretty concerned about the health effects this was having on me, my family, and my neighbours. I talked to others, but the attitude seemed to be that we lived in an industrial city and pollution was a price that we had to pay.

But then, unexpectedly, many began voicing concern about Hamilton's pollution. New attitudes emerged. The politicians became nervous and defended the companies. I remember the mayor, Vic Copps, saying, "When I see smoke coming out of a chimney, I see money." I was appalled. He felt he had to defend the steel industry and other industrial concerns from so-called "tree huggers" because the companies were the economic heart of Hamilton, but he was ignoring the well-being of his constituents.

It was not long before another environmental issue exploded onto the city's political scene. A small number of activists, myself among them, began talking about the polluted state of Hamilton's harbour. Someone suggested we start a group to agitate for better water quality, and we adopted the name Save Our Bay (SOB). In those days there were still people around who remembered swimming in the bay in the 1920s and 1930s, so the campaign caught the imagination of old and young alike. Many people wanted the bay cleaned up, and before those of us from SOB knew it, there were demands from across the city to do something about water quality.

The harbour was a mess. Sewage was treated before it was dumped into the lake, but the city and province allowed industry to dispose industrial waste into the bay — slag from steel production, spent acid from the pickle line that made corrugated steel, and all sorts of other pollution. It wasn't just SOB members who demanded this stop. Unions, church groups, community groups — eventually, everyone wanted the pollution of the bay to stop. In time, Hamilton City Council responded by passing resolutions, but not before assigning hundreds of acres of water lots to the steel companies so that they could continue to dump slag.

I tell these stories not to besmirch the reputations of long-dead politicians, but to illustrate the wanton disregard for the environment that was common in those days. I happened to live in Hamilton, a city of heavy industry, but similar problems existed across the country and people began to take notice. Attitudes about pollution and the environment changed in the 1960s, and they changed remarkably quickly. It took time for some politicians to catch up with the people, but the attitudes of others, like the oil companies of Alberta and their supporters, like Stephen Harper, are still back in the days when pollution was seen as a cost of generating wealth.

Water quality has improved across the county over the last fifty years. Notwithstanding the tragedy of Walkerton, every municipality in Ontario has a state-of-the-art water treatment program to treat sewage. Industry has become much more responsible in recycling its waste, and the water quality of our lakes and rivers has improved. It is not perfect. We still cannot swim in Hamilton Harbour or Toronto Harbour, where I now live, but the water quality of Lake Ontario has improved, and rarely are there swimming bans or pollution warnings. The most serious water pollution problem in Toronto and other GTHA municipalities is storm water run-off that washes surface pollutants from yards and streets into the rivers and streams, but even that is being dealt with. Municipalities are building holding tanks where storm water can be stored until it can be treated by the sewage facilities.

Garbage was another huge problem. In the late 1980s landfill sites in the GTHA were rapidly filling. Politicians were in a dead panic because they could not find a "willing host" to take Toronto's garbage. The Bob Rae government went so far as to study forty-four possible garbage sites in the GTA, but never found a willing host. For a time Toronto trucked garbage all the way to Michigan, until David Miller finally closed the deal on a landfill site south of London, Ontario, willing to take Toronto's garbage. But that is not the good news. Today Toronto and most of the municipalities in the GTHA recycle about 45 to 50 percent of all garbage and again that is a remarkable accomplishment.[2]

But the most serious pollution problem of the GTHA is air pollution. We have been doing better than other places in Canada, but the seriousness of global warming and the impact that it will have dwarfs any other environmental problem that we face today.

AIR POLLUTION AND THE GTHA

It is important to recognize that the reduction of all forms of pollution only came because of public concern. The politicians were not the leaders; they responded to public demands to reduce pollution. The environmental movement helped to make us aware of the problems, and scientists have played a major role in helping us understand why air pollution is causing climate change and what the long-term impact will be if nothing is done, but it was the change of attitudes of the population that made this possible. Improvements have been made, but to go the last distance and reduce greenhouse gas emissions by 80 percent by 2050 will be an enormous challenge. I believe we can do it, but we need a plan, we need commitment from the public, and, most important, we need the political will to make it happen.

Air pollution is a major health hazard across Canada. A University of British Columbia study found that there were 21,000 deaths each year across Canada as a result of air pollution. This is nine times the 2,400 people killed in traffic accidents.[3] Air pollution is causing an epidemic of deaths and health problems in this country, particularly in densely populated urban areas, and yet we accept it as normal — just as the people of Hamilton once accepted the pollution of their harbour as normal.

In the GTHA, air pollution remains a serious problem, but there are some hopeful signs. A Toronto Board of Health study conducted in 2004 found there were 1,700 premature deaths and 6,000 hospitalizations every year as a result of air pollution in the city. In 2014, the study was repeated and found that it had fallen to 1,300 deaths and 3,550 hospitalizations. And yet this is still alarmingly high. By comparison, in 2014 Toronto had sixty-three traffic fatalities and fifty-seven homicides.[4] Despite this, the health hazards of air pollution are virtually ignored by the media, while homicides are front page news.

But what causes air pollution anyway? We know that it is the burning of fossil fuels, but what is the source, and where is it burned?

Table 5: Sources of Greenhouse Gas Emissions for the City of Toronto[5]

	1990	2004	2011
Electricity	21.4%	23.2%	18.6%
Natural gas (heating buildings)	32.0%	32.4%	34.2%
Transportation (cars, trucks)	26.7%	30.5%	36.0%
Other	19.9%	13.9%	11.2%
Total	100%	100%	100%
Tonnes of GGE produced	27.3 million	26.6 million	23.2 million
Change from 1990	—	-2.7%	-14.9%

The City of Markham in the outer suburbs did a similar study in 2011 and came up with these figures for their municipality.[6]

Table 6: Sources of Air Pollution Emissions in Markham 2011

Residential	48%
Transportation	36%
Commercial	12%
Industrial	3%
Solid waste	1%

There has been a great deal of publicity about the pollution of cars and trucks, but what is surprising about the findings of these studies is that the air pollution generated from heating and cooling buildings is as great or greater than transportation. To its credit, the provincial government is trying to improve public transit and reduce air pollution from vehicles, and we are going to look at that in the next chapter, but very little is being done to deal with the pollution that comes from heating and cooling buildings.

This is a key problem that significantly changes the way that we have to deal with air pollution. In the case of water pollution, we could demand that industrial and municipal water treatment facilities clean up their act. Garbage is a problem for municipalities to solve. But if we are to reduce the threat of climate change, we will have to change how we heat and cool our buildings and how we move around our city. This will mean a change in the lifestyles of many. It will be up to each of us.

GTHA municipalities have begun to play a role in the issue of climate change by writing reports. Some are excellent while others are mediocre, but the problem with most is they do not spell out plans of how greenhouse gas emissions can be reduced. Mississauga has joined the Greater Toronto and Hamilton Area Clean Air Council, but all they do is write reports highlighting the problems. The city has adopted "Green Development Standards,"[7] based on Leadership in Energy and Environmental Design (LEED), a type of environmental building code, but that is already a standard adopted by Ontario. They are doing very little to reduce greenhouse gas emissions in Mississauga.

All of the other large municipalities in the outer suburbs have followed this practise as well. Vaughan, Brampton, Pickering, and Markham have published environmental studies that focus on their cities. Markham's report is particularly good because it deals not only with environmental sustainability, but it includes things like affordable housing, poverty, youth unemployment, transportation, and other issues. It is an excellent report, worthy of careful study, but like others, there is little on how Markham can reach its goals of reducing air pollution and creating a more sustainable city.

The Hamilton report on air pollution, called "Clean Air Hamilton," I found particularly interesting because it illustrates how this industrial city is much different than Toronto and the bedroom municipalities in the outer suburbs. This is a table that comes out of that report.

Table 7: Total Hamilton Greenhouse Gas Emissions, Corporate and Community, 2010

Industrial	48%
Steel Industry	38%
Transportation	5%
Residential	5%
Commercial	3%
Municipal	1%

This does not mean that Hamiltonians produce much less pollution from their buildings and cars than Toronto or Markham. Instead, it illustrates the huge amount of air pollution produced by industry in the city. If Hamilton is going to reduce greenhouse gas emissions, the city will have to try to get industry to change, something that the politicians have been very reluctant to do in the past.

Hamilton's current leaders have tried to keep the issue of air pollution before the public. The city formed a citizens' group that regularly reports on air quality. Those reports have more detail than any of the others that I have reviewed, with discussions of different types of chemicals and the impact of air pollution on the neighbourhoods of the city, but again there is no real strategy of how the pollution can be reduced.

Industrial air pollution regulations are a joint provincial-municipal responsibility. The Ontario government worries that if standards are too high, it will discourage industries from locating in the province. If we are going to do anything about pollution, we have to get beyond this. We need a comprehensive strategy to combat greenhouse gas emissions or we will never meet the challenge of climate change. The province has to become part of that strategy, but so do municipalities, neighbourhoods, and individual citizens.

I offer two different examples of municipalities that are doing good things to reduce pollution. One comes from the City of Toronto, the environmental leader not only in Ontario, but a leader in North America. The other is from Guelph, a small Ontario city not even in the GTHA. Both examples show what a municipality and its citizens can do if they really want to deal with air pollution, greenhouse gas emissions, and the challenge of climate change.

Toronto, the Environmental City

Toronto has long had a good environmental record. A high proportion of the population uses public transit and there is a good system of parks. The ravines, an outstanding natural feature of the city, are protected, and although the waterfront was degraded for decades, in recent years major strides have been made to reclaim it through Waterfront Toronto, an agency funded by all three levels of government.

Toronto continues to nurture its urban forest, despite former mayor Rob Ford's efforts to cut the tree planting program. There are over ten million trees in the city, many of them giant, mature trees, providing shade and protection to the buildings and streets. The city has an active program of replacing trees and improving the health of trees damaged by poor soil, ice storms, drought, disease, air pollution, construction, and environmental hazards. The city also puts much work into educating the public in the care of trees on their own and public property.

It is only recently that the benefit of trees has been recognized. Trees absorb and store carbon, the most damaging of the greenhouse gases. They retain water and help to stop flash floods. Trees moderate the temperature of the city both in summer and winter, improve air quality, and a green canopy of trees in neighbourhoods improves the quality of life for everyone. Dollar for dollar, the planting and care of trees is the most effective anti-pollution expenditure that a municipality can make. Many of the communities in the outer suburbs would benefit from active programs for the planting and care of trees.

A more dramatic example of Toronto's environmental record is found in its use of district heating and cooling. These systems use different technologies, but they all work on the same principle. Water is heated or chilled in a central facility and sent underground to buildings through a network of insulated pipes. There are huge advantages to the system. Individual buildings do not need to establish their own heating and cooling plant. A centrally controlled system is less expensive to run, more dependable, and creates less pollution.

There are many district heating systems around the world. As early as 1911 the University of Toronto established a system of heating buildings from a central heating plant. A number of years ago the city and the Ontario government played a leading role in establishing a system to heat large institutional buildings such as hospitals and government buildings. Today, the system heats 140 buildings in downtown Toronto.

The Toronto district energy system started as a way to heat buildings, and has now been expanded to cool buildings, using an innovation called Deep Lake Water Cooling. Cold water is pumped from deep in Lake Ontario, off Toronto Island. The water is brought into the city via insulated pipes and the cold is drawn out of the water with heat exchangers. That cold is used to cool buildings. Afterward, it is used as potable drinking water. The system was brought online in 2004 and now is operated by Enwave, a sustainable energy company.

District heating and cooling systems are very cost effective and have great environmental advantages. They are efficient, use less energy, and reduce emissions from refrigerants and heating. There are initial costs with the construction of the network of pipes, but that outlay is recovered over time with the reduction of heating and cooling costs.

David Miller was elected mayor of Toronto in 2003. He is a committed environmentalist and his leadership made a difference. In 2007 the city published a report called "Change is in the Air,"[8] which Miller described as a "framework" for a clean air action plan "for meeting our greenhouse gas and air pollution reduction targets."

Today it is disappointing to look over the action plan because it is obvious that Toronto is not going to meet many of the targets set out in the report. As examples, the action plan calls for an energy retrofit of 50 percent of single family homes and small businesses by 2010, and a financing plan for the energy retrofit of high-rise condos. The report claims that the bike network will be completed by 2012, and an aggressive expansion of the Deep Lake Water Cooling system in the downtown core. Again, that did not happen. Rob Ford was elected in 2010, and the mayor, along with his councillor allies, cut the program drastically.

There are elements of it, however, that have been implemented. Mandatory green building standards is one. The Toronto Green Standard, as it has come to be called, came into effect in 2010. It is a two-tier set of green performance measures, along with supporting guidelines, for both private and public new buildings. The standards work with regular development approvals and the building inspection process.

Tier 1 sets out required environmental performance measures. This includes a design development stage and an energy report. In the design stage, the buildings must be shown to be 15 percent more energy efficienct than the standard required by the Ontario Building Code. The efficiencies are found in things like thermal windows, insulation, heating systems, and so on. The focus is on reducing energy consumption.

Tier 2 is a voluntary compliance program where it must be shown that there is a 25 percent energy reduction over the Ontario Building Code. Tier 1 is required for the building to be approved for construction. Tier 2 is encouraged by the refund of city development charges if targets can be reached. This can be a considerable amount of money for the developer.

But the real savings are in the long-term reduction of energy costs, and the results of this program are impressive. A recent city evaluation of new buildings found that all of them achieved 25 percent efficiency improvements; 53.5 percent of the buildings evaluated achieved 30 percent or better. These efficiency improvements reduce air pollution, but also create huge savings for the owners of the buildings because of the buildings' reduced energy costs. The long-term benefits are enormous.

Another environmental innovation that Miller helped to implement is called Tower Renewal. Almost all of the older high-rise towers are energy hogs. They leak energy through inefficient windows and doors, and their heating and cooling systems are outdated. The City of Toronto set aside $10 million for a loan program that the owners of these buildings can use for energy refits. To date, the city has funded about ten high-rise apartment buildings a year. It takes about six or seven years for the loans to be repaid out of energy savings, but those savings will benefit the tenants and owners for decades. The problem is that there are hundreds of buildings in the city that need energy retrofits and the program does not begin to fill that need.

It is these types of programs that will reduce energy costs and will help to reduce greenhouse gas emissions. Virtually every building in the GTHA is heated by natural gas, a fossil fuel. The cooling of buildings now means that peak energy consumption in Ontario is in the summer. Any reduction in energy use will result in the reduction of greenhouse gas emissions, as well as the costs associated with consumption of fossil fuels.

Private companies are moving into the area of energy retrofits. They will carry out a feasibility study of a building, called an "energy audit," establish a plan, and even arrange the financing. Once an agreement is made, they then will install new equipment, like a heating system, insulation, windows, and doors. After the costs have been paid for and a profit out of the energy savings, future savings go to the building owner. These companies even provide a guarantee. The problem is that they mainly work on large buildings like hospitals, universities, and large commercial and industrial buildings.[9]

Given the economic incentives, the question, then, is why don't all developers build the most energy efficient buildings possible, and why don't the owners of older buildings do energy retrofits to reduce costs? The unfortunate reality is that it is not always in the interests of developers to reduce costs.

Developers, in most instances, sell their buildings to condo owners or corporations after they are built. Installing energy saving materials and devices increases the costs of the buildings, costs that will be soon recovered by energy savings. But when the developers sell the units, the saving will be realized by the condo owners, not the developer. That is why developers are reluctant to install energy saving technologies. They have to pay for the energy saving materials, but the benefit goes to the new owners. Miller and others realized this and required developers to meet Tier 1 standards and encouraged them to meet Tier 2 standards.

The second obvious question, then, is why other municipalities have not followed Toronto's example by requiring these standards in new buildings? Toronto is in a very favourable position. Developers are clamouring to build in the city, and they are willing to meet higher standards in order to get their projects approved. Outside Toronto, municipalities compete for development, and the local politicians do not want to scare them away by requiring expensive energy standards.

The province could enforce these standards through the building code. Why won't they do it? The Ontario government is very cautious of the developers. The development industry remains one of the most powerful lobby groups in the province.

David Miller was an environmental mayor who made a real difference. He sponsored a number of innovative programs. The green roof bylaw was the first in North America; it remains a very good program, reducing the heat of central core of the city on hot summer days. But the greatest disappointment is that Miller resigned too early. Had he run for one more term, he would have had the ability to implement many of the proposals in his action plan.

Politics makes a difference and Rob Ford and his followers have significantly changed the direction of Toronto. John Tory has been silent on these issues, and that suggests that environmental issues are not part of his political agenda. Today the city is seen as an environmental laggard, not an environmental leader.

The Guelph District Energy System

Guelph is a small city of 120,000 people, just to the north and west of the GTHA. It has a university, whose origin was as an agricultural college, a number of small manufacturers, and it is the centre of Ontario's co-operative movement. The university's Agricultural College and the co-ops are closely linked. The city has benefitted from a long tradition of working together to solve community problems.

Like those in the GTHA, the people of Guelph and its city council became concerned about climate change a number of years ago. They recognized that 50 percent of the city's greenhouse gas emissions were created from the heating and cooling of buildings, but unlike other cities, they began to work on a practical plan to help solve this problem. Their solution was a community-wide district energy system.

In 2006 the city adopted an ambitious plan to heat and cool homes, as well as institutional, commercial, and industrial buildings, with a district energy system. This is not a small project; it will heat and cool at least 50 percent of all of the buildings in the city by 2031. The Guelph system dwarfs Toronto's Enwave system, which focuses exclusively on the high-rise buildings in the downtown.[10]

Guelph was able to put this project together because it was led by a city-owned corporation called Envida Community Energy Inc., which worked in partnership with Guelph Hydro, another corporation owned and controlled by the municipality. The first phase is a co-generation project that produces electricity by boiling water with natural gas. The waste heat that is normally exhausted into the atmosphere is captured and used to heat water for the district energy system. This combination of the production of electricity and district heating increases the efficiency of the system to 80 percent.

Hot water is pumped to the buildings through a network of buried, insulated pipes. In warm weather, chilled water will be fed into the system for air conditioning. The hot water will also be used to warm tap water, and old lead pipes that present a health hazard will be replaced as the system is constructed. The district energy system is much more efficient than furnaces or air conditioners located in buildings, and will decrease costs significantly. The system will use 50 percent less energy and produce 60 percent less emissions in the city.

The involvement of Guelph Hydro is a key element in the promotion of the district energy system in that city. It was explained to the public that this was an extension of existing services, like electricity, water, waste collection, and sewage. Guelph Hydro has the ability to finance the expansion of the system. They manage the construction of the district energy system and their employees administer and monitor the system. This combination gave the public confidence. Another political plus is that everyone can take advantage of the system. Priority would be given to downtown businesses and a large industrial park, but everyone benefits. That has helped the plan gain political support.

Finally, the system was promoted as an economic development project that would bring employment to the city. A recent annual report of Guelph Hydro says: "This infrastructure will help the community be more energy efficient, dramatically improve the municipality's carbon footprint, and attract residents, businesses, jobs, and investments to our forward thinking community."

In the future it is likely communities will develop district energy systems using electricity, not natural gas. Ontario is rapidly approaching the point where we produce more electricity than we can use. Even today there are often times when the city has excess power. Electricity can be used to heat or cool water very efficiently, and that water can be pumped through the insulated pipes to heat or cool buildings. A system such as this will be non-polluting.[11]

The benefits of district energy systems are so compelling that we simply must implement them across the province, and hopefully across the country. Not only will it significantly reduce pollution from buildings, but it will make our cities more affordable and create jobs.

THE ELECTRIC CITY

The dream of environmentalists is to drastically cut our creation of greenhouse gases and eliminate the threat of climate change. The only realistic way that we can do this is by creating an electric city, where the burning of fossil fuels are eliminated or significantly reduced. In the past an idea like this would be the preserve of dreamers, but now it is possible.

The expansion of our use of electricity is emerging as a practical way to reduce costs, increase affordability, and, at the same time, reduce emissions of greenhouse gases. Despite the recent fall in the cost of oil, in the long run the price of fossil fuels is expected to rise as costs of exploration, extraction, and refining of oil rises and demand in the developing world increases. Meanwhile, alternative energy supplies are increasing, with the development of solar panels, windmills, and energy storage systems that save power when it is plentiful and turn it into electric power when it is expensive. This in time will drive down the costs of electricity.

District energy systems are another practical way to reduce costs and at the same time reduce greenhouse gas emissions. It will be costly to build these systems, but the energy savings in time will recoup those costs. In the long run, district energy is the most practical way to reduce emissions from buildings. It would take some years to build the district systems that would provide heat and cooling for all buildings across the GTHA, but our commitment in the Kyoto Accord was to reduce greenhouse gas emissions 80 percent by 2050. We should try to reach that goal even if others abandon it. If we can do that, it would not only significantly reduce air pollution, but in the process it would reduce the costs of heating and cooling buildings for owners and tenants and make a more affordable city.

The retrofitting of buildings will do the same. It will reduce pollution, make the city more affordable, and at the same time produce scores of green jobs.

These two systems have one other benefit: they are cash positive. It will cost money to build district energy systems and to retrofit buildings, but after six to eight years of reduced energy costs, that money will be paid off, and savings will be substantial in subsequent years.

The other promise of the electric city is the conversion of our transportation system. The extension of the GTHA transit system, run by electric power, is well underway, but an even more significant development is electric cars and other vehicles. Again, this is driven by the need to cut fossil fuel consumption. As an added bonus, in the long run it will be much less expensive to run electric vehicles.

The arrival of the electric city will bring enormous benefits. Think of the 1,300 premature deaths of Torontonians from air pollution, and the 21,000 deaths every year of Canadians. And think of the economic benefits. There will be far more jobs in green industries like district energy systems, renovating buildings, and generating electric power from solar and wind than will be found in a policy that ignores the costs of air pollution. Those who think only of the short-term economic pain from reducing air pollution, and ignore the long-term economic, social, and health benefits, distort reality.

Transit follows the same pattern. Again the investments will be considerable, but the long-term gains will be enormous. That is what we look at next.

FOUR

THE PROMISE OF TRANSIT

There is no doubt that we will need much better public transit if we are to build a more sustainable GTHA, and it has to be a top item of the New Urban Agenda. Change will be difficult. Car culture is a fundamental part of our way of life, and cars will not be given up easily. But the benefits will be enormous.

The provincial government began the debate with the publication of "The Big Move," their proposal on transit.[1] At the same time, they created a government agency called Metrolinx to implement the recommendations. The report is an ambitious plan; one of the few government documents that propose very significant changes that will have an impact on everyone who lives in the GTHA. The costs are estimated to be $50 billion over twenty-five years, but cost is not the problem. The real risk is that after all of the money is spent, and new transit lines are built, very little will change.

"The Big Move" makes for fascinating reading. It is written in an accessible style where the problems are laid out, followed by the benefits and solutions: first the bad news, then the good news. Let's follow the same format.

FIRST THE BAD NEWS

- Today the average commuter in the GTHA spends eighty-two minutes a day in travel time. That could hit 109 minutes by 2031 if nothing is done to combat gridlock.

- "The Big Move" estimates congestion costs the Toronto-area economy $3.3 billion a year, a figure that will rise to $15 billion in 2031 if significant action isn't taken. Recently, Metrolinx revised this figure to say gridlock was a "$6 billion congestion crisis for business and quality of life," every year. The impact on every individual is $1,600 a year.[2]

- People in the GTHA have become increasingly dependent on private automobiles for mobility. Car trips are increasing at a faster rate than the population. Between 1986 and 2006 the number of trips made by automobile in the GTHA grew at 56 percent, compared to a population increase of 45 percent.

- Currently, more than two million automobile trips are made every day during the peak travel periods in the GTHA, with that number forecast to approach three million trips by 2031 unless there is better transit.

- The average car on the GTHA's roads transports just under 1.2 people during the peak period, consuming a tremendous amount of energy and wasting significant amounts of road space to transport empty seats. At full capacity, a standard forty-foot bus is about ten times as space-efficient as a typical North American car.

- Average commute times by car are still considerably shorter than by public transit,[3] and will continue to take much less time even if the full Metrolinx plan is implemented.

- Eighty-five percent of car drivers in the GTHA never consider public transit. More than 70 percent of Torontonians drive to work.[4]

- About one-third of all household income goes toward transportation in Canada. A car costs between $8,000 and $15,000 to own and operate a year.

- One study found that each hour spent in a car on a daily basis is associated with a 6 percent increase in the likelihood of obesity. It is also related to diabetes and heart disease. By contrast, every kilometre walked per day was associated with a 4.8 percent reduction in the likelihood of obesity.

- Emissions from motor vehicles have an impact on respiratory and cardiovascular ailments and cancers.[5]

- The largest (man-made) contributor to the greenhouse effect is carbon dioxide gas emissions, about 77 percent of which comes from the combustion of fossil fuels."[6]

- Today, TTC and GO Transit systems are designed to take people primarily to and from Toronto's downtown, but only about one in six jobs in the GTHA are located in the city core.

- The GTHA's public transit system is currently comprised of nine separate local transit agencies and one regional transit provider. This patchwork of systems is poorly integrated, making travel across boundaries by public transit inconvenient, frustrating, and costly.

- Until recently, each system had its own separate system for paying fares and each had its own fare structure. This has meant, for example, that people who travel from a local bus in one city, to a GO train, and then to the subway in Toronto need to pay three different fares, or have three different transit passes for their trip.

- There is an assumption that driving on roads is free, compared to public transit, which is paid for out of the fare box, but both are heavily subsidized by the public. A study by the C.D. Howe Institute found, "Gas taxes, vehicle licences and other revenue from drivers ... only covered 53% of roadway expenses across Canada during the 2009/2010 fiscal year."[7] The rest comes from various levels of government.

- The TTC covers 72 percent of its operating costs out of the fare box. This is more than any other transit system in North America. Other operating costs are paid for by the municipality. Most capital costs for transit in Ontario (those are costs for equipment, vehicles and new lines) are paid for by provincial government grants.

- Cars take up much more space than any other form of transportation. The average car is ten feet long. When it is being driven, it needs the space of several car lengths in front and behind, depending on the speed of the vehicle.

- Parking takes up enormous room in our cities. Even just to sit there, the average car takes up about 100 square feet, and the average parking space is 120 square feet.

- One of the biggest subsidies to employees is free parking. Even many public institutions like universities provide free parking for employees. This encourages people to drive to work.

THEN THE GOOD NEWS

- Implementing "The Big Move" will cost $50 billion — $2 billion a year over twenty-five years. The Ontario government has already committed $16 billion and will pay the rest with provincial tax revenues over the next twenty-five years.[8]

- The plan is to build over 1,200 kilometres of rapid transit, more than triple what exists now. Over 80 percent of residents in the GTHA will live within two kilometres of rapid transit.

- The Presto Card, a smart-card system owned by Metrolinx, has been adopted by GO Transit and all nine municipally owned transit systems across the GTHA. Ottawa Transit has also adopted Presto. There was resistance from the TTC, but that has now been overcome, and it is expected the card will be fully implemented in 2015. This will make it easier for passengers to move between the different systems. The Presto Card can be used for additional services, such as parking, and in the future it could be used to implement a payment system based on the number of kilometres travelled on transit.

- The transportation system will be fully integrated across the GTHA. It will be easy to make a decision on how to get somewhere, or ship something, thanks to seamless integration, accurate and timely information, and prices determined in a transparent manner.

- The GO train service on the Lakeshore rail line from Oshawa in the east to Hamilton in the west will provide all-day service with extra trains at rush hour. Each station will be a hub with transit lines like buses and LRT coming into the hub. Union Station in downtown Toronto will be the central hub, of the entire system.

- Light Rail Transit (LRT) lines will be built in more densely populated parts of the GTHA and bus service improved.

- Average commute times in the GTHA will decrease by 2031 despite an expected 50 percent increase in population. More residents will be able to access jobs and services by transit.

- Public transit will compete effectively with the automobile with service that is fast, convenient, integrated, comfortable, safe, reliable, and inexpensive.

- In twenty-five years the distance that people drive every day will drop by one-third. On average, one-third of trips to work will be taken by transit, and one in five will be taken by walking or cycling. Sixty percent of children will walk or cycle to school.

- The TTC had a record number of riders in 2013 and it is expected that the numbers will rise again every year in the foreseeable future. This suggests that people are adapting to a lifestyle of transit, but this success has led to unprecedented congestion on many routes.

- The Downtown Relief Line will be given priority in Toronto. (John Tory, the new mayor, proposed his SmartTrack plan in the election, and the priority of the Relief Line is now unclear.)

- Seven thousand kilometres of new bike lanes, trails, and pathways for pedestrians and cyclists in the GTHA will make walking and cycling safe and will encourage healthy lifestyles.

- Greenhouse gas emissions per resident will decline dramatically and our air will be cleaner.

- Reducing our dependence on non-renewable resources will help reduce the costs of transportation.

- Union Station in downtown Toronto is Canada's busiest passenger transportation facility and a National Historic Site. Over 240,000 users pass through Union Station every working day, amounting to over 65 million per year. The station is being totally renovated and modernized. In the next twenty-five years, Union Station will see a quadrupling of passenger traffic.

- Metrolinx is building a rail link from Union Station to Pearson International Airport, called the UP Express. It will open in 2015 in time for the Pan American Games. The $456 million cost will be paid for by the Ontario Government and recouped from ticket sales.

- Key major transit stations will become mobility hubs, where transportation modes come together, including local transit service and cycling, and pedestrian networks, with secure storage facilities for bikes and car-share drop-off areas.

- These hubs will become locations for major services and facilities, such as office buildings, hospitals, educational facilities, sporting and cultural venues, and government services. They will also offer amenities to travellers such as heated waiting areas, traveller information centres, cafés and restaurants, and services like daycare, grocery stores, and post offices.

- Metrolinx is building parking garages at all of the GO train stations in the outer suburbs.

- New residential, commercial, and employment developments in municipalities will be built within walking distance of a transit stop with frequent service.

- All transit corridors in the regional rapid transportation network shall be assessed for their potential for higher density mixed-use development.

TWO CHALLENGES

Any program that promises so much — and has such a high price tag — is bound to create political controversy, and "The Big Move" has done that. In the municipalities outside the City of Toronto, the reaction has been close to enthusiastic, and why not? The Ontario government is promising to build transit with no cost to the municipalities. But the reaction of people in Toronto has been quite different.

Toronto has had public transit for more than 150 years, and it has always been a major political issue in the city. "The Big Move" was developed after extensive consultations with the public and politicians and staff of the municipalities. In Toronto the most important group that determined the new transit lines that became part of the plan was not the TTC, it was Mayor David Miller, Adam Giambrone, then TTC chair, and their political advisors. Their proposal was for seven Light Rail Transit (LRT) lines, and the name "Transit City" was given to the plan.

Miller and his people knew a lot about transit, and the technology that they loved more than any other was LRT. This is the technology in vogue in European cities. It can move a lot of people because, although their trains are like streetcars, they are much larger and longer. LRT lines are built along streets at grade on a dedicated right of way. Tunnelling is not necessary, so the cost is much less than it is for subways. Planners point out that because the line is at street level, the LRT gives easy access to riders and stimulates retail along the streets. The technology is even a good fit with Toronto's existing streetcar system, with dedicated streetcar lanes already built along Queen's Quay, Spadina, and St. Clair.

After the original announcement in 2007, the province reduced the number of Transit City lines from seven to four, over Miller's objections, but planning went ahead and all seemed good to go. Then Rob Ford was elected mayor. On inauguration day in 2010 the new mayor declared, "The war against the car is over!" And then, "Transit City is dead!"

Ford is a man of the suburbs, and he believes streets should be the preserve of cars and trucks. LRT are like streetcars in his mind; they slow traffic, and he wanted them off the street. In Ford's view, subways were the answer to Toronto's transportation problems.

The saga of how Ford tried to convert the Sheppard LRT line into a subway, regardless of the cost, is a fascinating element in the story of how he lost the confidence of Toronto City Council. The level of incompetence he showed in this debate, along with revelations about his personal life, led to council stripping him of power. In time, council reinstated Transit City, with one major exception: the Scarborough subway.

The second challenge to implementing "The Big Move" was mounted not by a politician, but by an urban think tank called the Neptis Foundation. Their report was authored by Michael Schabas, a transit expert originally from Toronto, who has had experience in transit planning in cities around the world. Although it was a much more serious and substantial challenge, it did not create the political waves of Rob Ford's attack on Transit City; however, it ended with a similar fate: it gathers dust on a library shelf. For those who want to seriously understand transit in the GTHA, it is a must read.[9]

This is the Neptis summary of their transit study:

> The report ["The Big Move"] shows that while some projects represent good value for money, several can be modified to improve cost effectiveness. A few projects should be reconsidered in their entirety. The advice to Metrolinx is to consider a "course correction" to ensure that "The Big Move" reaches its important goals and makes the best use of its funds.

The report does not attempt to scuttle the plans for transit, but to make "The Big Move" more effective. It warns that the plans as they are now will not achieve the Metrolinx objective of doubling transit ridership. It points to a number of ways that "value for money can be substantially improved" with specific modifications. Finally, it warns that, if there is not a reconsideration, the public may lose confidence, and the whole transit plan could unravel.

Ford's critique proved to be shallow and self-serving, but the Neptis study is a concern. It is based on careful research and the conclusions are drawn by an expert with years of experience in transit planning. The report is detailed and as factual as the information provided to Schabas allowed. Until the Neptis report's publication, the chief critique of "The Big Move" has come from politicians and journalists. That is like having the person on the street evaluating Einstein's physics. They might have some interesting insights, but transit planning on the scale proposed in "The Big Move" is complicated. In order to understand the full details and impact of this massive investment, we need an evaluation by someone steeped in the field.[10]

Unfortunately, there is no indication that the Neptis critique has changed the Metrolinx plans one bit.

WHO IS RESPONSIBLE FOR WHAT?

One of the major problems with transit in the GTHA is understanding what level of government is responsible for what services. It is confusing to say the least.

Up until 1995 the rule of thumb was that the province paid the capital costs for most transit. That included building subways and buying new buses and streetcars. The local municipalities paid the costs of operating the system. Transit in the outer suburbs, however, was so inadequate that the province decided they had to intervene, and they founded GO Transit in 1967. The province still owns GO, but today it is operated by Metrolinx.

After 1995, with the provincial election of Mike Harris's Conservatives, all transit costs were offloaded to the municipalities, with the exception of GO. Unfortunately, local governments do not have the tax base to pay the costs of new equipment. The operating costs of transit in the suburbs were so high that virtually no investments were made for eight years. Transit declined everywhere in Ontario, particularly in the GTHA.

With the election of the Dalton McGuinty Liberals in 2003, the decision was made that the province would make major investments in transit. The commitment of the province was then, and continues to be, to fund and build the rapid transit infrastructure in the GTHA. This includes improvements to the GO system, LRT, and other rapid transit systems in Hamilton and the outer suburbs, and subways and LRT lines in Toronto. The bus service remains the responsibilities of the municipalities.

We are developing a hybrid transit system across the region, and that is part of the confusion. In Toronto, the TTC will operate all of the transit. Outside Toronto, GO will be operated by Metrolinx while the local buses will be operated by the municipalities. In York and Durham, the region will be the operator, but in Peel, it will be the local municipalities. There is even some confusion which level of government will run the new rapid transit lines. When I talked to Bob Bratina, the former mayor of Hamilton, he still did not know who would operate the new LRT service that is being planned for the city.

Adding to all of the confusion, sometimes the politicians do not even seem to know what they are talking about. During the 2014 Toronto municipal election John Tory advocated SmartTrack, his plan for transit. Much of that plan is for transit operated by the province, not the city at all.

Still, with the exit of Rob Ford as mayor and the defeat of Tim Hudak's Conservatives in the last provincial election, there is a general acceptance of the provincial plan for rapid transit, although there is still no consensus around bus service. In fact, there has been little discussion about buses in the great transit debate. And yet, if we are to solve the problem of gridlock, get people out of their cars, and become a transit-based city, good bus service is essential, because it is buses that provide transit to local communities and neighbourhoods. This is particularly true in the sprawling, low-density suburbs of the GTHA.

Let's look at each of the different types of cities and try and understand the type of transit that they need.

TRANSIT PLANS FOR DOWNTOWN TORONTO

The chief focus of the provincial government and Metrolinx has been to solve the problem of gridlock. For Toronto that is primarily a problem of jammed expressways and too much traffic on the downtown streets. It is people from the outer suburbs who are the prime users of the expressways. Seventy percent of the people driving on the Gardiner and Don Valley Parkway live outside Toronto.

Transit in the downtown core is excellent and it has attracted increasing ridership in recent years. The biggest problem is that the system does not have enough capacity to serve the number of passengers. At rush hour the King and Queen streetcars are crammed with people, and as they approach the downtown there is not enough room on the cars for new riders who want to board. The Yonge Street subway trains between Union and Bloor are crammed at rush hour. It often takes riders two or three trains before they can get into a car. I was on a train in February 2014 and the woman standing beside me told her friend that one day the previous week it took five trains before she could get into a car.

The Downtown Relief Line is now being floated as the solution to this problem. It was never part of "The Big Move," or David Miller's Transit City. Again, this should worry us, because this problem was never anticipated by the planners or politicians. The Downtown Relief Line proposal is a plan to build an entirely new subway line that would begin at Pape Station and arc into the core of the city. The subway would join the Yonge Line at the King Street Station and continue west until it finally terminates somewhere around

Ossington Station. This would relieve the congestion in the downtown. The initial cost estimate is between $6.2 billion and $8.3 billion.

Even with the Downtown Relief Line it is unlikely that the problem of congestion will be solved unless strong measures are taken to discourage traffic. Densities are increasing dramatically. Many people want to get out of their cars but it will take an improvement of transit in the downtown for that to happen. That means increasing investments in subways, LRT, buses, and new protected bike lanes.

TRANSIT IN THE INNER SUBURBS

The biggest critique of "The Big Move" is that it pays little attention to the transit needs of the inner suburbs. The people who live there need good transit more than any other group in the GTHA. They have lower incomes and many do not own cars, yet the focus of the provincial plans is gridlock on the expressways that will help higher income people from the outer suburbs. Even the Miller Transit City proposal did little for the transportation needs of people in the inner suburbs. Olivia Chow in the 2014 election talked about the importance of providing more buses on the routes in the inner suburbs, but she was the only one talking about this issue.

The other problem or bias of Transit City is the love of LRT by both planners and some politicians. It is an excellent technology, but it is not appropriate for much of the inner suburbs. Constructing LRT lines takes a long time, and it is expensive. Not as expensive as subways, but then no one, other than Rob Ford, argues in favour of subways for low-density communities. Yet there is another transit system that is less expensive than either subways or LRT that would give excellent service to these communities, and it can be easily adapted to the existing TTC system.

Many South American cities are building high speed bus systems because they are much less expensive to build than subways, and they can move a lot of people very quickly. The buses run on a dedicated roadway, usually in the middle of the street. The vehicles are electric, powered by overhead wires, like the power system of Toronto's streetcars. The vehicles are large, usually articulated buses with two units coupled together so they can carry a lot of passengers. Another benefit of buses is that they are frequent and reliable, so customers can depend on them. People will use transit if it is reliable, but will soon abandon it and go back to their cars if they have to wait for long periods. Reliability is essential if we hope to build a strong passenger base.

I have travelled in South America and have seen these buses in operation. What is impressive is how fast they travel. That is because of the dedicated bus lanes. Except at major intersections, they don't have to worry about other traffic. The other reason they are fast is that the buses do not make as many stops as our normal bus service. In that sense, they are more like our subway system, where each station is a distance apart.

This system has all the characteristics of good transit appropriate for low- or medium-density suburbs. It is fast, with regular service, and, if the buses are powered by electricity, they are non-polluting. Each route in Toronto would terminate at a subway or LRT stop where the passengers can transfer to continue their journey. But, most important, a system such as this is relatively inexpensive to construct. The most expensive feature would be the construction of the dedicated bus lanes. The overhead wires for electric power are not expensive to install. The buses could even run on ordinary streets without a dedicated lane. All that would be needed is the overhead electric wires.

One special problem in designing transit for the suburbs is that virtually all suburbs have meandering roads. There are crescents, dead end streets, and roads that curve around until they come back to where they started. Suburban communities are built like that in both the inner and outer suburbs in the GTHA. They fulfil a dream for those who hate straight roads and houses that line up neatly on uniform lots, but they are a nightmare for a transit planner trying to design efficient bus routes.

But, in fact, all of our suburbs have an important feature that makes transit considerably easier. If you look closely at a map of any suburb in the GTHA you will notice that the housing surveys are boarded by straight roads. These are the concession and side roads laid down by the surveyors who were marking out the land for farming in the early nineteenth century.

As I write this, I have a street map of Scarborough open on my desk showing an area south and east of the Town Centre. Lawrence and Ellesmere run parallel east and west. The side roads are Brimley, McCowan, Bellamy, Markham, Scarborough Golf Club Road, and Orton. Every one of these roads is straight, but the land that they enclose is filled with the houses built along the curving suburban streets.

Dedicated bus lanes could be built in the centre of streets like Lawrence and Ellesmere or on any of the side roads. They are wide enough to handle the buses and still provide lanes for cars. There could be bus stops at each of the major side roads or every second one. People living in the houses of the suburbs would walk or ride a bicycle out to the bus stops, and be whisked away by the fast buses that connect with subways or LRT lines. The apartment buildings in the suburbs, where many low-income people live, are all located along major roads. They would have excellent transit at their doorstep.

This type of layout exists all over the inner suburbs of Toronto — Etobicoke, North York, as well as Scarborough. It also exists in the outer suburbs, although in some places the roads are farther apart. We need to give silent thanks to the nineteenth-century land surveyors because they have made the planning of good transit infinitely easier.

TRANSIT IN THE OUTER SUBURBS

Before the provincial Liberal government began its efforts to improve transit in the outer suburbs, service was terrible or even non-existent. For the last decade, transit has been gradually improving. The most hopeful sign is that people are using it, as this table illustrates. [11]

Table 8: Local Transit Ridership by Regions and Cities

	Riders 2006 transit (000)	Riders 2013 transit (000)	Change %	Per Capita Ridership 2011
Durham Region	6,942	10,626	+53.1%	17.5
York Region	17,108	22,709	+32.7%	22.0
Brampton	10,139	19,406	+91.4%	37.1
Mississauga	29,022	35,789	+23.3%	50.2
Hamilton	21,165	21,847	+3.1%	42.0
Toronto	444,544	528,000	+18.8%	189.2

There are a few obvious things that leap out of this table. One is the far greater use of transit by Torontonians than the residents of other cities. That is something we have known for a long time, but what is surprising is the growth of transit in the outer suburbs. This suggests that, if better service is delivered, ridership will grow. The question, then, is how to improve the service so that people get out of their cars. Again, the answer is rapid bus service in dedicated lanes along the arterial roads in suburbs taking riders to the GO train service and new rapid transit infrastructure that will be built in the future, like LRT.

Let's begin with York Region because they are building something that is remarkably like my suggestion for the inner suburbs. Along Highway 7, dedicated bus lanes are being built in the centre of the road that will connect Markham and Vaughan; later they will be extended west, all the way to Brampton. Another dedicated bus lane will be built along Yonge Street as far north as Newmarket. Both of these lines will connect with the Yonge Street subway, and the Highway 7 line will connect with the new extension of the University subway line that will terminate at Vaughan Metropolitan Centre.

Unfortunately, these high-speed buses will be powered by diesel, rather than electricity, a serious mistake in my opinion. In the long run, electric power will be less expensive, and the elimination of pollution from diesel buses will make electric buses worthwhile. Fortunately, these buses can be converted to electric in the future at a reasonable cost.

Today the York Viva system provides bus service east and west to suburban communities flanking Yonge Street. When those routes can be converted to high-speed buses on dedicated roadbeds then the more densely populated parts of York Region will have an effective, reliable transit system. The system will be almost as fast as commuting by car and much less expensive. Only then will large numbers of suburban commuters abandon their cars.

Peel Region is another matter. Mississauga and Brampton suffer more from traffic gridlock than any other part of the GTHA, and that will continue because development pressure is to the west of Toronto. Former mayor of Mississauga Hazel McCallion, in her own irascible way, claimed that she advocated improvements in public transit for twenty years. Now, she says, "Let's get on with it." But her support of low-density housing in the past contributed greatly to the problem.

The major transit solution for Peel and Halton Regions to the west, and Durham to the east of Toronto, is to improve the GO Lakeshore train service. In Peel, another GO line goes from Union Station, through Brampton to Georgetown and further west. Already GO has converted these lines to regular, all-day service, with the number of trains increased at rush hour.

As well, Metrolinx is planning improved local transit. The major project in Peel is an LRT line along Hurontario Street from Port Credit to Brampton, connecting with the GO rail stations at either end. Linked to this is a plan to transform Hurontario Street into a high-density avenue with shops and condominiums, replacing the strip malls and empty parking lots.

All this is to the good, but will it get people out of their cars? The populations of Peel and Halton are growing rapidly. For many it is a long way south to the Lakeshore line or north to the Brampton/Milton line. It will not be very convenient to drive down to a GO station, park, and then take the next train into Union Station.

A better option for many would be to give priority to a rapid transit route along Dundas or Burnhamthorpe that takes passengers to the Kipling or Islington TTC subway stations. That would be faster and more convenient for many commuters going into the city. The TTC system also gives a much broader choice in their final destination. Not everyone wants to go to Union Station in downtown Toronto.

But key to building a good transit system that serves the needs of the riders is to provide good service right into the suburban developments. The way to do that is fast bus service travelling in dedicated bus lanes, like I proposed for the suburbs of Toronto. Arterial roads mark the boundaries of these housing surveys. Those roads can be the way to move people down to the GO lines or to rapid transit along Dundas or Burnhamthorpe. Once that type of local transit exists, people can leave their cars at home.

When looking at the transit needs of the outer suburbs, it becomes clear that "The Big Move" plans alone will not get people out of their cars, and it will not solve the problem of gridlock. It is an important first step, but good transit has to reach well into the suburbs, and that means local governments must provide dependable, fast bus service along the arterial roads, and they will have to continue to provide subsidies out of tax revenue.

That will be difficult and expensive. Burlington, in Halton Region, is an example. Today only 2 percent of the city's commuters use the city's transit system and 90 percent of the seats on the buses are empty. The fare for adults, seniors, and students is $3.25. Only small children get a discount.[12] It will be a long time before Burlington will be able to pay for transit out of the fare box. York Region's Viva Transit System only recovers 38.9 percent of the operating costs out of the fare box, and the TTC only receives 72 percent of its operating costs from riders.

Building an effective transit system in the suburbs will be expensive, and it will take time. That is the price we will pay for low-density sprawl.

HAMILTON PROJECTS

Traffic is a problem in Hamilton but there are many who refuse to admit it. When I lived in the city in the late 1960s and early 1970s I was a young man and I owned a snappy new car that I was very fond of. First I lived near Stoney Creek in the east end of the city, and later I lived near the university in the West End. Often I would drive the twinned one-way streets of King and Main through the heart of the city. Like everyone, I found if I kept my speed at thirty-five miles per hour (we used miles not kilometres in those days) I could hit every green traffic light and sail along at a good, steady rate.

It took time, but eventually I came to understand that this one-way street system had done great harm to Hamilton. Rivers of cars were streaming through the older, downtown neighbourhoods, making the streets difficult to cross for those on foot, and bringing pollution. It was as if two slow-moving expressways had been built right through the centre of the city, cutting communities in two and isolating others. I would say to people, "What can we do about the one-way street system?" and they would look at me like I was crazy. Even my friends were not willing to recognize it was a problem. Today that has changed. Some of the one-way streets in Hamilton have been converted back to two-way streets, but the King–Main one-way pair remains, with all of its problems.

I had hoped that the Metrolinx plan for Hamilton would solve the one-way street system. It may, but it will take some time. The province has focused on integrating the city's transportation system into the GO Lakeshore train service in an effort to try and take Hamilton's commuters off the road. The city already has GO trains that operate out of the station on Hunter Street. A second station on James Street North offering all-day service will be opened in 2015. It will use the rail line in the city's North End. These trains will go east all the way to St. Catharines and Niagara Falls, stopping at important centres.

I talked with Bob Bratina, the former mayor of Hamilton,[13] and he expressed enthusiasm for the new GO train service. He told me that this has already spurred development in Hamilton's downtown, and he expects that it will do much more to improve the entire north end of the city.

Metrolinx has also proposed to build four LRT lines in Hamilton, but Bratina is much more cautious about supporting them. Hamilton is different than the municipalities in the outer suburbs. It is an older city, and has had public transit as long as Toronto, but traffic gridlock on the scale of Toronto simply does not exist. The current bus system works reasonably well and many people rely on it. Four LRT lines seems almost like an expensive extravagance given the size of the city and the lack of gridlock.

The one LRT line that will have the greatest impact is proposed to be built along Main and King Streets, from Eastgate Square, near Stoney Creek, through the heart of the old city all the way to McMaster University. It will cost between $875 million and $1 billion. "It will be the biggest investment in the history of the city," Bratina told me, a little in awe. It also could be a way of dealing with the one-way twins of King and Main Streets, if they are turned back into two-way streets, but there is no mention of that in the Metrolinx plan. That will be a decision left to Hamilton City Council.

Many planners, like Ken Greenberg, see LRT projects as a stimulus to redevelopment, but Bratina is much more cautious. "It could lead to rejuvenation, but I'm not convinced the rail line from the Eastgate [Square] to Wellington Street will do that. The bus is operating very well there, but in the west, through the downtown, it may well do that."

He read to me the conclusions of a McMaster University study. "LRT has the potential to work in Hamilton ... but it will be a long, challenging, and costly process."[14] That prediction is enough to make any politician cautious, even one as optimistic as Bob Bratina. "They are saying that congestion is the number one problem, but we don't have that, and we don't have people with the ability to pay. A guy in Hamilton, with a total family income of sixty or seventy thousand dollars, can drive anywhere with his old beater in twenty or thirty minutes."

I believe improved transit will have a long-term benefit to everyone in the GTHA, including Hamilton, but then I'm not a politician worrying about the guy driving around town in his old beater, who is having a hard time supporting his family and paying his property taxes. That's where the rubber hits the road.

THE MISSING DISINCENTIVES

My greatest fear about the implementation of "The Big Move" is that transit improvements will be built at great public expense, but people will still not be lured out of their cars to use the system. This would be like hosting a party, going to great expense to buy food and drink, and having no one show up. The new transit system will cost a huge amount of money, and if it solves none, or only some of the problems it will have been a waste of precious resources.

The numbers are sobering. We are more dependent on cars today than twenty years ago. Cars transport an average of 1.2 people during peak periods. Eighty-five percent of car drivers never consider public transit. Commute times are considerably less by car than by public transit when travelling outside of the downtown core.

Cars are convenient and comfortable, and despite the lengthening commute times, they remain an attractive way to get around, especially for people who live in low-density suburbs. The other side of the equation is that public transit can be a problem. I usually enjoy travelling by the subway or bus in Toronto, but my schedule allows me to arrange my time so that I use transit at non-peak times. Occasionally I travel during rush hour on the Yonge Street subway line, and I find a terrible crush. Squeezing into a subway car along with thousands of others is not fun.

As distasteful as politicians find it, I believe there must be disincentives if we are going to pry commuters out of their automobiles and into transit. Disincentives are not a new idea. We put taxes on alcohol and tobacco in an attempt to reduce consumption because they can be harmful to individuals and society. These taxes are an attempt to control behaviour through price. They do not work terribly well. Alcoholism remains a serious social problem, and people still use tobacco despite the taxes and the knowledge that smoking leads to serious health consequences. But we know that prohibition is even worse, because it has little effect on consumption and encourages crime. High taxes on these products are felt to be the best of the alternatives because it discourages consumption and still allows individual choice.

The best-known disincentive designed to discourage the use of cars is the Congestion Charge of London, England. Following the initiative of Mayor Ken Livingstone, London County Council passed legislation to place a charge on cars driving in the Financial District and the West End of the city, the most congested parts of London. When the charge was introduced in 2003, it cost ten pounds sterling to drive cars in the designated area. Today it is over eleven pounds. A discount for electric vehicles and hybrid cars was introduced to encourage the sale of cars that produce less air pollution. More recently the London Congestion Charge has been revised to take into account to engine emissions.

Livingstone proposed that the area included by the Congestion Charge be widened to the west. That was rejected when Boris Johnson was elected mayor, but the original area where the Congestion Charge applies has been maintained. The plan remains controversial but has considerable support from Londoners. It is estimated that the Congestion Charge has reduced traffic by 25 to 30 percent and improved air quality in the centre of the city. A few other large cities have adopted the system, including Stockholm,[15] Singapore, and Milan, along with a number of smaller centres. These cities have adopted congestion charges because they work.

As Edward Keenan, a columnist for the *Toronto Star* points out, "It's pretty clear looking around the world that only one thing works to reduce the amount of traffic on the roads: charging people to use them." He goes on to quote sources for this, including a RAND Corporation study. He also points out that none of the leading mayoral candidates in 2014 were in favour of tolls, and therefore, congestion will continue.[16]

Toronto could implement a plan such as this by placing tolls on the Gardiner Expressway and Don Valley Parkway because the city owns those expressways, and they are predominantly used by people from outside of the city. But it would be very difficult politically because car culture is so prevalent that any challenge to the right of people to drive on any road will be unpopular.

There are other alternatives that may be less controversial. Reducing the number of parking spots and increasing the cost of parking in areas of the city where we want to control the traffic would help to reduce cars. Closing streets, restricting traffic lanes, and encouraging — or banning — employers providing free parking for employees are all effective disincentives to driving, but nothing would be as effective as tolls, and that is what we should support.

THE CYCLING, WALKABLE CITY

If there is one area of public policy that reflects the poverty of politics of Toronto, it is cycling. Rob Ford despised cyclists and actually went so far as to cast blame on them when someone was killed on a bicycle. "Roads are for buses and cars. That's all," he said. The former mayor is not alone in his views. An online commentator wrote, "Bicycles should be treated as toys and kept off major streets." Mayor John Tory outlined what he called a "modest" network of bike lanes, but his lack of interest after the election speaks volumes.[17]

These attitudes have virtually brought the City of Toronto cycling program to a stop because suburban councillors are reluctant to support them. In 2001 a bike plan called for 495 kilometres of bikeways. Today, thirteen years later, only 114 kilometres have been installed.[18] Virtually all of those bike lanes are only white lines painted on the pavement. The only exception is Sherbourne Street, where a dedicated lane was constructed, but even that does not have a protected barrier between the lane and the street.

Part of the 2001 plan proposed to build protected bike lanes along Richmond and Adelaide Streets through central Toronto from Bathurst Street to Sherbourne. It was stubbornly resisted by suburban councillors, and only in 2014 is the plan being implemented. The protective barriers are little more than posts that collapse if hit by a car. It is difficult to get a bike lane approved in the downtown and practically impossible in the inner suburbs because the councillors from the suburbs see bikes and bike lanes as a challenge to cars. Toronto is the only city I know that has taken out a major bicycle lane, the one on Jarvis Street.

Jan Gehl, the Danish planner and architect who did so much to make Copenhagen and other cities bicycle-friendly, had this to say about cycling in this city: "Toronto is excellently suited for a high-quality bike system. It is relatively flat and reasonably well-connected in the old city. The streets are wide, so there's room for bike lanes. It would be a much more lively city, more sustainable, and more healthy." He also pointed out that what is needed is a complete system that links all of the lanes and makes travel on the lanes continuous.[19]

The painted lines on the pavement indicating a bike lane are little more than a suggested priority. I often ride my bike downtown, and it can be a frightening experience. Over and over again I have heard people say that they would cycle to work if there were protected, dedicated bike lanes. It is simply too scary to cycle on Toronto streets when there is no protection from speeding cars.

Toronto's short-sighted policy on bike lanes and cycling reflects how dominated we have become by an agenda driven by those who believe in cars. The use of bicycles and the promotion of walking in the city would help to solve traffic congestion in the city, not hinder it. These are the words of the City of Toronto's chief planner, Jennifer Keesmaat: "It's not a zero-sum game. When you take someone out of a car and onto a bike you've actually just freed up a tremendous amount of space in the street infrastructure."[20]

Fortunately, not all GTHA cities are following Toronto's lead. Hamilton is building an extensive system of bike lanes. Cannon Street has a two-way protected bike lane that goes right through the lower city and connects with a bike lane on York Street in the West End. There are lanes for cyclists on Hamilton Mountain and in the suburbs. The Clairmont Access and Sydenham Road in Dundas have cycling lanes up the Escarpment. The city is actively promoting cycling with copies of a map with the cycling routes, bike racks on the buses, and enclosed bike parking. This is a city that has enthusiastically taken to cycling.

Toronto is way behind other cities, and yet walking and cycling make up nearly one-third of all travel in the downtown. The numbers are on the rise. If some of the streets were reconfigured to provide protection to cyclists, and sidewalks were improved and widened, it would encourage even more people to walk and cycle every day.[21] This promotes a healthier lifestyle and a less-polluted city, while at the same time it helps to solve the problem of gridlock in the city.

That is what many other cities are doing. Copenhagen is the cycling capital of the planet, with 55 percent of commuters going to and from work and school by bicycle. The city is supported by a system of bike lanes that are given priority with specially designed cycling stop lights and snow removal. Copenhagen, before cycling was introduced, had streets with four lanes for cars, much like Toronto today. Two lanes were taken out on many streets, bike lanes were built, sidewalks widened, and trees and shrubs planted. There was opposition at first but now so many people travel by bicycle in Copenhagen it has helped to make traffic flow more easily. Parking has been removed, opening up squares, and streets for pedestrians, open air cafes, and other uses. Public support for cycling is at an all-time high.

Montreal and New York have aggressively expanded their bike lanes, and this is making a major contribution to the calming of traffic in those congested cities. Rahm Emanuel, the newly elected mayor of Chicago, has promised to build one hundred miles of protected bike lanes in his first four years of office. A bike lane will be within a one-half mile of every resident. It looks like he will fulfill that promise. Vancouver, a smaller city than Toronto, has more kilometres of bike lanes. They have adopted a plan to have 50 percent of commuter trips by bicycle by 2040 and are aggressively pushing ahead.

Metrolinx understands the importance of cycling and has proposed to build seven thousand kilometres of new bike lanes, trails, and pathways in the GTHA. Much of that is planned to be built in the outer suburbs where there is strong support for recreational cycling, but the real challenge is to build lanes in the densely populated parts of the city to encourage people to commute by bicycle.

The political climate in Toronto, dominated by councillors from the suburbs where the car is king, suggests that this is not going to happen unless there are changes to our political leadership.

TECHNOLOGY, INNOVATION, AND QUALITY OF LIFE

The Metrolinx plan relies on old technology. The conversion of the GO system to electric, and the upgrading of the Lakeshore and other railway lines will cost billions. LRT, subways, buses, and trains are all technologies that have been around for decades. New technologies are being developed and invented for public transit, but Metrolinx and the politicians have no interest in them

Vancouver, by contrast, promoted the SkyTrain, a system that uses a type of monorail technology developed by Bombardier, a Canadian company that is a leader in the field of public transit. Planners in Toronto universally seem to be opposed to this technology. Even Steve Munro, the most knowledgeable citizen critic of transit in Toronto, dislikes monorail. The only serious criticism that I heard in my talks with experts came from Ken Greenberg. He told me that he preferred LRT technology because it helped to bring life back onto the street.

Despite all this, there are some important features of monorail technology. The lines are considerably less expensive to build than subways because there is no tunnelling, but the trains can travel at comparable speeds. Monorail is an elevated system, the pillars are spaced apart, reducing costs, and the lines can be built along existing streets. Some capacity to handle traffic is lost on these streets, but that is compensated for by the trains carrying more passengers. The stations are more expensive to build than LRT stops. Passengers have to get up and down to the elevated line, but they are less expensive than subway stops. Like subways, the trains are non-polluting because they are run by electric power, and they have the added advantage that they do not require drivers. They are run safely and efficiently by computers.

When I visit Vancouver I enjoy riding on the SkyTrain. The rail lines wind through the city streets, and the trains provide good views of buildings in the downtown core and the suburbs. The mountains gleam off in the distance, the sea is not far away, and on the way out to the airport the monorail soars over the Fraser River. Toronto does not have the mountains, the Pacific Ocean, or a river the size of the Fraser, but there are some pretty spectacular sights in our city. A technology like this would help to showcase Toronto — better by far than the dingy views offered through a subway car window.

Transit should serve the practical purpose of moving people, but there can be other things to consider. In the early decades of the last century, Hamilton had two funicular, or incline, railways that went up the Escarpment from the downtown to the Mountain brow. The reason they were built was to move horses and wagons up the steep climb. Once cars and trucks came into use in the 1920s and 1930s, the use of the inclines declined and both were closed down.

But there was another reason for the incline railways. Visitors came to ride them and experience the spectacular sight of the city, its harbour, the Dundas Valley, Lake Ontario, and beyond. Tourism was a secondary reason for the inclines, but it did much to promote the city and it brought enjoyment to a lot of people.

Today, cities with mountains or hills are bringing back their funiculars. Niagara Falls has one for tourists. Quebec City has a spectacular funicular that gives sights of the Lower Town and the St. Lawrence River. There are several in Hong Kong, Europe, South America, and Mexico.

Tourism is a good reason to bring back the incline railways in Hamilton. Another is cycling. There are bike lanes that go up the mountain, but you have to be a strong rider to make the climb. An incline railway that could carry bicycles and had an enclosed compartment for people would be a wonderful addition to Hamilton's network of bicycle lanes.

An incline railway would promote the city and add to the convenience and enjoyment of cyclists. It would also be a way to encourage people to bike to work or school, and add to the quality of life of all Hamiltonians. I am not old enough to remember the old inclines, but when I lived in the city I would often hear older people brag about the wonderful Hamilton funicular railways. Reinstalling them might add a little to the tax bill, but think of the enjoyment it would bring.

And wouldn't it be nice if people in Toronto could stop constantly worrying about taxes and think for a moment about how we could build some infrastructure we could enjoy. What if a SkyTrain was built along Dundas Street from the western reaches of Mississauga, heading east, stopping at all of the arterial roads as it goes through Toronto, connecting with the Bloor–Danforth subway at the Junction, continuing east to downtown Toronto with stops at University, Yonge, and Jarvis, and then extending further east, past Parliament, over the Don River, connecting with Kingston Road at Woodbine, and then going all the way east through Scarborough, over the Rouge River to Pickering, Ajax, and Oshawa.

This type of plan sparks the imagination. We could call it the "Heritage Route," because Dundas Street and Kingston Road were the first of the old settler's roads laid out following the orders of Lord Simcoe well over two hundred years ago. Admittedly, it is a wild and extravagant scheme, and I am sure that the transit engineers and politicians would reject it out of hand, but if we are going to build a system that will be successful in transforming transportation, and convincing people to feel positive about public transportation, we have to begin to think in imaginative ways. That's what builds a great city.

A CULTURAL CHANGE

We have become so accustomed to car culture that we no longer see how our city streets and public spaces are dominated by vehicles and the problems that they bring. An American commented, "Driving to and from work in the United States is the most ritualized tasks performed by the largest number of U.S. citizens each day."[22] The same is true in Canada, particularly in the GTHA.

We have a deep attachment to our cars that goes well beyond convenience. To adapt ourselves to a city of transit, and reduce the number of cars, will require a change in our lifestyle as profound as those brought by the suburbs in the 1950s, but it can be done.

Cars, transit, cycling — these form the front line of the urban political battlefield in the GTHA. But there is a new consensus emerging in the cities of North America and Europe that says that we must rein in the use of private cars because they are bringing serious harm to our cities, the environment, and the health of our people.

The way to do this is now clear: vastly improved, low-cost transit, reducing traffic in densely populated parts of the city, protected bicycle lanes, and a improved pedestrian experience. These are items that are at the top of the New Urban Agenda. What could be more important than living in a pollution-free, safe, healthy, affordable city?

Good planning, many believe, is the sensible way to achieve these objectives, but as we shall see in the next chapter, it's not so easy.

FIVE

THE PROBLEMS WITH PLANNING

Land-use planning has been a hot political issue for decades. Back in the 1980s, when housing suburbs were being thrown up in Peel and York Regions at a furious rate, there was a type of cowboy capitalism controlled by hard-driving developers who made fortunes by buying both land and political influence and converting that combination into houses that they sold at high prices.

Today, the development industry has been transformed into a form of corporate capitalism. The companies have become professionalized, staffed by real estate lawyers, architects, and planners. But still the most important ingredients are land and political influence, and developers don't appreciate it if community members or politicians interfere with their plans. Like those that came before them, the developers have to bring money, organize political support, and take risks, but that can still be parlayed into millions.

In the last ten years the development industry has shifted away from building houses. Instead, the industry focuses on high-rise condo construction. Although there are a few exceptions, most of the projects are simply stacked housing units with retail at the ground level. There is little interest in sustainable development that looks to the future, or building affordable housing, or creating mixed-use developments. It's "buyer beware" in the world of condo housing.

The provincial government has legislated a planning system that is supposed to protect the public, the environment, and provide the type of housing we need. Various policies are in place, ranging from official plans to building codes. Approvals have to be sought from municipal governments, and a system of inspection is in place. The developers follow the rules (usually), but the public is still not getting the type of housing that it needs. There is virtually no new housing for low-income families, and the input of communities is largely ignored.

Problems with the developers continue, but it is more than that. There are serious problems with the political decision-making process around approvals. It's a complicated story with many different elements, but let's begin in Toronto, in the midst of the condo boom, where the pressures are the greatest. That way we can see how the planning system works — or doesn't work. Here are three examples of recent projects.

EXAMPLE 1: HOW BAYVIEW AND SHEPPARD GOT A MEGA-DEVELOPMENT

In 2005 Verdiroc Development Corporation, an associated company of the politically powerful Greenwin Construction Company, was given approval by the Toronto Planning Committee to build a 280-unit condominium on the north-east corner of Bayview and Sheppard. The approval was given only after broad public consultations and close examination by the politicians and the city planning department.

Verdiroc did not like this decision. The company appealed to the Committee of Adjustment, asking to increase the number of units to 481, an increase of 201 units. This application was turned down and Verdiroc appealed the decision to the Ontario Municipal Board (OMB).

Unless the application was opposed by the city, the OMB would automatically approve the expanded project. Councillor David Shiner, a supporter of the project and Verdiroc, made a strong representation at city council arguing that the city should not oppose the application and won the vote. As a result the OMB approved the increase of the project to 481 units, and Bayview and Sheppard got a mega-development.

EXAMPLE 2: TEN YORK STREET, DOWNTOWN TORONTO

Ten York Street is a huge new Tridel condo development in downtown Toronto that was proposed in 2013. It is a seventy-five-storey building, with 774 units ranging in size from one, two, and three bedrooms and 344 parking spaces.

The prices for the condos start at $345,000 and go up to $1 million. This is the promotional hype the developer uses to describe the project.

"Chic, timeless, sophisticated, Ten York is a glass vision in the sky.... The location of Ten York is enough to inspire wonder and awe all on its own. An architectural marvel, this statuesque beauty soars dramatically up from a triangular-shaped wedge alongside Toronto's major city artery."[1]

The project is in the heart of the downtown, a block from Queen's Quay and the waterfront, and a short walk to the Air Canada Centre and Union Station. The property is a narrow, triangular shape, isolated by very busy roads. It sits, literally, in the middle of the Gardiner Expressway. Immediately to the north are the elevated lanes of the expressway. To the south is an offramp that goes down to York Street. At ground level the north side of the property is defined by Lakeshore Boulevard and streams of traffic westbound, and on the south by Lakeshore with traffic heading eastbound. On the east is the busy arterial road of York Street. The Tridel website illustrations show no hint of the Gardiner.

I attended a community meeting held to discuss the project hosted by Tridel. Also at the meeting were Adam Vaughan (then the Toronto city councillor for the ward), city planning staff, and at least three hundred people who lived in the immediate area. The residents were concerned with the number of new people who would come to live in their neighbourhood and the traffic that they would generate, but it was the height of the building more than anything else that local residents asked questions about. Would the seventy-five storeys overshadow the other buildings in the neighbourhood and cause wind tunnels and loss of sunlight?

There were even alternative suggestions for the site made at the meeting. One young mother, with a child on her lap, said she thought the land should be used as a park for children. To me, that seemed the worst possible outcome. The air would be virtually toxic with all of the traffic, and to get to the park people, with children in tow, would have to cross lanes of heavy traffic.

The Tridel employees who attended the meeting, I am sure, were never concerned about the opposition of the residents. Toronto's Official Plan for the downtown and central waterfront designates it as a "regeneration area intended to provide for a broad mix of commercial, residential, light industrial, institutional and live-work uses." The building fit all of those criteria. More important, the zoning for the area has no height restrictions.

There were at least two other meetings where the public could voice their objections to the building, but nothing slowed down the approval process. Adam Vaughan attempted to get the developer to include office space in the building — in his view, the tall buildings downtown should be mixed use, with residents, work space, and retail in the ground floor. In that way, there would be twenty-four-hour life in the building and the surrounding streets. Tridel tried to include some office space, but I was told by one of Vaughan's staff that, "They couldn't get it to work."

Finally, after all of the discussion, the Toronto and East York Community Council gave approval to the building and that decision was ratified by city council. Construction is now underway.

EXAMPLE 3: THE MIRVISH/GEHRY DEVELOPMENT ON KING STREET WEST

David Mirvish is the son of the greatly admired Ed Mirvish, who created Honest Ed's, a truly iconic department store in Toronto. After making a fortune in the discount retail trade, Ed went into the theatre business. He bought the Royal Alexandra Theatre on King Street in 1963 and saved it from demolition. The theatre was refurbished and has become one of Toronto's, and Canada's, leading theatre venues. Later, Ed's son, David, joined him, and the two built a formidable live entertainment business.

As part of their business, over the years the Mirvish father and son bought property along King Street west of the Royal Alexandra Theatre. At the corner of John and King Streets they built the Princess of Wales Theatre. The Mirvishes brought Broadway-style theatre to Toronto and people were delighted. Ed died in 2007, but his son continues the business and now owns and operates four theatres in the city.

In September 2012 David Mirvish announced that he had engaged celebrity architect Frank Gehry to redevelop his King Street properties into a major new condominium project. Gehry had grown up in Toronto and trained as an architect at the University of Toronto. He moved to Los Angeles and became one of the world's leading architects, with projects in cities in several countries.

In the original proposal the Mirvish owned buildings on King Street would be demolished, including the Princess of Wales Theatre but not the Royal Alexandra. In their place, three condo towers would be constructed of 82,

84, and 86 storeys. Altogether, the project would have 2,700 condo units. It would have a six-storey mezzanine open to the public, which would house shops, a satellite campus for the Ontario College of Art and Design, and David Mirvish's private collection of modern art.

This massive new proposal for the entertainment district just west of the business district immediately attracted a mix of negative comments. The restaurant owners along King west of John were outspoken in their opposition. They said that the new towers would create wind tunnels and break sightlines. At a neighbourhood meeting to discuss the project that I attended, there was universal opposition. Residents cited traffic congestion, overcrowded streetcars, and the fear of an increase in property taxes. Some said the need was for affordable housing, not expensive condos for the wealthy.

David Mirvish spoke at the meeting saying in effect that the buildings, designed by the world famous architect, would bring prestige to the city, and his art collection would be a marvelous contribution to Toronto's culture. But the people at the meeting were not buying it. They didn't like the density and traffic that the buildings would bring, they objected to the height of the buildings, and they did not like the fundamental changes it would bring to their neighbourhood.

But Mirvish proceeded with his proposed development and applied to the city for the zoning changes. The city planning department, after studying the proposal, made it clear that they were opposed to important elements of the project. They said that the new buildings would not fit into the existing neighbourhood, and they were concerned that the project would demolish four designated heritage buildings. But it was density that the city found most objectionable. Jennifer Keesmaat, the city's chief planner, explained that the project was too dense, too tall, and, architecturally, the design was, "Trite.... We don't think we, as a city, have an obligation to absorb this much density."

But the Mirvish redevelopment of King Street had its defenders. Christopher Hume, the influential urban critic of the *Toronto Star*, wrote: "Keesmaat has succumbed to the same timidity that has kept Toronto from achieving greatness it so badly wants.... How sad that a city awash in countless nearly identical glass towers ... would fail to grasp a unique opportunity to do something truly remarkable, something that would turn heads around the world and help bring Toronto into the 21st century."[2] Later he wrote that Toronto lacks "boldness and imagination." It "squashes creativity and innovation and favours the same-old, same-old."[3]

The controversy took a twist when Adam Vaughan set up a fourteen-member working group to see if a compromise could be reached. After months of meetings, in May 2014 it was announced that the project had been substantially redesigned and reduced by 30 percent. Rather than three high-rise towers, it would have only two, 92, and 82 storeys. In the redesign, the Princess of Wales Theatre was saved, along with other buildings. Both Keesmaat and David Mirvish hailed the deal as a great improvement.

This project reflects a fascinating debate about the aesthetics of our buildings, density, height, public services, and the type of downtown that we are building. In the recent past, our arguments about cities focused on the destructive impact of suburban sprawl. Now the concern is about too much density. Sprawl results in the destruction of good farmland, traffic gridlock, and the inability to provide affordable services. Too much density, critics are saying, often leads to the demolition of old buildings, leads to congestion, and will overwhelm city services.

PLANNING — A TORONTO COUNCILLOR'S VIEW

Conflicts like this are going on between residents and developers across the GTHA, but the most intense and difficult are in downtown Toronto. We need new housing because more people are settling in the region. People want to live downtown; the developers are meeting this wish by providing high-rise condos, but local residents want to protect their neighbourhoods. The biggest unresolved question is: Are we getting the housing that we need? It is a classic conflict between people with different interests. At the centre of these controversies are local politicians.

Adam Vaughan is now the member of Parliament for Trinity–Spadina, but previously he was the city councillor for Ward 20 in the heart of downtown Toronto. When he was councillor he was one of the busiest people I knew, with a long list of development proposals that he was shepherding through the system. I have known Adam for many years and managed to get an interview with him in his city hall office not long before he announced his intention to run for Parliament. We talked at some length about the problems that he saw with the planning process as it is practised in Ward 20.

Adam knows a great deal about development and planning. His father practised as an architect in Toronto, and in the 1970s became a city councillor. Before Adam was elected, he was a media personality, commenting on city politics for local television channels. When he became a city councillor, he quickly became involved in ward politics. Ward 20 is a densely populated part of the city that stretches on either side of Spadina from the Waterfront to the Annex north of Bloor.

This is how he began to express his frustrations with the planning process: "The only thing I hate more than sprawl is density. Winner takes all. There is very little finesse. It's either horizontal sprawl or vertical sprawl. There is very little between the two extremes."[4] He went on, sharing his views on developers and municipal politicians:

> The development industry is the most powerful influence on local politics. It is not that they can buy elections and decisions, but they certainly can influence them and get candidates elected and so on.... And don't forget, the development industry is powerful in local elections, but it is also extraordinarily important in provincial elections.
>
> We often blame the developers and it's equally unfair to always blame the OMB but it is also unfair to always blame the politicians. The problem is that when you have blurred rules and accountability, the most powerful forces are the ones who get their way.

Still, Adam is a strong believer in good planning:

> If you do planning properly your budget problems start to disappear. It's when you do bad planning that these problems arise. Jane-Finch is a really badly planned neighbourhood, and the social consequences of that are high crime rates and all of the rest. Jane-Finch is landlocked. There are social outcomes, health outcomes. It is built in such a peculiar way that you don't actually have the density to put in higher order transit.... People need a car to do virtually everything and that undermines the chance for transit to work up there.
>
> If you build it differently, like the St. Lawrence Neighbourhood, that is an integrated community with integrated services and integrated transportation policies and an appropriate amount of density and an appropriate amount of recreational space, and

you have an appropriate educational component, that neighbourhood is self-sufficient and still low income. So good planning is the best way to solve the budget problems, and bad planning is the way to create them.

As a councillor, Vaughan was very active in trying to shape developments in Ward 20. The area has more development pressures than any other part of the city because it is in the downtown core. He was always kept busy tracking the development applications, meeting with residents, and negotiating with developers. Over time he developed innovations to help his constituents keep up with what was happening. Perhaps the most interesting was his system of online maps of the ward that provided detailed information on virtually every development in the approvals process.[5]

Public meetings with residents about developments were essential in the way that he did planning. He was there, he explained to me, to allow residents to voice their concerns and then to take those concerns to the developer and the city planning department to see if they could be resolved or accommodated in some way. In his view, he was not so much the advocate of the residents — although he often found himself in that role — as he was a facilitator, trying to find the best way to help fit the new building into the existing community. It was a role that took good political judgment and infinite patience.

One objective that he developed after he was first elected as a councillor was to build sustainable neighbourhoods for a mix of family types and a variety of incomes. That has not been easy. The developers make more money with small apartments because they can fit more units into the building, but the problem is that those types of developments lead to a mono-culture of residents, usually young singles. Vaughan is proud of the fact that since he was elected councillor more than one thousand two-bedroom units have been built in his ward.

Ken Greenberg, the architect-planner, strongly supports this type of mixed development. "Rather than building enormous buildings filled with tiny units for a transient population, we should be building larger units for families, including the working population. Housing for older people, young families — we should be creating neighbourhoods with diversity."

It is not surprising that when he ran for Parliament Vaughan said that his first priority in Ottawa was to create a good affordable housing program. Although he struggled to integrate new buildings into existing neighbourhoods, he had to cope with provincial and city land-use policies, developers who want to earn maximum profits, and residents who want their concerns heard. He is faced with pressures from all sides. His greatest frustration is with the OMB. These are his words:

> You don't get to finesse the final decision because of the OMB. That is the final layer of accountability and that is the test you are up against. You make bad decisions in an attempt to avoid the (development being referred to the) OMB or you make bad decisions because of the OMB.... As a result, we don't have a very sophisticated planning process. It delivers us a whole string of unintended consequences.

THE ONTARIO MUNICIPAL BOARD

If there was one universal opinion shared by the people I talked to about planning in the GTHA, it was unhappiness with the Ontario Municipal Board. They list a number of reasons.

One of the most frequently heard complaints is that the OMB is an unelected body that can overrule the decisions of elected politicians who are directly accountable to their constituents, and that is undemocratic. This is not exactly fair. The OMB is responsible to the provincial government, who are elected by the people of Ontario. But what the critics are saying is that land-use decisions, by their nature, are very controversial, and it should be local politicians, who are responsible directly to the people, who should be making planning decisions, not an unelected body like the OMB, insulated from the political controversy.

Another complaint I heard was that the OMB most frequently sides with developers, ignoring politicians and local governments. That is a serious accusation, and it would take considerable research to prove conclusively if it is true, but developers have deep pockets and the ability to hire the best legal firms in the province. Community groups, on the other hand, have to fund their own appeals. It's not an even playing field.

But the real problem with the OMB, and the one that Adam Vaughan was alluding to, is that planning in Ontario has become distorted because local politicians and municipal planning staff have to anticipate what could happen if the development is appealed to the OMB. Once that appeal is made, it is expensive for the city and very time consuming. More important, the developers negotiate knowing that if they do not get what they want from the politicians and planning department, they can always appeal to the OMB. That weakens those who are trying to protect public interests or create a planning system that is predictable.

This is what Ken Greenberg says:

> The OMB has set itself up as a planning board for Toronto. Basically with impunity, it overrules the city and makes up its own policy, and these are people who are not qualified. They're not elected. They're not accountable. It's gone away beyond what is reasonable.... We have a legal profession in this province that to my knowledge doesn't exist anywhere else. Batteries of lawyers in all the big law firms who don't appear in courts. They only appear at the OMB.
>
> What is more, preparing for an OMB hearing, and pursuing it is enormously expensive. This disempowers communities and it is a drain on city resources. As a result, city staff are reluctant to deal with things because they know they're not going to make the final decisions anyway. So what's the point?

Greenberg is in favour of dismantling the OMB and turning all of those powers over to the municipalities. He would like to see a system where the local government is required to write an official plan clearly designating where new development should go. The plan would stipulate, in detail, what should be allowed and what should not be allowed.

He points out that this is the way that land-use planning is done in every other major city in North America. It reduces the controversy and provides a stable, predictable environment for the residents. What is more, he says, this would be good for the development industry because it would provide predictability.

I talked to John Sewell, the former Toronto mayor, about this. He was the chair of the Royal Commission on Planning and Development Reform in Ontario and has strong opinions about planning. Like others, he does not like the existing system, but he believes we still need some type of appeal body for planning decisions. This is his solution:

> The easiest thing to do is to say to the OMB, look OMB, you have three functions and when someone comes to you — you have three decisions. One: is the development in conformity with the official plan? Secondly: is it in conformity with provincial policy? Thirdly: was the process relatively fair? If the answer to all three is yes then the project should be automatically approved. If the answer to any one of the three questions is no, then the project should not be approved and [it should be] turned back to the local municipality. That then makes the OMB a real appeal body.

City politicians have also become involved in this issue. On February 6, 2012, Toronto City Council voted 34 to 5 to petition the Ontario government to exempt Toronto from the Ontario Municipal Board. After that vote, Councillor Josh Matlow was quoted in the *Toronto Star* saying: "We've heard time and time again from our residents that there's an inequitable playing field.... Developers simply have a better chance at the OMB because they have the financial resources, the ability to get planners and lawyers, anything they need to be able to argue their case."[6]

Despite the widespread opposition to the OMB by municipal politicians, the Ontario government refuses to eliminate it, or even lessen its powers. One reason is the political power of the development industry, but another is that provincial leaders are concerned that development would be killed by "Not in My Back Yard" (NIMBY) local politicians if they had sole control over development approvals. To the province, any form of development is good, because it is economic growth. The most important issue a provincial government is judged on at election time is one how much economic growth they have produced.

THE OFFICIAL PLANS AND ZONING

Land-use planning, as the name suggests, implies making plans that will be in force over a long term, which will provide predictability and stability for neighbourhoods, and also give developers a guide to where new development will be allowed. In Ontario, municipalities are required to prepare official plans, and that, supposedly, is to provide their blueprint for the future.

You can find Toronto's Official Plan online,[7] and all of the other GTHA municipalities I have checked also have put their plans on their websites. Official plans are worth reading if you have interest in the shape of your local municipality. I say "shape" because the Toronto plan, which I have read, provides stirring statements and images, but the problem is that it lacks important details. These are some samples from the text:

> The Official Plan is about making the right choices and shaping Toronto's collective future. The plan is about getting the fundamentals right. It is about having a clear vision for the city — grounded in durable principles that assure a successful future....[8]
>
> The plan is about the big picture. It spells out a clear direction for Toronto. It is the road map to our future, providing the basis for building a city wide consensus around change.[9]

I like all of that. The words stir the blood and make you think of "the shining city on the hill," as Americans like to say, but the problem is that the Official Plan never gets much beyond those types of statements.

There are some things put in the plan to reassure the citizenry. It says, for example, that about 75 percent of the city's geographic area will not experience much growth in the next thirty years.[10] But what does that mean? Well over 50 percent of the land of Toronto is taken up by streets, ravines, and parks, and so is not threatened by redevelopment.

It is a lovely document, grounded by principles of diversity and opportunity, beauty, connectivity, and stewardship, but it is not very reassuring. In land-use planning, you want details. People need to know what will happen on their street, in their neighbourhood, and possibly on the main street where they do their shopping. That level of detail gives predictability and forces developers to conform. This Official Plan does not do that.

If you want to get beyond the general statement you have to look at zoning. As the city website says, "Zoning bylaws regulate the use, size, height, density and location of buildings on properties and affect every property in the city."[11] Toronto now has computerized all of the zoning bylaws and put them online. The program is a remarkable example of how complex, detailed information can be made available to the general public in an understandable way. The only problem is that in Ontario — particularly Toronto — zoning still does not give predictability.

"LET'S MAKE A DEAL PLANNING"

Let's assume that you are a homeowner and want to put an addition onto your house. Before you begin construction, you better find out what the zoning for your street allows. You also should check the other city building bylaws to make sure your plans do not violate them. If you know your plans are within the rules, have someone familiar with the process prepare some drawings, go down to city hall to apply for a building permit, and staple the permit to the wall for everyone to see. You are finally ready to begin construction. Oh, and before you begin you better talk to your neighbours and tell them what you are doing or you might find yourself with a stop work order because you violated some rule.

Small fry, like homeowners, violate zoning bylaws at their peril, but the rules do not apply to the big developers. An example gives the best illustration of how the system works.

The residents of St. Nicholas Street, a quiet, tree-lined street with elegant Victorian houses just off Yonge near Wellesley in downtown Toronto, opposed a high-rise development on their street. The developer's proposal was to tear down a former church property and build a forty-four-storey condominium.

The zoning for the neighbourhood was for single-family dwellings; the development was a gross violation of the zoning bylaw. The neighbours, believing the zoning would protect them, objected. They pointed out that not only was the project a violation of the zoning laws, it was completely incompatible with the character of the neighbourhood, and the increased densities would attract traffic and create parking problems. In their view it was a case where the development violated the principles of good planning.

Nevertheless, their objections made little difference in the final outcome of the project. The local councillor negotiated with the developer to reduce the height of the building from forty-four storeys to twenty-nine, along with other minor concessions. Calling it a victory, the councillor presented the project to city council. The project was approved and went ahead.

Many in the neighbourhood felt they had been betrayed and manipulated. They came to believe that the original height of forty-four storeys was proposed only so that the neighbours would feel their concerns were addressed when the developer reduced the height. They remain very unhappy but have no ability to change the decision.

The developer and the politician in this case used section 37 of the Ontario Planning Act to change the zoning on the property. Many new developments violate the existing zoning bylaws. The allowable height of the building is usually what needs to be amended, but it could be other details. In return for changing the zoning, benefits are received by the municipality from the developer, either in cash or "in kind," such as the creation of a public park, space in the new building for the public, or some other benefit.

This has led to a system where councillors negotiate with developers in private to increase the density of a proposed building. After the negotiations, a so called "compromise" is announced to the public as *fait accompli*. The new deal has to be ratified by city council, but that is not a problem. Toronto councillors rarely get involved in the local affairs of another councillor. A ward is viewed as a councillor's preserve — you stay out of my turf on planning issues and I'll stay out of yours is the rule at city hall.

The St. Nicholas Street development is only one example of, "Let's make a deal planning." In this case, the so-called benefit to the community was the reduction in height of the building, but in most cases the developer pays money or provides community amenities in return for increased densities. From 2004 to 2009, a total of 1.17 million square meters of "large" projects were approved in Ward 27. Under section 37 agreements, a total of $26,488,000 in cash was received by the city and an additional $11,700,904 in benefits from this ward alone.[12]

Some would argue this is good. The city always needs money and this is a way of improving community amenities, but it plays havoc with the planning system. The buildings do not conform to any vision for the city or the neighbourhood. Planning has become ad-hoc, at the whim of developers and individual councillors, and the residents are subject to whatever deal can be cobbled together. "Let's make a deal planning" defies the whole notion of planning. But the developers do not object to paying the money. Increased densities mean increased profits — enormous profits at that.

Ken Greenberg is very disturbed at this type of planning:

> We are getting applications for projects now that bear no relation-
> ship whatsoever to any plans that have been prepared over the
> years or any zoning. Big, ninety-eight-storey buildings. And so
> people don't have any confidence in who is shaping the city, and

what the priorities are at play. It seems that anything can happen on any given day, and this is not a healthy thing.

John Sewell expressed consternation when I brought section 37 amendments up with him:

> Cash for zoning! Councillors go into a room with the developers and come out with cash. And there are no rules! There are literally no rules about how much money you should be asking for. And the city councillors will tell you that. "There are no rules." Well why not? It's a total crap shoot and it looks as though the councillor is being bribed. Go into a private room with a developer and come out with money. What else would you think? And then that councillor decides where the money is going to be spent. It's shocking!

Certainly the city benefits from the money, and the local residents can use the amenities that are added to the project, but it is the optics, the lack of accountability or rules. More important, as Ken Greenberg points out, it leads to a lack of confidence in the planning system. The little guys have to follow the rules, and the big guys make their own rules.

ZONING AS FORCED CONFORMITY

Relatives of mine live in the East End of Toronto in a neighbourhood that has come to be called Little India. On warm, sunny weekends some residents of the neighbourhood spread wares to be sold out on their front lawns. It is a colourful sight, with sari textiles fluttering in the breeze, brass pots, and odd brick-a-brac. The sale of these objects is illegal because it violates the zoning bylaws.

I have worked at home since I started earning my living as a writer. It was a natural development that began when I was a student many years ago and had a desk in my bedroom; today I have converted a spare room in our house into a modest home office. The activity was not illegal when I was a student because it was a part-time activity, but now that I am a professional writer I wondered whether my home office violated the zoning bylaw. That's why I phoned the bylaw officer and enquired. The answer was not at all clear. It depended on the neighbourhood I lived in, and there were various other stipulations that I found confusing. I think I am okay, but I confess I am not entirely sure.

It is not that I worry that the bylaw officer will show up one day and demand that I shut down my cottage industry as a writer. All my neighbours know I work at home. If I was to ask, they would probably say it is good to have people around the neighbourhood 24/7, but I wonder if the merchants selling goods in Little India would be treated with the same toleration.

Zoning attempts to separate different types of uses of property. The most familiar zoning rules are the separation of industry, commercial, and residential buildings, but zoning is also used to restrict the height of buildings, setbacks, separation between buildings, and so on. One of the most controversial set of zoning bylaws in different GTHA municipalities is the ones dealing with basement apartments and rooming houses.

It is now legal to subdivide a house for a separate apartment, but it cannot contravene the building and fire codes. Rooming houses are legal in the former City of Toronto, but illegal in most of the inner suburbs. All of these rules are attempts by politicians to keep low-income residents out of neighbourhoods of single-family houses. Politicians justify the laws by saying that they are the result of safety concerns — and there is some truth in that — but more often they are a way to keep unwanted people out. It is a form of discrimination against the poor.

Some planners have advocated that we should get rid of all zoning restrictions altogether. When Barbara Hall was mayor of Toronto (1994–97) she took the lead in eliminating all zoning in areas of the city around King, Bathurst, and Spadina, and another area around King and Parliament. Actually, restrictions were kept on the height of buildings, but that was the only zoning restriction. The experiment came to be called "The Two Kings."

Ken Greenberg, who lives in one of these neighbourhoods, sees The Two Kings as an outstanding success. It has led to mixed-use communities where high-density residential living coexists with offices and other workspaces, and the streets host a great mix of retail. Some of the buildings were designed from the beginning to have floors of offices and floors of residential units. Greenberg points out that the simple change in the zoning bylaw has enriched the neighbourhood and led to a diversity of uses.

This is his succinct summary of zoning and what we should be attempting to achieve with these planning tools:

Zoning, which started off as a way of separating things, is gradually morphing into a way of connecting things. This corresponds with our better understanding of how cities work.... We should be zoning for diversity not separation.... We should be requiring a mix of living and working and shopping and other supporting institutions and amenities. That is what makes sustainable neighbourhoods.

PROVINCIAL POLICY STATEMENTS

During the Harris Conservative years there was very little interest in planning. If there was any restraint on the development industry it came from the municipalities, not the province, but with the election of the McGuinty government in 2003, land-use planning again became a priority for the province. Its approach has been to set down clear land-use policies designed to slow suburban sprawl and require the municipalities to follow them.

Two provincial policy statements are having a significant impact on the entire GTHA, particularly those municipalities in the outer suburbs that have greenfields (undeveloped land). The first policy, released in 2005, was the "The Greenbelt Plan." It was designed to protect environmentally sensitive land on the Oak Ridges Moraine and Niagara Escarpment from development.[13] It builds on policies developed by earlier governments and protects nearly two million acres of land. Some maintain that it has been a success, protecting farmland and woodlots across a vast area of southern Ontario, but others are more skeptical.

Many who know the area and the pattern of recent development in York and Peel Regions point out the greenbelt policy has forced development south of the Oak Ridges Moraine. This has done much to stop sprawl north of the city. It has also had the unintended consequence of increasing the cost of developable land across the GTHA. My own assessment is that this policy has been a great success. We need to protect agricultural land and geographic features like the Escarpment and the Moraine. Much of the drinking water of the GTHA comes from these areas. That alone is reason to protect them.

The second policy statement, called "Places to Grow," was released in June 2006. It encourages "intensification," requiring new development to have population densities of fifty people and jobs per hectare. A minimum of 40 percent of all new residential development must occur within the existing built-up area of the municipality, and greenfields development are to be complete communities supporting transit, bike paths, parks, and a mix of different types of housing, retail, and jobs. The policy advocates development around existing towns and cities, and that, in turn, will make it possible to provide affordable transit to those communities. It also requires that farmland be protected. [14]

The criticism of the Liberal government land-use policies is that they are great on the plans, but fail in implementation. Others say the plans do not go far enough. I talked to John Sewell about the policy statements and he was very critical:

> I think the government should lay down policy in which municipalities have to make land-use decisions.... I like the idea of the province setting out good clear policies. [The problem is] I happen to think it is not a good plan.... It should be much stronger, much tougher. When they announced it, they said this plan allows up to twenty-five or thirty years of traditional suburban growth. Come on! That's not intensification. [15]

Ken Greenberg has a mixed assessment of the policy:

> What is fascinating is that in all of the 905 communities there are initiatives around urbanization. From Mississauga to Markham to Vaughan to Burlington, you name it, there is a recognition that those places have to change.... The principles are the city becomes denser. It becomes more diverse in its uses, and I would include all forms of employment but also life-cycle housing. So housing [is available] for different income levels including the working population, housing for older people, and housing for young families. If you go out to the furthest fringes of urbanization in the GTHA, you will still find them building low-density, auto-dependent suburbs of the most unsustainable kind. I crudely say we are sucking and blowing at the same time....

Municipalities are key decision makers in the planning process. Provincial law requires them to make their decisions "consistent with" provincial policy. This is another big change. Before 2004 municipalities were only required to "have regard to" provincial policy. This sounds like a minor thing, but it has been very important. The province was signalling that they were going to play a much more important role in planning and municipalities would be required to follow provincial policy. Despite this, sprawl in the GTHA continues.

PLANNING AND THE PUBLIC DOMAIN

The major problem with the planning process, as it is practised in the GTHA, is that land-use planning serves the needs of the developers, not the public. In Ontario we have a development approvals system, not a planning system. Local councillors, city planners, and the public are forced to look at each new application in isolation, always with the concern that the OMB can overturn their decision.

But what about the new ideas that have emerged from "humanitarian planning," which emphasizes the importance of improving the public domain. In the GTHA there is little thought to these issues. We still ignore the lessons that have been learned. Ken Greenberg has thought a lot about this issue because it is the focus of his architectural and planning practice. This is how he describes it:

> This is all about balance between the public and private spheres. [In Toronto] we have one that is operating at very high intensity. That is the private sector, but we are starving the public sector [the public sphere of the city]. In Ottawa, Amsterdam, Calgary, Montreal, and Edmonton, where I have been working, there is an understanding that they have to transform the public sphere to make the city more inviting and more in tune with public needs. Here in Toronto we're still arguing about it.

This is a very telling critique of planning in Toronto, and I think it applies to the entire GTHA. Planning should be more than the approval of individual buildings. In other cities the emphasis is on planning public spaces. Times Square in New York City has been cut off to traffic. People amble along talking to friends in the centre of what used to be a busy street filled with traffic. Ottawa has had the Sparks Street Mall for decades. Vancouver has reserved a huge strip of land for walkers and cyclists along English Bay and False Creek.

Virtually every European city restricts traffic in the core and some cities have turned whole districts into car-free areas.

Toronto does have areas such as this. The Distillery District and Toronto Islands are both car free, but in both instances that is because of historical circumstances not good planning. Queen's Quay west of Bay Street is being reconfigured to restrict car traffic to two lanes and allow for walking and cycling paths. Waterfront Toronto has planned and paid for that, not the City of Toronto.

It is the private sector that is leading the movement to enhance downtown Toronto and that has led to some great designs. Many buildings have become semi-public spaces. The Eaton Centre is an example. It was built as a downtown shopping mall and is still owned by private companies, but it has been created as a space accessible to the public. From the day it opened it became one of Toronto's top tourist attractions, and even today it attracts one million people every week.

I like going to the Eaton Centre because I find the architecture attractive, and the throngs of people are always of interest. Of course, it is a place of commerce — "a temple of capitalism" as one of my friends calls it. The intent is to attract customers into the shops, but the successful, attractive public spaces in every city are dominated by shops, restaurants, markets, street vendors, and the like. That is what gives cities their life. The Eaton Centre is successful in melding the public and private.

Many of the new office buildings in the downtown core do the same. The large bank buildings along Bay Street and the PATH system that connects these and other buildings, are good examples. The upper floors of the buildings are private offices, but the ground and lower levels are semi-public spaces with a mix of shops, banking facilities, and food courts.

The reason why some buildings work well is that there is a happy convergence between the interests of the owners and the public. The owners want to get people inside their buildings to attract them to the shops, while people like myself want to enjoy the space. But unfortunately, that is not always the case. Often the interests of the public conflict with private interests, and in our society private ownership always trumps public need.

We need to rebalance the public and private spheres of our cities across the GTHA. In designing and evaluating buildings we have to look at more than whether the buildings will be an economic success for the developer. It is as if we have forgotten the big questions: How does the building fit into surrounding buildings and streets? Is it aesthetically pleasing, using interesting materials and design? How does it contribute to the local community and the city?

And good planning involves more than a focus on buildings. It includes a conscious design of public spaces — "the spaces between the buildings," to use Jan Gehl's phrase — so that they work for the people who use those spaces. The enhancement of our streets, the retail districts, and the neighbourhoods of our cities must become a major focus of the planning system.

MIXED-USE PLANNING

The developers have enormous control of the planning system, and if we want to shape the GTHA into the type of city that suits our needs, we have to take back control of planning. That is what is being done in other cities. The term used to describe this is mixed-use planning.

Vancouver is the one North American city where mixed-use planning is highly developed. It emerged because geography hemmed in the city between the mountains in the north, the U.S. border to the south, and the ocean to the west. Complicating this was the need to protect agricultural land and access to the water. Because of the scarcity of land, planning in Vancouver has long been a burning public issue.

Downtown Vancouver has become a densely built forest of high-rise buildings that include apartments, offices, work spaces, and retail. Affordable housing is an important component of the residential development as well as housing for families and single people. No expressways were built in the downtown because of the scarcity of land, and planners have always given priority to transit over private cars.

The planning system in Vancouver requires developers and planners to look at the entire population and try to create buildings and complexes that satisfy different interests and needs. It is not to say that all problems have been solved in Vancouver, but it is a type of planning that has led the city to be called the most livable on the continent. The GTHA would benefit enormously if mixed-use planning was adopted here.

The principle that planning of this type follows is that all developments should result in communities of diversity and variety. There should be housing, retail, and work space. They should have an affordable housing component with a mix of people of different incomes, ages, and family size. Services and even entertainment facilities should be designed into complexes. The site should be pedestrian- and cycling-friendly, and have access to parks, and good transit.

But change is coming. Waterfront Toronto has been following mixed use planning principles and will be creating new communities with greater diversity. The redevelopment of Regent Park and Alexandra Park will result in a great mix of income, family size, age, and ethnicity. Even the private sector is changing: Honest Ed's property at Bloor and Bathurst will be redeveloped following mixed use principles. It is no accident that it is being designed and built by an architect and developer who are both from Vancouver.

There is much that we should be concerned about with planning in Ontario and the GTHA. We have created a regulatory system and development industry that is market driven and concerned with the bottom line — profits of developers. The focus is on the approval of individual development applications, but there is little interest in the public domain, community, developing mixed-income housing, or building condos appropriate for families.

We are not building the housing we need at the prices we can afford. There is more than enough good housing for those with high incomes, but new housing for those with middle or low incomes is simply not being built. This is becoming a crisis that we ignore at our peril.

Our planning system, from official plans, section 37 applications, zoning, and appeals to the OMB, must be redesigned to create a more open, predictable system that can be clearly understood by the public. This does not mean that NIMBY movements will reign or development will be shut down. That is not happening in other cities where a more predictable system exists.

The public has the right to know what is going to be built in their community and they should be involved from the beginning, a new development when an application is filed for to the final construction phase, to ensure that the needs and ideas of the community are taken into account. Meaningful public participation, more than anything else, will ensure that we get good development. Unfortunately, that is not happening in the GTHA.

SIX

DEVELOPMENT AND THE GTHA CITIES

What most concerns me about the way we practise planning is that it results in new development that does not serve the needs of the people. In part this is a criticism of the developers. They have used their political power to protect and promote their interests, but their raison d'etre is to construct buildings, sell them off, make a profit, and move on to the next project. It is our responsibility — the responsibility of the public and the politicians we elect — to protect the public interest, and we have done an abysmally poor job at that.

Let's start this discussion by looking first at the record of the developers in both the past and today and then go on to look at each of the four types of cities in the GTHA in order to define what type of development we should be encouraging.

DEVELOPERS, APPROVALS, AND "THE BIG PIPE"

Before suburbanization took hold in the GTHA, it was small independent builders who provided most of the housing. A builder would buy a vacant lot, build a house, and then sell it to make a profit. Sometimes the future home-owner would buy a lot and then hire an architect and builder to build the house.

With suburbanization and the building of houses on a large scale, small builders were forced out of the business because they didn't have the resources and access to capital that they needed to carry large projects through to completion. Soon a small number of developers came to dominate the suburban housing market.

A good example was Bruce McLaughlin, who operated in Peel. He started as a house builder after the Second World War. Soon he became convinced that suburban development would spread west from Toronto and so he bought farmland along Highway 10, or Hurontario Street, in what is today Mississauga. He organized the money through Canada Mortgage and Housing Corporation (CMHC), hired professional help and workers, and built suburban houses on that land. It made him a millionaire many times over. McLaughlin showed that, while the ownership of land was essential for a successful developer, there was also much more to it. Getting the approvals to build was another necessity, and that meant a developer needed political influence.

It was in York Region that this system of depending on politics developed into a serious scandal. In 1988 Jock Ferguson and Dawn King, freelance journalists, published a series of articles about development in York Region in the *Globe and Mail* called "Behind the Boom."[1] Their articles revealed how a small number of developers of suburban houses became multi-millionaires with the help of municipal councillors and officials.

In York Region, approval to connect to sewers was an essential part of land development. Once that approval was granted, the others flowed in a matter of course. In York, that meant the land had to be granted the right to connect to the York–Durham Sewer Pipe, known locally as the "Big Pipe." As Ferguson and King described it, "In the world of the developer, a man without sewers is nothing."[2]

Decisions to connect to the Big Pipe in York Region were controlled by the local council and were hotly contested. An approval or rejection made all the difference, deciding whether the developer could make a fortune or end in bankruptcy. Developers had a number of costs before they could apply to connect to the Big Pipe. That meant they had to borrow the money to pay those costs. In the 1980s, interest rates were very high and the faster the loan could be paid off the more money could be made. Everything depended on getting the approvals as quickly as possible. As it turned out, some developers could get approvals much faster than others.

Ferguson and King showed that three developers were consistently successful in getting approvals for their land. They were Marco Muzzo, Alfredo De Gasperis, and Rudolph Bratty. They operated independently, but also as a type of syndicate to help each other. All three were smart, knowledgeable, hard-driving men who knew how to wield power to get what they wanted. Together they developed about twelve thousand acres in York Region in the 1970s and 1980s.

The three of them learned very quickly that the key to making money in the land development business was getting approval to hook up to the Big Pipe, and that took political influence. This is how a former developer and competitor described what happened: "I used to think [Muzzo, De Gasperis, and Bratty] were very smart to guess where the pipes were going. But I realized that where they buy their land is where the pipes will go."[3] These were men who had influence with those who made the decisions and those were the local politicians.

Gaining political influence was, and still is, a very important part of the development business. The three developers regularly wined and dined the politicians, engineers, planners, and anyone else who had influence over the approval process. They held regular poker games for those in the municipal departments, and, most importantly, they made generous campaign donations.

In time there were accusations of corruption. During a judicial enquiry into the construction industry in the early 1970s, Muzzo testified that paying bribes was standard practise in the industry, but claimed he never knew what he paid for. He was never convicted in the enquiry. Bratty and De Gasperis were never implicated in wrongdoing.[4]

The mayors received most of the attention because they controlled the staff and had influence with other councillors. Many of the pro-development councillors had their entire campaign expenses paid for by the developers or the companies that they controlled. (In 1988, the provincial government legislated a limit of $750 for contributors, but before that there was no limit.) Ferguson and King reported that some councillors had received envelopes stuffed with cash, and one municipal employee of the region received a loan of $80,000 that was never repaid.

And the members of the syndicate did not ignore the provincial politicians. In the early 1980s they gave substantial contributions to the Progressive Conservative Party, but in the 1987 election the Liberals were on the rise and the developers quickly switched their allegiance to the Liberal Party. In that election De Gasperis, Muzzo, Bratty, and their companies were by far the largest contributors to the Liberal Party, donating an astounding 71 percent of all the money that the provincial party received in the election.

The result was inevitable. The three received quick approvals to hook up to the Big Pipe and had their developments quickly approved by the councils. Lorna Jackson, then the mayor of Vaughan, told the reporters that she was offered bribes by developers twice. Some on her council were guided by the following principles: "One — what's good for me. Two — what's good for my friends, and three — what's bad for my enemies."[5] The public good was not part of the equation.

There were police investigations in Vaughan, but the province refused to get involved. The rumours of scandal hurt the Peterson Liberal government and contributed to the election of the Bob Rae NDP government in 1990, but even then nothing was done. The onset of the recession in the early 1990s hurt the development industry across the province, but the members of the syndicate continued to prosper. Now they have passed from the scene, but their children continue of be active in the land development business.

The development industry remains a powerful force in virtually every municipality, and they are extremely influential with the provincial government. That continues to this day.

PROBLEMS WITH THE DEVELOPERS — YET AGAIN

For all of the excitement about the new lifestyle that is emerging in downtown Toronto, all is not nirvana in the world of condominiums. Although many of the high-rises are less than ten years old, the complaints are mounting.

The price of the new units is the biggest concern. Some say the high rate of profits of the developers is driving up the price, but others say that it is strong demand that is responsible. The number of individuals and young couples seeking out the downtown Toronto lifestyle is one reason. Offshore money is also contributing to high prices. Money from Europe, the Middle East, and the Far East is flowing into the city to buy condos. These investors see owning property in a secure country like Canada as a sound investment, but it is driving up prices.

The developers, of course, love the high prices, but that is putting condos out of the reach of low- and even middle-income individuals, couples, and families. The other concern is the fear that a housing bubble is being created that could burst at any time, much like the housing crisis that made a major contribution to the 2008 recession in the United States. The federal government has tried to moderate the price increases by requiring a higher down payment, but prices continue to drift upwards.

Shoddy workmanship is another complaint: windows that leak, burst plumbing, poorly installed drywall, and so on. Many units were built very quickly by developers and contractors who want the job done as inexpensively as possible. It is no wonder that there are serious problems, but it is the new condo owners who have to pay the costs, not the developers or contractors.

Legal agreements are yet another problem. The contracts between the developers and the buyers are highly technical, and all but a few lawyers specializing in real estate understand the problems. The aim of the developers who hired the lawyers to write the contracts is to reduce their liability and shift the costs and future problems onto the purchasers.

Many buyers complain about the closing dates because they were caught making a down payment on the understanding that occupancy was a certain date, only to find out that the building isn't completed on time and they have to wait months before they can move into their condo. The legal agreements give them no ability to seek compensation.

There is yet another set of problems that in the long-term will prove more serious than any of the others. Virtually all of the new buildings are unsustainable. Energy costs for heat and cooling of the buildings will continue to rise and some buildings will deteriorate quickly. This is a consequence of the design of the buildings and the materials used.

The most serious concern is with the glass buildings. They make spectacular looking towers. From the outside they gleam in the sunlight and inside are floor-to-ceiling glass walls that give remarkable views. As a selling feature, these have proved to be irresistible to many buyers, but as a construction technique they are fraught with problems. This is the estimation of Adam Vaughan, who was a Toronto councillor representing a downtown Toronto ward when he made this comment.

> A forty-five storey building is extremely inefficient, especially the glass buildings. In forty years, when the skin of that building wears out, fixing that building is a very expensive proposition. And with a group of absentee [condo] owners and low-income owners, the capacity of a condo board to fix those buildings is impossible.

> People are just going to walk away from them. Reskinning the
> building is what you have to do. And you have energy problems.
> You have to re-engineer the building to use low energy.

Energy is a particular problem with the glass buildings because they are like greenhouses. They trap the heat, which pushes up the costs of air conditioning. Heating is another problem. Even thermal pane windows cannot stop cold from migrating into the building. Most of the condos have balconies. Again that is an important sales feature. The floor of the balcony is concrete that extends into the condo and becomes the floor. In winter those concrete balconies conduct cold into the unit.

None of these things are of concern to the developers. After they sell the units, the problems with building design, energy inefficiencies, and poor workmanship become the problems of the condo owners. What the developers are concerned about is creating a building whose units will sell as quickly as possible. There are environmental buildings codes, but little enforcement. What will happen to the glass buildings is anyone's guess. Maybe they will be reconstructed or maybe, as Adam Vaughan suggests, the condo owners will simply walk away from them because the energy costs and the cost of re-skinning the building are prohibitive.

Until recently there have been few rental buildings built in the GTHA. Condos are preferred by the buyers because they give the buyers equity, but the real reason they are built is that this type of a financial arrangement gives a huge advantage to the developers. A comparison between a rental building and a condo illustrates the point.

A rental building has to be financed entirely by the developer. A huge mortgage has to be arranged to cover the costs of the land, design, and construction. That means the developer will be deep in debt before the building earns one dime. The risk is considerable.

Condominiums are financed in a much different way. The developers put up money to buy the land, get the architectural drawings completed, and work through the approvals process. That money is certainly at risk, but after the early process is completed they begin selling the condos. Once they have enough sales to cover the costs, construction begins. Developers are using the purchaser's money to cover the most expensive stage of the project, and that reduces their costs and risks enormously.

But this type of arrangement does one other thing for the developer. Once the building is completed, the developer has covered all of its costs and made a profit. There are some remaining obligations, but essentially it is finished with the building and can move on to the next project. In a rental building, on the other hand, it will be years before the developer gets all of its money back, and it has the added problems of dealing with the tenants.

More than one expert told me that the quality of new rental buildings is much better than that of condos. The reason? The developer plans to stay as the owner of the rental building for a long period of time so it ensures good building techniques are used that produce energy efficient buildings. That will help keep costs low in the future. The builders of condos don't care. That's someone else's problem. They have made their profit and moved on.

Today in the high-rise development business the political problem of approvals is not as important as it once was in York Region, but politics still shapes the industry. The planning system has been designed to favour developers, as we have seen, and efforts to change the Condominium Act to strengthen the rights of buyers has been resisted by the provincial Liberal government.[6] We need better regulation and enforcement of things like the building code and much better protection for consumers. Will that happen? Developers still have enormous political influence at both the provincial and municipal levels.

Let's look at development and planning issues in the four cities of the GTHA. Only then can we understand the planning priorities of the New Urban Agenda.

DOWNTOWN TORONTO

Because of the intensity of development, the problems of shoddy workmanship and energy inefficient buildings are particularly acute in the downtown. But there are another set of planning issues that are often ignored. They have to do with the public domain, and the responsibility for that does not rest with the developers, but with the city.

Enhancing the public domain will take a long time to implement. It took forty years to transform Copenhagen, and it will be just as long in Toronto. But change must come. These are some ideas: Major shopping streets could be closed to traffic, allowing access only to pedestrians, transit, and delivery vans.

Restaurants, shops, and bars could take over parts of the sidewalk. On certain days, some streets could become open-air farmers' markets. An extensive system of protected bike lanes will be designed throughout the downtown and extending into the suburbs. Public art could migrate out of the museums and onto the street. Alleys could be turned into walking streets. Heritage buildings could be given much stronger protection from demolition and the city can encourage developers to use new, innovative designs and building materials.

There are any number of exciting new ideas that can be developed to turn downtown Toronto into an attractive centre for people. It is not only the streets and back alleys that will be refashioned, but the look of the buildings, and the use of interesting materials will enhance the city in the future. We have begun to learn that design is tremendously important in the process to transform our city, and we have some of the most gifted designers in the continent living and working right here, but it will not be easy, as Kristyn Wong Tam, the councillor for Ward 27, found out.

Not long after she was elected in 2010, she proposed converting parts of Yonge Street in the downtown into two lanes for traffic, widening the sidewalks, and providing space for shops to show their wares, and tables for restaurants and cafes. Her plan was immediately attacked by then-Mayor Rob Ford and his supporters because it would slow traffic. It was politics that caused the problem here. The councillor compromised and the narrowing of the street was permitted only during a summer festival, but the issue is not settled.

This was one of the opening skirmishes in the struggle to take back the public domain in the downtown, but it won't be the last. I predict this will be one of the defining political issues of the next decades. The people who will make it happen will be the new generation coming to make their home in the downtown. They will understand that we need a city for people, not cars.

INNER SUBURBS

Today there is little development in the inner suburbs, and those buildings that are going up, such as those on Yonge Street, and Sheppard, are expensive and geared to those with high incomes. About thirty thousand new immigrants a year are settling in the inner suburbs and the housing that they can afford is very limited. Very little affordable rental housing is being built in the city, and the programs to rehabilitate the existing high-rises are totally inadequate. That spells a serious crisis on the horizon.

This is the failure of our development industry and the policies that shape it. We are not building the housing needed by the people. The developers defend themselves by saying that, with building costs, they cannot construct condos or apartments at a price that those with low incomes can afford. From what I know of the industry, I think they are right. The politicians don't even bother to defend themselves, and the rest of us simply ignore the problem. As a consequence, things are getting worse — much worse.

Past waves of immigrants that settled in Toronto lived close to the downtown, because that was where they could find inexpensive housing. Jews settled along Spadina, Poles and Ukrainians in the West End, the Italians and Portuguese along College Street. Soon they established synagogues and churches. Specialty shops sprang up. Communities were created where the newcomers could find people with the same language, background, and culture as their own. All of that helped them feel at home and eased their problems of integrating into a new society. Today, it is more difficult for immigrants living in the isolated high-rise towers of the inner suburbs. There are few supportive networks for them in the surrounding communities. Even our bylaws conspire against them.

Amanda Kwan recently wrote an article in the *Globe and Mail* that included this description:

> On a stretch of Kipling Avenue between Finch and Steeles there are 19 postwar apartment buildings on the east side of the street forming a superblock of concrete towers. "If each tower has 1,000 people, just on average, that's 19,000 people," says Pritanti Patel, who lives in one of the high-rises. "But none of them has a medical clinic." That's because these apartment neighbourhoods are zoned only for residential uses.[7]

Not only are there no medical clinics, there are no grocery stores, drug stores, or clothing shops. Residents have to travel blocks just to buy a loaf of bread, though most of them would not want the white bread that is the favourite of many Canadians. These buildings are filled with new immigrants; people of very diverse backgrounds. The buildings are packed with children and most families do not own cars. The neighbourhood has become a trap for those who live there, and all because of zoning bylaws. Fortunately, as Amanda Kwan points out in her article, this is about to change. Planners and politicians have come to understand that this type of zoning is simply not appropriate and must be adapted to meet the needs of the new residents.

These high-rises and the vast suburbs of single family houses suffer from a lack of focus. They need to be redesigned to create hubs, or village centres, with shops, public services, offices, and other places of work. Rigid zoning has isolated people in the suburbs by creating acres and acres of housing. Retail, often big box stores, is concentrated along highways or arterial streets, and then there are separate areas for offices and factories. Our suburbs need to be transformed so they become more like diverse towns, with a central core of shops and services where people can walk to do their shopping and schools nearby so that children can walk or ride their bikes.

It is American planners like Andrés Duany and Elizabeth Plater-Zyberk who advocate these types of changes.[8] They have been very critical of the suburb, pointing out that car dependency is so complete in these communities that every adult needs one just to do the simplest of tasks. Even the children are completely dependent on cars because they need adults to drive them. Toronto's inner suburbs, with their high level of low-income immigrants who cannot afford cars, have produced isolation for whole communities.

Variety and diversity are needed in all neighbourhoods. That is what makes for a healthy, vibrant lifestyle. Again, it will take time to transform our suburbs, but as new development is planned, like affordable housing, there will be opportunities to redesign the suburbs and make them much better places to live.

OUTER SUBURBS

When cities in the outer suburbs like Mississauga, Brampton, Vaughan, Markham, and Pickering were taking shape, development was driven by demand for single-family houses. Hazel McCallion, the long-time mayor of Mississauga, was called the "Queen of Sprawl" because she was a strong supporter of suburbs. In 1985, Lorna Jackson, then the mayor of Vaughan, told the *Star*, "The general consensus is to allow mainly single-family dwellings. We want low-density and so do the ratepayers."[9] That was a typical view of that time.

But now that desire for low-density suburban sprawl has come to haunt these communities. The vast acres of suburban housing with no community centres, shops, and gathering places have created places with no focus. People are more affluent, but the isolation may even be worse because transit is very inadequate. Costs are rising rapidly. Municipalities have discovered that it is very expensive to service low-density housing and property taxes are on the rise.

For years, Hazel McCallion bragged that taxes were low in Mississauga, and her city had no debt. That was true, but the reason was not good management, as she was suggesting. It was because the city charged high development fees and they were used to keep taxes low. Today, Mississauga is completely built out and development fees have almost disappeared. Now the city has high taxes relative to Toronto, and they are bound to go up. This is the great contradiction of the suburbs. The residents want low-density communities, but they also want good services and low taxation. It is impossible to have all three. The very sprawling nature of the suburbs makes it costly for the municipalities to provide good services.

However, there is one possible answer to this conundrum. If some of the property in the suburbs can be redeveloped into high-density buildings, with condos, retail, and offices, they will bring in development fees and higher property taxes. Those buildings are much less expensive to service. Those revenues, then, can be used to lower taxes for the homeowners. The irony is that people moved to the suburbs to get away from the city, but now they want to intensify and become much more like the city.

Today, all of the suburban municipalities in the GTHA are bent on attracting these types of developments, and they are having some success. In Markham, developers have built a series of mid-rise condominiums and row-houses west of Unionville GO station. Commercial developments with shops, movie theatres, restaurants, and other amenities are being built in the complex that will bring activity and a sense of community to the complex. A large area north of Highway 407 is designated as high-density housing with shops and other amenities.[10]

Vaughan is developing a new city centre near highways 400 and 7. It will have a TTC subway stop. The plan is to create a network of streets with "multi-use office towers, residences, open green space and urban squares, pedestrian shopping areas and restaurants, along with walking and cycling paths. All coexisting with some of the most technologically advanced sustainable buildings in the world."[11] Or at least this is the promise that is on the City of Vaughan official website. The plan even calls for "affordable housing units in these new developments to ensure the area attracts a demographic mix."[12]

The City of Mississauga, as usual, is unique in the ambition and scope of its plans. In the last decade of her reign as mayor, Hazel McCallion became the defender of high-density urban redevelopment. Once she demanded the construction of highways and expressways so people could commute to work. In the last few years she became a promoter of transit. Even Hazel had learned that low-density sprawl was unsustainable and policies had to change.

This proposal to transform the outer suburbs into cities with both low-density suburbs and high-density concentrations of condos, offices, and retail was driven in part by costs, but it also reflects a change in tastes. Just as people coming to live in the condos in downtown Toronto wanted the high-density urban experience, many people across the outer suburbs want a similar type of housing, only they preferred to live outside the city.

It is this change in how people want to live that is transforming all of the cities in the outer suburbs, and the movement is just beginning. It will only be successful if the new development provides housing for all income groups, and the only way that can happen is if there is an effective affordable housing program developed by senior levels of government.

I believe that in time this type of housing can lead to a transformation of the suburbs into affordable, mixed-use communities with densities that vary from high-density enclaves of high-rises to low-density suburbs. It is still early to predict, but it could prove to be as important for the GTHA as the redevelopment of downtown Toronto.

Mississauga City Centre is the best example of the new city that the political leaders hope to build. In 2010 a new plan was adopted to build a high-density community south of Square One, with hotels, condos, offices, and shops that will be the new heart of the city. The emphasis will be given to create walkable streets with restricted traffic. The area will be serviced by LRT.

There are other opportunities in Mississauga. Along Hurontario Street, Metrolinx will be constructing an LRT line that connects to GO trains. Mississauga planners hope that will lead to a complete transformation, changing Hurontario from a street lined with strip malls, gas stations, and shopping plazas into a high-density avenue lined with shops, low-rise apartments, and offices. On Lake Ontario, two hundred acres of land will be redeveloped into a mixed community with access to the water and the Waterfront Trail. Dundas Street will ultimately be redeveloped with an LRT that links into the TTC subway at Kipling Station, and the hope is that it will lead to the transformation of that street.

Ken Greenberg, the planner, has done work in Mississauga and remains optimistic that this municipality, once the Canadian model of suburban sprawl, can be transformed. This is what he told me:

> What's so interesting in these transformations is that the greatest weaknesses become the greatest opportunities. And so the parking lots will gradually turn into city blocks with mixed-use development and an ever increasing amount of mix. For the office developers now, the attraction is to be in a mixed-use neighbourhood. To attract and retain employees, they don't want a parking lot in the middle of nowhere. They want to go out to a restaurant or a café. They want to pick something up on the way home, they want daycare, they want to be part of a neighbourhood.

GREENFIELDS DEVELOPMENT IN THE OUTER SUBURBS

When the province first announced the "Places to Grow" policy statement, they still allowed for some low-density suburban development.[13] This was done to blunt criticism from developers and suburban councillors. The question now is should there be any more greenfields development allowed in the GTHA? These are the points in this controversy.

Durham councillors voted in favour of developing 2,192 hectares of land for housing. The plans would have violated the provincial government's greenbelt legislation and guidelines on density. Only Steve Parish, the mayor of Ajax, voted against this proposal. In the end, the Ontario Cabinet rejected Durham's plan for the development,[14] but this issue is not resolved. Members of Durham council are still determined to develop the land.

Markham developers speculated on two thousand hectares of agricultural land north of the city and immediately south of the greenbelt. The developers wanted Markham City Council to designate this land for urban development. A group of local citizens called "Environmental Defense" opposed the designation. They argued that this "food belt" land would be lost permanently to urban sprawl. They gathered the support of environmentalists like David

Suzuki and took a poll of Markham residents that found 83 percent of the people supported the food belt and opposed the development. Markham council, however, voted to designate the land for development. This issue is not over. Accusations are mounting that some councillors had voted on the motion but should have declared a conflict of interest.[15]

The City of Vaughan, in York Region, is engaged in a controversial issue over a new official plan that would allow development on rural agricultural land. A group of citizens called "Sustainable Vaughan" are opposing the suburban expansion arguing that there must be a major discussion in the city about urban sprawl before council makes a decision. They say that Vaughan should be intensifying all new development because a new subway and high-speed dedicated bus lanes are on the way.[16]

Even in the northern part of York Region, near Lake Simcoe, demands for development have appeared. Georgina's Official Plan suggests the community should grow by thirty thousand people and Sutton is proposing a one thousand home subdivision. Both of these projects are on land that is included in the greenbelt, but are exempt from protection.[17] It is unclear whether the province will allow these developments to go ahead.

Much of the development pressure in the GTHA is still to the west of the City of Toronto. All of the land in Mississauga has been developed, but there are some greenfields left in Brampton. It is the northern part of Halton Region where the development pressure is greatest. Milton is the fastest-growing town in Canada. According to the 2001 census, it had a population of 31,471, and by 2012 the town clerk estimated the population to be 95,000 people, a three-fold increase in eleven years.

The Town of Milton has done everything right. It has followed the "Places to Grow" provincial guidelines. The new developments have higher densities than the old suburbs, but the homes are built on greenfields and they sprawl across beautiful countryside within sight of Rattlesnake Point, a high promontory on the Niagara Escarpment.

All of these possible greenfields developments beg the question: do we need them? The market is shifting away from suburban housing to high-rises. Certainly there is a lack of affordable housing and condos and apartments for families, but that does not mean that pristine farmland should be converted into suburban houses. The evidence is in. Sprawl is unaffordable and leads to an unsustainable lifestyle and should not be supported.

HAMILTON

There have never been the development pressures in Hamilton that Toronto and its suburban communities have experienced. House prices remain more reasonable. The MLS average price for houses in Hamilton in September 2014 was $411,579, compared to $563,000 Toronto in June of the same year. [18] Rental accommodation is also considerably less expensive. A number of young people have moved to the city to take advantage of the affordable housing.

Affordability is one of the great strengths of Hamilton. That, along with the unionized wages of the industrial work force, has meant that the city remains more prosperous than many other centres in the GTHA. But there still is a high level of poverty, particularly in the downtown.

Many new homes have been built in the satellite suburbs of Dundas, Ancaster, and Stoney Creek. Building around existing town centres that had a core of retail stores and other services has given these suburbs a ready-made sense of community. That contrasts sharply with the outer suburbs around Toronto, where the housing projects were often built in empty farmers' fields, with arterial roads marking the boundaries. Much of this vast suburban sprawl around Toronto still suffers from a lack of community, while the Hamilton suburbs are much better integrated with the existing towns and the city.

Like Toronto, all of Wentworth County was amalgamated by the Harris Conservatives in 2001 into one municipality called the City of Hamilton. There was considerable opposition to this by residents of Dundas, but it has not led to the type of dysfunctional government that Toronto has experienced. I talked to former mayor Bob Bratina about this and he conceded there were problems:

> Small towns like Carlisle and others are huge rural areas and then there is this intense urban area of Hamilton. Some people have no wish to ever go to downtown Hamilton, but we have worked it out.
>
> There was a serious tax problem where council was split. The rural areas said that they did not have the services and were paying for the services of the downtown.... In the end they voted unanimously because the councillors knew that they had to compromise and they did.... The Ivor Wynne Stadium issue was another deeply divisive issue, but in the end they voted unanimously for it.

There are different reasons why Hamilton is able to find consensus while Toronto remains deeply divided — the city is smaller and does not have the pressure-cooker big city politics of Toronto, but it may be simply the personalities of the leaders. Bob Bratina is an inclusive type of politician who consults with others while Toronto politics has become polarizing and confrontational.

One thing that Bratina shares with his predecessors, going back at least as far as former mayor Vic Copps, is concern about the deterioration of the downtown. Copps tried to solve it with a huge urban renewal project in the city core that only compounded the problems, and increased the decay. Bratina dreams of high-rise development in the downtown and some development is already happening. Like a good promoter, he is always talking up the advantages of the downtown of his city:

> If we can put a building on all of those empty lots downtown, it will relieve the tax burden of everyone.
>
> I told the homebuilders, "Why don't you build in the downtown because there are no development charges." And they say, "Oh, nobody wants to live there." A year later I go back with the same speech and there are condos being built.
>
> Builders think there is no demand downtown but every time a builder gets a lot in the North End [traditionally a poor part of the city] and puts up a house, it's sold. If you drive around in the North End you will see all of this infill. They are sold before they are finished.
>
> I asked the fire chief, "How many more firemen do you need if we put more people downtown in condo towers?" and he said "None." But if you build a new suburb you have to build a new fire hall and put six more guys in it. When you build downtown all the services are there. All you have to do is plug them in.

There are a number of encouraging things about Hamilton that make it distinct and auger well for its future. The low cost of housing makes the city much more affordable than any other city in the GTHA. The existing GO train service as well as the new service that will be opening on James Street North will make Hamilton a much more attractive place for people looking for reasonable housing in the region. And there are strong indications that developers are interested in the city centre.

The city has a number of older neighbourhoods with fine, late nineteenth- and early twentieth-century houses. In Toronto these gems would have been snapped up in the gentrification movement, but in Hamilton they remain the homes of people with modest incomes. A number of people from Toronto and other GTHA centres have moved to Hamilton to take advantage of the housing.

The most interesting recent development in Hamilton has been the art scene. The city still has a distinctly blue collar, working-class feel about it. In my view, that is one of its charms. But a number of years ago artists began to settle in the city's North End along James Street North, an old section of the downtown that was experiencing decay. The artists rented or bought vacant stores or buildings on James Street that they used as studio space or art galleries. Restaurants catering to the health food crowd opened along with an artist's co-op. The old residents welcomed them or watched with interest.

At some point someone came up with the idea of a Friday night art crawl. It includes galleries, restaurants, and ends in the pubs and local taverns. Often the discussions spill out onto the street. Soon murals appeared on empty walls. There were talks about art and people worked on computer graphics. Others were attracted and the number of artists grew.

The city saw what was happening and encouraged the movement by blocking off James Street North on nights of the art crawl. Then they licenced street vendors, serving not the usual hot dogs that you will find in Toronto but more exotic food. An art scene had emerged on Hamilton's working-class streets and the city now proudly boasts about it. That is a sign of a healthy city.

This is no small thing. The low cost of housing, studio, and store space was the catalyst that helped to create a new, vibrant industry that is employing young people and providing support for an alternative way of living. The artists did it themselves, but the city encouraged the movement and that was a very important element of its success. There are many places in the GTHA that would benefit from understanding this experience.

Hamilton's great opportunity is in the transformation of its downtown. The art movement has begun the needed changes, but what it really needs is more people living downtown. The conversion of the Royal Connaught Hotel into condos is a beginning, but much more housing in downtown is needed. If the province and federal governments establish a good affordable housing program, and if Hamilton City Council insists that the new housing be located in the downtown, it will encourage other private-sector development. This will give life to the core of the city that is essential if it is going to change.

Then the possibilities will become exciting for Hamilton. Gore Park has some unique buildings that date from the middle of the nineteenth century. If they were renovated with an eye to historical restoration, it would create a distinctive shopping area. There are many old neighbourhoods in the city. The North End is a wonderful working-class community, not unlike Toronto's Cabbagetown before it was gentrified. The waterfront is being transformed into a series of parks, and when the waters of Burlington Bay are cleaned up, and become swimmable again, the city will have reinvented itself.

I believe that Hamilton holds great promise. With the Mountain, the bay, Lake Ontario, access to the Niagara Peninsula, the Escarpment, and Dundas Valley, it has the most spectacular location of any city in Southern Ontario. It also has a strong mixed economy, and its housing is affordable. Much of this has been achieved because it has been able to avoid the problems of the big city. The question remains, however, whether Steel Town can go the next step to become sustainable.

THE OPPORTUNITY TO REBUILD OUR CITY

This review of development in the GTHA points out many problems but the one thing it reveals is that our most pressing problem is the lack of affordable housing. This is something we can change.

Some will see a development program as a burden — another cost that they will have to pay for out of their tax dollars. I see it as the greatest opportunity that we have to transform our city into a truly wonderful place to live, with strong integrated neighbourhoods that meet the needs of everyone. It is one item that is essential in the New Urban Agenda.

SEVEN

AFFORDABLE HOUSING AND REBUILDING THE CITY

In this country housing is thought to be the preserve of the private sector. The development industry is expected to deliver the housing that we need while municipalities regulate the industry for the benefit of the public. That is how it is supposed to work, except it fails miserably to provide affordable housing for people most at risk, those with low or middle incomes.

Other developed countries face the same problem, and they have responded by implementing government-led housing programs to benefit those who need help. Canada has done that in the past, but since 1995, twenty years ago, Canada and Ontario have not had an affordable housing program. Today, we are the only developed country in the world that does not have comprehensive housing policies, and many are suffering as a result.

I believe we can have a housing program that meets the needs of low- and middle-income people. It will take good planning, and some seed funding from government, but it can be largely self-funded. The benefits of such a program will be enormous. Not only can we provide good housing for a lot of people, but it will help to transform the GTHA into a sustainable city by increasing densities, making transit and other services more cost-effective and efficient, and help hundreds of thousands of individuals and families.

Who knows, it might even bring some moderation to the bloated prices of the housing market.

PAST AFFORDABLE HOUSING PROGRAMS

The only way to understand today's affordable housing crisis is to appreciate something of the history of housing in this country. During the Great Depression in the 1930s and the Second World War there was virtually no new housing constructed in Canada. In the Depression few people could afford to buy houses; during the war the government did not allow private housing to be built because all effort had to focus on fighting the war. By 1945, with the return of the soldiers from overseas, hundreds of thousands of people across the country had no place to live. The Canadian and provincial governments became involved in a variety of programs to stimulate the building of housing.

By far the most important of the government programs was through the federal government agency Canada Mortgage and Housing Corporation (CMHC).[1] Money was made available at low interest rates to developers and contractors to build houses. That was a key part of the stimulus that created suburbs across Canada. Later, money was made available to build high-rise apartment buildings, and, as a result, today we have scores of apartments in the inner suburbs that provide much of the affordable housing stock of the city.

Part of the CMHC program was targeted at low-income families. Public housing projects exclusively for poor people were built across the country. In Ontario the first and still the largest of these projects was Regent Park, built in late 1940s in the heart of Cabbagetown in downtown Toronto. In time many such projects were built across the province. It was not long before the problems of public housing became apparent. This is housing expert Michael Shapcott's explanation: "When Regent Park was originally built it replaced a horrible, abysmal slum…. It was only later that we realized that the social segregation that was created in that environment was a recipe for disaster for that neighbourhood."

Poverty rates of people living in the projects were so high that public housing came to be seen as ghettos of the poor, with high concentrations of social problems like crime, delinquency, unemployment, high youth school drop-out rates, alcohol and drug problems, and so on. The social stigma of living in projects like Regent Park added to the problem and made it hard for all residents, particularly young people, to break out of the poverty cycle. Critics came to call the program a form of warehousing the poor.

The negative reputation of this type of public housing is one of the reasons why it has been so difficult to establish an effective affordable housing program in Ontario. Politicians did not want to be seen as supporting public housing because of the failures and criticisms. What is forgotten is that coming out of this experience was the creation of one of the most innovative housing programs not only in Canada but across the developed world.

In the 1970s, with the support of New Democrats, the Liberal federal government helped to establish housing co-operatives and non-profit housing, sponsored by churches, unions, and other community groups. The provinces joined in the program and helped with the funding.

The federal government provided start-up funding through CMHC. As part of the requirements, the co-ops and non-profits agreed that a percentage of the units — usually between 15 and 20 percent — would be reserved for low-income residents and the rest would be rented at market value. The low-income residents would live in the buildings like everyone else, with the same rights as other residents, but they received a subsidy in a program called rent-geared-to-income. This helped provide stable funding to the project and it gave the low-income families the means to live in these new projects.

This program created more than 500,000 co-op and non-profit homes across the country, housing more than 1.5 million Canadians, 200,000 of whom were low-income residents. Much of that housing was built in big cities because that was where there was need. Toronto and Hamilton got their share. The residents were accepted by existing communities, the buildings were well administered, and the level of satisfaction of the residents has been high.

But government priorities change. The Brian Mulroney Conservative government (1984–1993) cut back finances to the program and the Chretién Liberals terminated the program completely when they came to power. Some provinces tried to carry on the program. In Ontario the housing program continued a little longer. The Liberal Peterson and NDP Rae governments in the late 1980s and early 1990s provided money for social housing. The Bob Rae government, in fact, increased the money available for affordable housing despite the recession.

When the Mike Harris Conservatives were elected in 1995 one of the first things they did was to kill the affordable housing program. Those buildings that were under construction were allowed to be completed, but all others were cancelled. Like the federal government, Ontario still does not have a policy to stimulate the building of affordable housing.

The Harris government did one other thing in the area of housing that has been very difficult for cities. They downloaded the cost of social housing onto the municipalities, but provided no funds to pay for them. There was a huge outcry from municipal leaders. Hazel McCallion and Mel Lastman led the attack, but it went nowhere. Harris was not going to back down.

This affected virtually all large municipalities in Ontario, but Toronto, because it was the largest and had the most social housing, suffered the most. Today the city administers ninety thousand social housing units. There are repeated news accounts that many buildings and units are in decrepit condition because there is little money for repairs. Despite this, today there are 165,723 people on the waiting list for social housing, most of them seniors and single-parent families. These are people desperately in need of affordable housing and rent-geared-to-income support because rents for private sector housing are so high.[2]

Every year, municipal leaders gather under the banner of the Federation of Canadian Municipalities and pass resolutions urging the federal government to create an effective affordable housing program. They know the need, and yet nothing is done. The reason is politics. The Stephen Harper Conservatives are believers in free enterprise and are not in favour of government-led affordable housing programs. But the lack of a housing program cannot be attributed entirely to a right-wing political agenda. There have been a number of failures of urban programs. Public housing is one and urban renewal is another. Even the co-op housing program has met criticism because only 20 percent of the people in the buildings are low income, but despite all of the failures, the lack of affordable housing grows and the need for a good program is more urgent.

THE HOUSING CRISIS

After the cancellation of the federal affordable housing programs, the housing industry in Ontario switched from building rental apartments to condominiums. In the last fifteen years, less than 10 percent of new construction has been for rental housing in Canada, according to Steve Pomeroy, an Ottawa housing expert.[3] This may be changing. News reports in 2015 say some developers intend to build rental housing, but it will take years before they are built and the new rental will be expensive, not the affordable housing we need.

There are essentially two different types of housing rental markets in Toronto:

one for those with low-incomes in the inner suburbs and the other for the high-end of the market, primarily in the downtown. In October 2013 CMHC published a comprehensive report on rental housing in the Toronto-Centred Region. They found a vacancy rate of 1.7 percent. It is difficult to find an average cost because there are so many different variables — from location, to amenities, to apartment size — but what is interesting is that the average cost had increased by 3.1 percent. That is higher than the rate of inflation.[4] Many experts believe that the cost of rents will go up in the future because of the shrinking number of rental units. According to the study "Where's Home?" published by the Ontario Non-Profit Housing Association, Ontario lost 86,000 rental dwellings between 1996 and 2006, either because they were converted to ownership or redeveloped.[5] The non-profit group concludes, "Growing competition for limited rental units will drive up rents, making it even harder for low- and moderate-income renters."

This is the summary of the affordable housing crisis by the United Way of Toronto called "Vertical Poverty":

> For years, the construction of new private-sector housing has been targeted almost exclusively at better-off families. Only limited numbers of new non-profit units have been built since the mid-1990s. There has been a significant loss of rental housing units, especially at the lower, more affordable end of the market, due to gentrification and other changes in property use. And the rising costs of owning a house have made the privately-owned high-rise rental stock a major source of relatively affordable housing for the city's low and moderate-income households. Families gravitate to the inner suburban high-rises because they are increasingly all that they can afford in the city.[6]

This report listed a number of serious problems faced by people that lived in the high-rise buildings in the inner suburbs. Many of the older rental buildings across the GTHA are now over fifty years old and in need of repair and renovation. They are expensive to heat in the winter and cool in the summer. Over the next few years it will be essential to renovate many of these buildings to keep them livable, if they are to be retained as rental housing stock.

A common complaint is that elevators break down on a regular basis. People with disabilities, the old, and families with young children are virtually trapped in the upper floors of these aging buildings when this happens. "Disrepair in units is rife.... Infestations of pests and vermin are common.... Nearly 20 percent said their buildings were beset with multiple kinds of pests and vermin. Drug dealing, vandalism, drunkenness and rowdiness are epidemic in some buildings."[7]

Essentially, low-income individuals and families have been abandoned by all levels of government in Canada to find their own housing in an increasingly competitive market. Meanwhile, those same governments provide huge benefits to people who own their own homes. There are first-time homeowner grants, and by far the biggest benefit is that capital gains tax is waived when people sell their principal residence. This is a gift of billions of dollars every year to upper-income home owners. Low-income renters even subsidize the property taxes of home owners. Rental apartment buildings are taxed at a rate three times higher than owner property.

A March 2001 Statistics Canada study revealed that in 1999 the median net worth (or assets) of homeowners was $248,400, but for renters was only $3,300. I do not know of a more up-to-date study that compares the assets of homeowners to renters, but a study in January 2013 found the average household net worth of all Canadians now tops $400,000. "About half of household net worth is attributed to real estate values."[8]

Affordable housing is one of those social issues that refuses go away. That's why I went off to talk to the housing expert Michael Shapcott hoping to find some answers. As a young man Shapcott helped to develop co-operative housing in Toronto, and today he works for the Wellesley Institute, one of the Toronto non-profit, non-partisan think tanks that provides research and policy advice to governments and the private sector.

In our wide-ranging discussion Shapcott emphasized the importance of politics when it comes to solutions for housing. Only the federal and provincial governments have the funds to deliver the programs that are needed. The private sector cannot be expected to subsidize rents, and municipalities simply do not have the money.

Politics may be central in the issue of affordable housing, but the social costs affect people and communities. These are some comments that Michael Shapcott shared with me:

> To me, housing is a right but it is also a basic need, and communities suffer when there is no affordable housing available because it means that they cannot attract workers, it contributes to poverty, and so on. We are a fantastically wealthy country, but the money is not going

where it's needed.... The majority of Torontonians want to live in a city that is more caring, but we don't know how to do that.

Our problem [the problem of housing advocates] is that we don't have a champion. We don't have political momentum around housing. We have a bunch of initiatives that are kicking around and for me that is a recipe for political disaster.... There is no political leadership that would allow for a united voice on housing issues.

I think municipal governments in the GTHA are well positioned to be the broker ... but they basically have deferred to the private development market, and private developers, not surprisingly, are interested in working on projects that have the fastest possible return. Putting resources into the neighbourhoods, into the hands of the people who can mobilize those resources and get stuff done. That's what we need.

Affordable housing is one of the most pressing problems that we face, and there is little doubt that it is linked to that other problem that simply will not go away in this wealthy country of ours: poverty. If we are going to begin to address social problems, good housing that is affordable to all people must be part of the New Urban Agenda.

As Michael Shapcott pointed out, only senior governments have the resources to deal with this problem, but politicians shy away from it because they have been badly burned by failed housing programs in the past. However, there have been government-led public/private partnerships that have been brilliant successes. They provide models of innovative ways to improve our cities and at the same time provide good affordable housing. What follows are three examples.

THE ST. LAWRENCE NEIGHBOURHOOD

The St. Lawrence Neighbourhood, east of Jarvis and south of Front Streets, is in the oldest part of Toronto, settled soon after Lord Simcoe named this wilderness outpost the capital of Upper Canada. By the 1960s it had become a deteriorated industrial area, with many of the buildings at the point of serious decay. Despite this, David Crombie and the group of planners he had assembled in the planning department decided to turn it into a residential area after he became mayor.

Virtually all of the land in the neighbourhood was owned by the city or could be acquired for a low price; this made the redevelopment project considerably easier. The new development was designed to avoid the mistakes of urban renewal, then the policy favoured by planners. The concept was to turn the area into a mixed-income neighbourhood with some assisted housing, co-ops, market housing, shops, schools, parks, and a community recreation centre.

Michael Shapcott, the housing advocate I talked to, was involved in this project. He told me, "The key to its success was to get the co-ops and the non-profits in there first. That made it into a mixed-income neighbourhood." Afterward, developers were attracted to build market housing along with shops and other amenities. From its inception this was to be a public/private project. The public, in this case the city, owned the land and did the design of the neighbourhood. Private developers constructed the buildings and sold off or managed the private sector part of the project.

Today, the St. Lawrence neighbourhood is viewed as an outstanding success and has become a model for designers, architects, and planners from across North America. The project avoided the problems seen in so many suburbs devoted to one particular type of housing. What makes it interesting is the social mix. People of different income levels, ages, ethnicities, races, and religions live side by side in harmony. The housing is a mix of low rise apartments and town houses. Shops, restaurants, and public amenities like a library, a theatre venue, and schools, all coexist happily. Employment opportunities exist in the community and close by. Even today, three decades after construction, it remains a place filled with children and activity. A real functioning community has emerged with pride in neighbourhood, and support mechanisms for young people, new immigrants, and those in need.

What also made the St. Lawrence neighbourhood a success was the financing. Initially, public money went into building affordable housing, but much of those costs were recouped by the sale of land to private developers. They were attracted to land close to downtown sold at a reasonable price. It was this public/private combination that contributed to its success.

The contrast between the family-oriented St. Lawrence neighbourhood and the single, one-bedroom developments in the rest of downtown is striking. The St. Lawrence neighbourhood is one of the few mixed communities of great cultural diversity in the downtown core.

WATERFRONT TORONTO

Another example of a successful public/private partnership is Waterfront Toronto. It is the largest redevelopment project in North America and promises to transform the waterfront and ultimately change the city and its downtown.[9]

The area under redevelopment extends from Coxwell Avenue in the east to Ontario Place in the west. The largest piece of the property that will be redeveloped is near the mouth of the Don River in the old industrial area called the Port Lands. Altogether, there are about eight hundred hectares of land in the Waterfront project, roughly the size of the downtown core of the city. Much of this land is brownfields, mostly vacant industrial land. Its greatest attraction is the fact that the land is on the shores of Toronto Harbour and close to the downtown, but for redevelopment, its greatest feature is that virtually all of the land is publically owned.

For decades there was discussion about what to do with these lands. Some wanted to continue to reserve it for industry, but as time went on it became clear that industrial companies were not going to build factories in the heart of the city. Some private developers were interested in the land, but the investment needed for infrastructure was so great that none of them could take on a project of this size — in many cases the soil was badly polluted and major investments would have to be made to clean it up. Infrastructure such as transit, roads, sewers, and water had to be built, and a project this size needed parks and other amenities. It became obvious that only government had the resources to redevelop a parcel of land of this size.

Public/private partnerships have been done in other cities of North America and there are many more example in Europe, but any project of this kind has real risks for governments and politicians. It takes time to redevelop the property and a large initial investment in planning and infrastructure is required before there are any returns. What if the voters turned against it before it was completed? But waterfront land in downtown Toronto had huge advantages, and even hard-headed analysis showed the benefits overshadowed the risks.

Toronto is seeing an influx of population and people need places to live. Because of its location, future Waterfront residents and employees could rely on transit. That would help reduce traffic gridlock and make the city more sustainable. A project of this size would provide the opportunity, and the money for new parks and recreational facilities. But the most compelling reason for the government involvement was that redevelopment would bring new tax revenue. This was especially important for the City of Toronto, dependent on property tax.

Because of the nature of Canadian politics it takes a lot to convince all three levels of government to act in concert, but finally in 2001 the governments of Canada and Ontario along with the City of Toronto came together to announce that they would co-operate in redeveloping the waterfront. They created a corporate structure that came ultimately to be called Waterfront Toronto. Each of the levels of government donated $500 million as seed money and contributed the land they owned in the area. At that time it was projected that the private sector would ultimately invest $30 billion in building 40,000 residential units that would house 100,000 people; 30,000 or more full-time jobs would be created along with 300 hectares of park open to the public.

It has now been fourteen years since that announcement, and if there has been one criticism it is that the project is taking a very long time to come to fruition. Those in the business are not surprised; delays are inevitable in redevelopment projects of this size and complexity. The detailed planning has gone ahead stage by stage. When plans come close to completion, Waterfront Toronto hosts public presentations. Local residents and people who will live or work in the buildings are brought together to add their voices and criticisms. That in turn leads to revisions of the plans. The level of public participation is one of the most remarkable elements of the project, and that has helped to make the planning process a co-operative effort rather than one filled with conflict.

The plan from the start was that Waterfront redevelopment would result in mixed-use communities, with good transit, spectacular parks, and other public amenities. There has been concern that the affordable housing component might be ignored because the housing was too expensive to develop. In October 2013 it was announced that between seventy and seventy-five units in a condo project called Bayside would be bought by the city for affordable rental housing.[10] Rob Ford, then the mayor, criticized this, saying that poor people shouldn't live in expensive Waterfront housing, but in the end the progressives prevailed.

It still appears that the vast majority of the project will be new housing for upper- and middle-income individuals and families. It will remain unaffordable to people with low incomes, other than a small number who win the lottery and get one of the affordable rental units. This is a public project, created by public money, and yet very few of those most in need will be able to take advantage of it. At least 20 percent of the units in the Waterfront should be affordable.

The Waterfront project is interesting not only because it will ultimately transform brownfields into useful, productive land again. There will be outstanding architecture, new technology, and the development of parks and public facilities, but unfortunately the project will do little to solve the affordable housing problems in Toronto.

REGENT PARK REDEVELOPMENT

If there was one neighbourhood in Toronto mired in problems in past decades, it was Regent Park, a huge public housing project. By the new millennium not only were there seemingly intractable social problems, even the buildings were deteriorating.

In the early 2000s, a group interested in city issues began to discuss how to redevelop the community. The key players in the redevelopment project became Toronto Community Housing, which administer the land and the public housing units, and the Daniels Development Group, a development company active in the Toronto housing market. They became leaders because they had a role to play in the redevelopment, but the new project also had strong support from key Toronto city councillors and that made a vital difference.

The opportunity that those involved saw was that Regent Park had relatively low population densities in comparison to the downtown and surrounding neighbourhoods. A plan was developed to demolish the existing buildings and replace them with a mix of high-rise and attached housing. Much of the new housing would be sold or rented, but those who were to be displaced would be moved to other buildings by Toronto Community Housing and had the right to return to Regent Park once it was redeveloped.

In the plan, 2,083 rent-geared-to-income units would be demolished and replaced with as many new units. Another 5,400 units would be built as condos and sold at market prices. This would increase the densities and provide the opportunity to build retail space and add new amenities. This includes a park, three new connecting roads, a new aquatic centre, athletic grounds, and an arts and cultural centre that came to be called the Daniels Spectrum, after the developer who made so much of this happen.

The project was designed to be self-sustaining and revenue neutral for the city. Toronto provided start-up funds. Conventional mortgages were arranged for the planning and construction phases and this money was recovered as the condo units were sold. The city would benefit in different ways. The money that was invested in the project would be returned relatively quickly, the city would get taxes on the market condo units, and the redevelopment helped to solve the problems of a community in need.

In 2005, Phase 1 of the Regent Park project began and the final completion date of Phase 5 is 2019. Already, the neighbourhood has been transformed. Some of the original tenants have returned and are living in brand new units; a number of new condo owners have also moved in, and the various athletic and cultural facilities are being used by people who live in the complex and surrounding neighbourhoods.

But this is just the beginning of transforming public housing units in the City of Toronto. There are now twelve Toronto Community Housing redevelopment projects underway in the city, and they all are following the public/private model that was pioneered in Regent Park. Demolition of buildings in Alexandra Park has begun and reconstruction has started. Work has begun in Lawrence Heights. All of the construction will replace the rent-geared-to-income units with new apartments and, in addition, there will be condos sold at market, increased densities, retail, and improved services and amenities.[11]

Other sustainability features will be built into the projects. This is part of the description of the design features of Lawrence Heights. "Greening will create an interconnected green network for the neighbourhood, linking parks, streets and open spaces together while creating an urban canopy."[12]

PUBLIC/PRIVATE PARTNERSHIPS

All of the projects described are public/private partnerships and that is the key to their success. If we are going to solve the affordable housing crisis and begin to transform our city, public/private partnerships are the way to do it. Only governments have the resources to provide start-up funding; that initial outlay can be recouped once the new condos are marketed. Financing the rest of the project can be raised from private sources like banks and other lenders.

For municipalities this is the way to transform deteriorating neighbourhoods and create development on underutilized land. It will increase densities, make municipal services more affordable and efficient, and provide new mixed neighbourhoods for families, seniors, people with a range of income, immigrants, minority groups, and those with special needs. The costs for the city will be recouped, and as a benefit, the tax revenue from the property will increase considerably once it is redeveloped.

For developers there will be real benefits as well. They will not have to risk their money to acquire the property, create the design, and go through the approvals process. That will be the responsibility of the city or public agency created to manage the project. The developers will make their profit in the construction of the building and selling or managing the market units.

This is how it can work:

- The public agency will be the proponent and driver of the project. That ensures that the public interests are primary.

- The agency will acquire the land, create the design for the new community or building, and select the private sector partner. This money will be recouped as the mortgages are raised.

- The private sector company will raise the money, build the project, rent or sell the condos at market prices, and manage the retail and other elements of the project.

- The public agency will select the tenants and manage the subsidy program. The percentage of subsidized residents could vary but something between 20 and 30 percent should be the goal.

Rent-geared-to-income is the best way to provide financial assistance to those who need help in projects such as this because it is flexible. Let's assume an immigrant family that has recently arrived in this country needs assistance. At first they may require a full rent subsidy, but as members of the family get jobs the subsidy would drop to the point where, hopefully, they are paying full market rent. Maybe at that point they may want to move out of the project to make the unit available to another family, or perhaps they could buy the unit and become condo owners. In other cases some families will need assistance for a longer period of time, maybe the rest of their lifetime.

By having a government agency as the proponent of the project there can be realistic planning of the housing needs of the community, and the project or individual buildings can reflect that need. Unlike so many of the condos going up in the downtown, the buildings will reflect the needs of the community not the need for profit. Because families are most in need of affordable housing, many of the units will be two and three or even more bedrooms, but there will still be the need for small units suitable for individuals.

The government agency managing the projects will be very important. In the case of Regent Park and other public housing projects, the agency was Toronto Community Housing. Sources tell me that was a workable arrangement, but what we really need are agencies with housing and financing specialists. Each municipality across the GTHA should have housing agencies like this. Waterfront Toronto is an example of a model that works. It has a diversified staff with many different talents, such as planners, architects, financing specialists, those who can negotiate with developers, others who can deal with the public and politicians, and so on.

Financing is a special problem and will be the one area most politicians will worry about because of the concerns of taxpayers. I believe that in most instances there needs to be an initial loan by the municipality or other governments that can be recouped at a later date, but the other possibility is that the agency set up to manage the project may be able to borrow the money. There are other financing options like bonds, debentures, or special loans that can be arranged.

Planning experts like Ken Greenburg believe that mixed-housing projects are the ideal that we should strive for in cities. This type of public/private development is the way to achieve that objective. In the process it will provide the affordable housing that we need and help us to rebuild our cities with higher densities, better services, and communities that work. That combination will lead to more affordable cities.

HOUSING ON THE AVENUES

All of the public/private housing projects that I am aware of have been developed in the downtown, but this approach could make a major contribution to transforming the suburbs in Toronto and the rest of the GTHA.

For some years now the planning departments of Toronto and other large municipalities in the outer suburbs have advocated that mid-rise housing developments of between eight and ten storeys should be built along transit corridors. This type of development would integrate with existing suburban housing and still would substantially increase densities. In turn, this would strengthen the existing communities, provide the densities needed to provide better services, and lead to an improvement in public transit.

Now that new rapid transit is in the final stages of planning and some projects are actually being built, the opportunity for this type of development is even more pressing, but nothing is happening. The reason is that the private sector cannot build affordable housing and still make a profit. The only way this type of housing can be built is with some form of public involvement.

New transit is the opportunity for new development, but it does not always happen. When the Yonge Street subway was built it did stimulate new development along the Yonge Street corridor, but on the Spadina and Bloor–Danforth subway lines, very little new housing or offices were built. The areas around the stations in Toronto's East End like Pape, Donlands, Greenwood, Coxwell, and Woodbine remain low-density communities of single-family houses.

It is not hard to figure out why. Developers do not want to build high-density projects in communities like those along the Bloor–Danforth line because there will be opposition from the residents. Even more important, it is difficult for developers to assemble enough land to make a viable project in communities where there are a number of small property owners. Governments spent a huge amount of money building subways, but did not reap the benefits of higher property tax revenue.

There are several opportunities for this type of redevelopment on the avenues in Toronto and across the rest of the GTHA. For example, along Eglinton Avenue a new LRT line is being built. There is vacant or underutilized land along this transit corridor, and a number of companies are proposing developments. East of Victoria Park on Eglinton, for example, there is an area that once was called the "Golden Mile." It has become a stretch of failed, or almost failed malls and enormous parking lots that mostly sit vacant. This property will soon have excellent transit and should be redeveloped with medium-density developments not unlike St. Lawrence neighbourhood. Integrated into this new development can be retail stores, parks, and amenities that people in surrounding suburban communities can use as well as the new residents.

In the outer suburbs there are even more opportunities for this type of public/private redevelopment. For example, Highway 7 has become the most important east–west transportation link between Markham, Vaughan, and Brampton. High-speed bus lanes will bring good transit along this corridor, connecting riders into the TTC subway system. More important, this is an employment growth area where new high-tech companies are settling. This area will need new affordable housing for the people coming to take these jobs. Like the Golden Mile, Highway 7 is lined with malls that have massive parking lots that can be redeveloped. The increased densities will also benefit surrounding low-density suburbs by bringing better services and amenities.

Highway 2 in Pickering, Ajax, and Oshawa is another area ripe for redevelopment. An LRT line is planned along this street, connecting it into the TTC subway system. Surrounding the gas stations, parking lots, and malls that line the highway is a considerable amount of vacant land.

The plan for the redevelopment of Hurontario Street in Mississauga includes the LRT and low-rise development. Mississauga planners believe that can be done solely by private sector money, and it may be true; the city has a vibrant economy. But studies show that many people in the outer suburbs are facing declining incomes. Affordable housing should become part of the housing mix across the GTHA and that can only be delivered by public/private partnerships.

Hamilton's former mayor Bob Bratina sees the new GO service that will create a major station and hub on James Street North as a great opportunity for the redevelopment of land in the city's north end, but that will not be enough to transform the downtown and turn it into a vibrant city centre. There is plenty of vacant land in the city core. Hamilton's politicians and citizens dreamed for years of redeveloping the downtown. That is what the huge urban renewal project in the 1960s and 1970s was supposed to do but failed. Bringing people to live downtown through these types of public/private partnerships that help to solve the affordable housing crisis is the way to do it.

Across the GTHA there are many opportunities to build mixed-income communities. But it will not be done if we rely solely on private developers. Public/private partnerships can make them happen, and in the process will strengthen our cities. More important, they will improve the standard of living of thousands of the most vulnerable people in our society. This is an opportunity we must not miss.

RETROFITTING THE HIGH-RISE

As discussed in Chapter 3, another pressing housing problem that we face is the retrofitting of the aging high-rise buildings that exist across Toronto and in many other cities of the region. If they can be improved and brought up to standard, the benefits will outweigh the costs. It will improve the lives of hundreds of thousands of people, particularly the many immigrant families who have settled there and are starting a new life in this country.

The City of Toronto has already started retrofitting these buildings with its Tower Renewal program. It is a program much like the public/private partnerships. Ten million dollars was set aside by the city and has been used to pay for the retrofits of the older apartment buildings. The money is provided in the form of loans to the landlord and repaid out of the money that is saved by the decreased costs of energy.

This is an excellent program, but it is limited. The city only has funds to retrofit ten buildings a year and the need is enormous. Energy retrofits are just the beginning of the work that is needed. Almost all of the building are over fifty years old. They have not had major work done on them since they were built, and many are in very bad repair. The buildings are still structurally sound and with proper renovation they will provide affordable housing for decades to come. It is essential that these buildings be improved because they provide homes for an estimated one million people. [13]

Several studies have found problems such as windows and doors that need replacing and kitchens and bathrooms that need modernizing. Virtually all of the buildings are leaking energy and some will need a new outer membrane in order to make them energy efficient. Material such as Styrofoam can be fixed on the outside walls of buildings and then covered with other material. This reduces heat loss in the winter and keeps the buildings cool in the summer.

In the west end of Toronto one older building was re-skinned with a Styrofoam jacket and given a stucco-like material over the top. That, along with new windows and doors and work on the balconies reduced energy costs by 40 to 50 percent. It also extended the life of the building by decades. [14] The repairs and upgrades of the buildings will be recouped over time from energy savings.

The green industry strategy of the Ontario government has been promoting this type of work as an incentive for our economy. They recognize that it will help build a strong sustainable economy, but there are two problems. Virtually all of these older high-rise buildings are privately owned and the owners, want to keep costs low to maximize profits. The other is the need for a company or public agency that can organize and finance a loan program.

Again, the answer is a comprehensive public/private partnership dedicated to this work. Part of that strategy will be a system of inspections of high-rise buildings that will require owners to develop a plan to bring the building up to modern standards both environmentally and in terms of improvements to the amenities. Once that plan is in place, and the financing organized, the owner could have the retrofitting completed by contractors.

No doubt there will be some landlords who will be resistant. They are earning a good income from the buildings and don't want anything to threaten their nest egg. In other situations the costs of the retrofit will be greater than the energy savings, but the building must be improved. In cases such as this, the public agency could take an equity position in the building and get the money back over a longer period.

There are huge advantages to a program such as this. There will be no costs to the taxpayers and a real benefit in new jobs. The province will have to amend its laws, and the municipalities will have to establish new building codes and inspections, but every city in the GTHA already has a system of building inspection in place. The most important result will be that a large amount of affordable rental housing will remain available, and it will be brought up to standards with improved amenities. This will improve the quality of life of many people with modest incomes. As an added bonus, it will significantly reduce our greenhouse gas emissions and help us achieve Kyoto Accord targets.

RETROFITTING THE GTHA FOR SUSTAINABILITY

Studies by municipalities on the sources of air pollution that we quoted in Chapter 3 showed that somewhere between 35 and 50 percent of all air pollution in our cities comes from the heating of buildings. High-rise, office, and industrial buildings make up one part of that pollution, but so do the hundreds of thousands of single-family dwellings in the GTHA. We have to find a way to reduce that pollution problem, and I believe the public/private partnership model can do just that.

The energy retrofitting of buildings is not only a way to reduce air pollution, it will also make buildings more affordable. Despite the recent drop in the price of oil, energy costs are predicted to rise in the future because of increased world demand for oil and gas, and if our buildings are inefficient, those costs will be a drain on our economy. By reducing our energy use with better insulation, windows, and doors, the efficiency of our buildings will improve, costs will be significantly reduced, and savings gained. If solar panels were added to houses as part of a retrofit program it would reduce energy consumption even more.

The economic model for this is already in place. Some solar panel installation companies will put them on the roof of your house without an upfront cost. They will cover the costs of materials and take their profit out of the savings that the solar panels create in coming years. Once these costs are paid for, all future savings go to the owner of the property. The same can be done with the costs of heating and cooling of the buildings. The upfront costs are recouped by the future savings.

Again, what is needed is an agency that can organize this, and again this can be a public/private partnership. It would provide the funds to pay for the costs of the retrofit and recoup its costs with the future savings. A PPP could even organize district heating and cooling for buildings in large areas, such as the one under construction in Guelph.

A program such as this would be a huge boost to our economy, which we need in this period of the lingering recession and high levels of unemployment, particularly of young people. A group called "Blue Green Canada" has analyzed such a program and claims that by slashing electricity and natural gas consumption by 25 percent by 2025 it would create 25,000 jobs in Ontario, would add $3.7 billion to the economy, and help cut the federal and provincial deficits by $2 billion annually. The high-rise retrofitting program would be much larger, and the job creation and economic impact much greater.

The benefits of a building retrofitting program are enormous. There would be no cost to the taxpayers and minimal involvement from government. It would be an opportunity to create employment, stimulate the economy, reduce the costs of living for people across the region, improve the environment and create a much more sustainable city. It would be foolhardy to reject it.

The prospect of retrofitting all of the buildings in the GTHA seems to be an impossible task. Certainly it will not be done overnight, but then it took fifty years to build the suburbs, and the downtown cores of our cities are still under construction. The retrofitting of buildings in the GTHA is as important as either of these two developments, and even more significant, because it will help to reduce the threat of climate change.

PRACTICAL PROBLEMS AND POLITICAL SOLUTIONS

High prices, our planning system, the development industry, and government inaction all have made it impossible, under the present system, to produce good housing at affordable prices. The problem is not building techniques, innovative technologies, or money. Most programs, as we have seen, can be self-funding out of energy savings using a little money and public/private partnerships. The real problem is that we lack the political will to correct the problems.

The tragedy is that hundreds of thousands of people in the GTHA and millions across Canada are suffering from this political sclerosis. In fact, all of us suffer because good programs will transform our cities, reduce social problems, make cities more affordable, and improve our quality of life. Everyone benefits. There is little doubt that we need a New Urban Agenda that can take advantage of technologies and all we have learned about cities, but the major doorstoppers are politics and politicians caught in the old ways of doing things.

What we need is a provincial policy statement designed specifically for urban areas that will force municipalities to make decisions consistent with principles of sustainability. The key areas that the statement should deal with are encouraging development along the avenues in our cities and the retrofitting of older buildings to make them more energy efficient. It should also have provisions facilitating or possibly requiring municipalities to establish public/private partnerships to encourage and fund these types of projects.

An urban policy statement could go well beyond this to require municipalities to create protected bicycle lanes for commuters, green roofs for buildings of a certain size, a minimum of tree canopy and improved building codes. If the provincial government could accomplish even part of this, it would reduce greenhouse gas emissions, and at the same time improve the standard of living for hundreds of thousands of people.

Politics is central to the problems and the key to creative solutions. As we will see this will be difficult to correct but it can be done.

EIGHT

LOCAL GOVERNMENT

The loss of prestige of local governments in the GTHA, and the rest of Canada for that matter, can be attributed to a number of things: poor leadership, domination of a corporate agenda, and the lack of meaningful citizen participation. But if there is one single issue that can be blamed for this change, it is the lack of revenue. Today, only 8 percent of all of the taxes collected in Canada are spent by municipal governments. Local governments simply do not have the funds to provide the services and infrastructure needed by the people.

It wasn't always this way. There was a time in the nineteenth century when municipalities were the most important level of government in the country. Property taxes raised more revenue than any other form of tax back then, and municipalities delivered the essential services that people needed, like roads, water, police, and transportation. Municipalities even provided support for the poor and destitute.

The crisis of the First World War led to the domination of federal and provincial governments. Income tax was introduced; other taxes followed. Today, the federal and provincial governments control the most lucrative taxes — taxes on income, corporations, and value-added taxes like the GST/HST. Meanwhile, municipalities have had to make do with property taxes as their most important source of revenue.

The federal and provincial governments need large revenues because they deliver important services like education, income support programs, pensions, and medicare, but today over 80 percent of Canadians live in cities, particularly large cities. These municipalities deliver a whole range of services, and the demands on them are rising as the population increases. That cannot be done without revenue.

In the early 1990s transfers from the federal and provincial governments provided 26 percent of local government revenues. After 1995, with download-ing, that shrank dramatically. By 2000 the federal government provided only 16 percent of local government revenues. More than any other thing, this has led to the crisis of municipal governments in Canada.

Any municipal politician in the GTHA will tell you that the most difficult issue that they have to deal with is taxes. Let's begin this excursion into local politics by examining property taxes.

THE GTHA AND PROPERTY TAX

Rob Ford won the 2010 Toronto mayoral election with simple slogans: "End the gravy train" and "We don't have a revenue problem, folks. We have a spending problem." His focus was on the spending side — stopping government waste — always a popular slogan because the blame is put on politicians and bureaucrats.

In the 2014 election the promises were the same. Across the GTHA all of the major candidates said that they would hold taxes at or below the rate of inflation. This leaves a serious problem. John Sewell, the former mayor of Toronto, expressed it this way: "Toronto does not have enough money to address its needs, whether it is the billion dollars needed to build better transit, build new affordable housing or expand city services in the fields of day care, youth recreation, or city planning."[1]

Still, the politicians play a rather disingenuous game around taxes. Before the last election, John Tory said political leaders had to find the "courage" to level with the public about taxes, but during the 2014 election when his oppo-nent Olivia Chow said that property taxes may have to be used to pay for a project, Tory attacked her in outraged tones for promising to raise taxes.[2] His "courage" fled when faced with the opportunity to attack his opponent.

Property taxes in Ontario are calculated on the value of the property. Each year the municipality sets a tax rate, which is a percentage of the value of the property. That tax rate, times the assessed property value, results in the taxes each property owner has to pay that year.

In the table that follows I have given the tax rate for residential houses for different GTHA municipalities so that we can make a comparison. Office buildings, parking lots, even pipelines all have different rates. To simplify things I have only given the residential house tax rate. Then I have multiplied that rate times $500,000 so that different municipalities can be compared.

Table 9: Tax on Property Valued At $500,000 in GTHA Municipalities for 2014

	Tax Rate	Tax
Ajax	1.310793%	$6,553.96
Brampton	1.263320%	$6,316.60
Burlington	0.910620%	$4,553.10
Hamilton	1.387211%	$6,936.05
Markham	0.831508%	$4,157.54
Mississauga	0.908370%	$4,541.85
Milton	0.777561%	$3,887.80
Oakville	0.874475%	$4,372.37
Oshawa	1.590670%	$7,953.35
Pickering	1.301837%	$6,509.18
Toronto	0.723008%	$3,615.04
Vaughan	0.862149%	$4,310.74

This table shows clearly that Toronto has the lowest tax of any of the municipalities. The reason is that the city has the good fortune of having scores of high-cost office towers and condos in the downtown. They are a cash cow for the municipality. Not only do they have a high value, which translates into high assessments, but office buildings, rental apartments, and industrial properties pay a higher rate of taxes than houses. For example, in Toronto the property tax rate in 2014 was 0.723008 but the tax rate for commercial property was 2.897807, over three times higher.

The two municipalities in the table with the highest property tax rates are Hamilton and Oshawa, both older industrial cities. But even this is not the full story. The value of property in Hamilton and Oshawa is, on average, less than Toronto, but the costs of municipalities to deliver services are about the same across the GTHA. As a result they must have a higher tax rate to pay the costs.

Mississauga, Brampton, Pickering, and Markham — the ring of outer suburban cities around Toronto — have both high property values and high taxes. The reason is that these municipalities are made up primarily of low-density suburbs, which are very expensive to service by their municipalities.

There are serious flaws with the property tax system. The assessment of property is supposedly based on market value, but it is still a subjective judgment. The system currently in use in Ontario assesses the value of the property on the first day of the year. Every assessment is based on a decision of assessors, and inevitably the assessed value of a property is the result of judgments that can be very difficult to justify. By contrast, income tax is objective — how much money was earned in a given year? All of the problems with the property tax system lead to complaints and grievances about the inequity of property tax and appeals clog the system.

One of the ironies is that, although it is homeowners who complain the loudest about municipal taxes, the system of property tax is a major subsidy to middle- and upper-class homeowners. The property tax system is regressive. It taxes lower-income people at a higher rate than upper-income people because those with lower incomes spend higher proportions of their income on housing.[3]

But lower-income tenants rarely complain about property taxes. The reason is that they pay their taxes indirectly through their rent and have no idea about the level of taxes they are paying. Homeowners, on the other hand, get a property tax bill every year and they can see immediately what they are paying and how this year's tax compares with last year.

A recent task force set up in Toronto summarized the property tax system in this way: "In one of the most successful, productive and economically diverse metropolitan areas in North America, if not the world, the City of Toronto ... is caught in a straitjacket of a nineteenth-century constitutional model."[4]

Despite all of these problems, Torontonians get excellent value considering the municipal taxes that they pay and the services received. Municipal leaders cry for the senior levels of government to pay more for local government, but unless there is a major restructuring of how tax money is raised and spent in this country, little will change. The Harper government in Ottawa is not going to give cities any more money, and the Ontario government is in financial difficulties, but in politics things often change. Both the federal Liberal and New Democratic parties have hinted they will provide more money to cities.

Toronto particularly needs more money. We have big-city problems and need good services to meet those problems. Table 9 shows the city has considerable tax room. One candidate in the last election argued that if everyone in Toronto paid fifty cents more a day in municipal taxes it would raise about half a billion dollars.[5] That would allow for improvements in services across the city and solve many problems. But don't expect it to happen soon. Politicians in the suburbs would mount a furious opposition to any tax hike.

HOW MUNICIPALITIES SPEND

Politicians have always milked the complaints about taxes, but can tight-fisted conservative municipal politicians make a difference in the level of taxes? In fact, municipal politicians have very little impact on budgets.

The total City of Toronto operating budget was $9.6 billion for 2014, but over 90 percent of the costs are legislated programs, or "core" programs. The city has no choice how to spend that 90 percent of the budget because they are required to deliver those programs by provincial legislation. Another 8 to 9 percent are what are called "traditional" services. These are services that the city usually delivers but that are not legislated. That leaves the councillors with from 1 to 2 percent of the budget as discretionary spending, about $90 million in Toronto. This is all that could be cut from the city's budget, and even if all of it was cut it would make very little difference to the individual taxpayer.

On the capital side of the budget, there is more flexibility. The municipality can even go in debt for capital spending, and that is exactly what Toronto council voted to do in 2013 when the majority of councillors supported the Scarborough subway. Rather than cut or even control the Toronto budget, Ford's term as mayor led to a much higher level of debt. It will take the next twenty-five years to pay this extra debt off. His claim that he saved the city $1 billion is bunk.

All of this begs the question: Why do we have so much controversy over the city budget every year if the debate is only over 1 or 2 percent of the total budget? Budget debates are little more than an opportunity for politicians to posture in front of the public as tax fighters. They are not the meaningful debates of politicians trying to seek out the best way to spend limited resources. The controversy reflects the public's deep dissatisfaction with government and the tax system, and the fact that many are finding it very hard to pay their taxes. This is especially true for retired people and others on fixed incomes who continue to live in their houses. Every year they see their property taxes going up, services not getting better, and yet their incomes remain fixed. That is what angers them.

Tax fairness is the core issue, not spending. We should be shifting away from property taxes and instead relying more on income and corporation taxes to raise the revenue we need for city government because it is a much fairer system of taxation. But don't expect it to happen. The senior levels of government protect their tax base, and though there are signs the province will give money to municipalities to help pay for infrastructure, cities are on their own to solve their financial problems.

The property tax issue is a difficult one for municipal politicians. Many voters think of little else. To get elected in many wards across the GTHA, the only thing that voters want to hear is that taxes will be kept low. For the politicians of the right, that is a promise that they want to make because they advocate limited government, but for progressives, it is a difficult because they know that the only way of improving services, which many need, is spending money.

The demand to keep taxes low has tilted municipal politics to the right everywhere in the GTHA. Conservatives control councils across the GTHA, and their agenda is small government and low taxes.

MEGACITY AND THE RISE OF THE CONSERVATIVES ON TORONTO COUNCIL

In the late 1960s the boundary of the City of Toronto was the old city, before amalgamation was imposed. The politics of the city at that time was polarized between groups called the "Old Guard" and the "Reform Group." The Old Guard supported a pro-development agenda. They were in favour of the Spadina Expressway, were pro-business, and advocated low taxes. The Reform Group wanted controls on development, opposed the expressway, advocated transparent decision-making at city hall, and community empowerment.

The Reform Group came to power in 1971 with the election of David Crombie as mayor. He was supported by reform councillors like John Sewell, Colin Vaughan, Allan Sparrow, and others. They created the most innovative municipal government ever seen in Toronto. In the process the province cancelled the Spadina Expressway, a decision that literally saved the downtown of the city. Development was brought under control by making all decisions open to public scrutiny and discussion.

Development and the Spadina Expressway were the two most important issues of the Reform Group, but there were a number of others. They saved the iconic Toronto streetcars, promoted transit, supported women's shelters, challenged the police over the bathhouse raids that targeted homosexuals, and provided cultural programs for theatre, film, and visual arts. Neighbourhoods were supported in many different ways, such as traffic calming, and new development projects, like the St. Lawrence neighbourhood, were promoted. The list of accomplishments is extensive.

The heyday of progressive politics in Toronto was in the 1970s and early 1980s, but even though more centrist mayors, like Art Eggleton, were elected in the 1980s and 1990s, the movement for reform and change had taken hold. There was no going back to the days of the Old Guard when developers got whatever they wanted and the police were allowed to hassle gays with impunity. But others at Queen's Park were watching and did not like what they saw happening in the city.

In the early 1990s there was concern that the two-tier system of municipal government was not working. Metro Toronto was particularly divided between the progressives of the City of Toronto and the conservative politicians that dominated the other municipalities of Metro, like Scarborough, North York, and Etobicoke. "Dysfunctional" was the favourite word to describe Metro Council, the raft of inadequate decisions that they made, and the constant bickering. To try and find a solution to this problem, the Bob Rae government (1990–1995) appointed Ann Golden, the head of the United Way and a Liberal, to make recommendations.

In the 1995 provincial election the Conservatives, led by Mike Harris, were elected. The Ann Golden report was tabled not long after their election. She recommended keeping the lower-tier municipalities in place and creating a second tier government that stretched across the entire GTA. It would create a huge upper-tier government made up of Toronto, Peel, York, Durham, and Halton.

The Conservatives floundered around on the issue of municipal governance for some months before choosing a totally different direction. Harris announced that all of the lower-tier municipalities in Metro Toronto were to be eliminated, and a single-tier City of Toronto would be imposed. This, the critics immediately cried, was "Megacity."

Megacity created a huge public controversy in Toronto, and it remains controversial to this day. The proposal was to amalgamate the six lower-tier cities in Metro into one government and one administration. One hundred and twenty councillors and six mayors were to be reduced to forty-four councillors and one mayor who were to govern a city of 2.3 million (now 2.6 million) people.

There was an immediate negative reaction to the proposal in Toronto. A public campaign against Megacity was launched by former mayor John Sewell and he helped found an organization called "Citizens for Local Democracy" (C4D). Sewell was a chair of the group. The co-chair, Kathleen Wynne, went on to become a school trustee, provincial Liberal MPP, cabinet minister, and premier of the province. The controversy went on for months, with accusations back and forth.

Megacity was an attempt by the Harris Conservatives to control the democratic process of local government in Toronto and stamp out the influence of the downtown progressives. Harris was responding to a real problem — what is the appropriate way to govern a large metropolitan area? But his solution was based on partisan politics — the desire to kill the progressive, urban, downtown political movement. The way that he did that was to produce a Toronto City Council controlled by conservative suburban councillors.

Recently I talked to John Sewell about this continuing problem and this is how he described it:

> You have one culture that comes out of the pre-1950s city. That kind of city is compact, [with] mixed uses, generally pedestrian oriented, fairly dense, and that has a certain kind of culture to it. And the post-1950 city is not compact. It is sprawling and car dependent.... It has its own culture as well. When you put them together and say they are going to have one kind of government structure, you have a total mess, where one side doesn't understand the other. They don't share values.

Since Megacity was imposed, Toronto has had four mayors. Mel Lastman and Rob Ford were Conservative and the core of their votes came from the suburbs. David Miller was a progressive. His core support came from the downtown. John Tory is also a Conservative but he also got Liberal support. In the 2014 election he swept most of the downtown and the Yonge Street corridor. Doug Ford, brother of Rob and sharing most of his politics, won much of the inner suburbs but not by enough of a margin to win the election. The polarization of the electorate continues.

This suburban/downtown split shapes every important issue on Toronto City Council. It has become a venue where suburban and the downtown councillors slug it out from different sides of the ideological divide, and more often than not the suburban councillors prevail because they have more votes than the downtown. The Harris Megacity revolution prevails, and council as a place where progressive, innovative programs flourish is no more.

LEFT, RIGHT, AND MUSHY MIDDLE

The political fault line between downtown and the suburbs is what shapes the politics of the City of Toronto. The downtown councillors tend to be from the left, or are more progressive. They support improvements in services and programs for those with low incomes and for the homeless, affordable housing, transit, and issues around quality of life and the environment. Not surprisingly, they have come to be called the "Left Wing Group."

The politicians from the suburbs gain their support from the home owners who get out and vote. New immigrants cannot vote because they are not citizens. These councillors support low property taxes. Like Rob Ford, they believe streets are primarily for cars, and they oppose issues like bike lanes, group homes in neighbourhoods, and affordable housing because they believe those facilities will harm property values. This group has come to be called the "Right Wing Group."

There is another group of councillors on Toronto City Council; they see themselves as unaligned politicians. They vote on issues depending on any number of different factors. They have come to be called the "Mushy Middle." Despite the derogatory term, it is the Mushy Middle who determine the outcome of many important issues on Toronto council because they are swing voters.

Toronto City Council is unpredictable because these political groupings are always in flux, changing depending on the issue. In David Miller's day, the outcome of issues was much more predictable because Miller watched the voting behavior of councillors very carefully and knew how to apply pressure in order to gain the votes needed to pass important motions. He used his influence like an orchestra leader and so lost very few votes. That is what made him an effective mayor.

Rob Ford, on the other hand, often lost motions. The main reason was that he did not know how to use the power of his position to get the votes he needed. For example, Ford lost crucial votes on the Sheppard subway and the Eglinton LRT. He did not meet with councillors to apply pressure, and when the issues came to council he was unable to counter the arguments of his opponents. His leadership of the council unravelled because of his drinking and drug abuse, but also because he did not know how to influence votes.

It is too early to see how John Tory will lead council, but he must find a way to deal with these different political groupings.

While Toronto Council is split between the Left, Right, and Mushy Middle, in the outer suburbs and Hamilton this polarization rarely exists. Development is still the most important issue, and councils consistently support the proposals of developers. Occasionally there are councillors who voice their opposition, but they usually find that they stand alone.

THE POLITICIANS AND THE ISSUES

Municipal politicians in Ontario run for election as individuals, and although most of them are members of one political party or another, they don't use their party affiliation to get elected. This lack of parties is a unique feature of Ontario municipal politics. Vancouver and Montreal have political parties, but in both cases those municipal parties are independent of national or provincial parties. In the United States, municipal parties are part of the Democratic or Republican parties, and across Europe a similar pattern is followed.

The reason Ontario has a non-partisan municipal political system goes back to the early part of the twentieth century and the struggle against corrupt political machines in American cities, but today the lack of parties in the GTHA has many unfortunate consequences. Affiliation with a party gives candidates an identity; it shows what policies candidates are in favour of and what they will support if elected. As Myer Siemiatycki, a political scientist at Ryerson points out, "It would require the skill and tenacity of a super sleuth to actually identify the record, position, and background of every candidate running for office."[6]

As a result, ward election contests today are almost devoid of city-wide issues. This makes it hard for citizens to figure out the approach candidates will support if elected. Incumbent councillors run on their record, they take credit for the accomplishments of others, and they blame the mayor or other councillors for the problems.

Once elected politicians constantly promote themselves. An incumbent councillor is a full-time politician with staff to handle constituency problems and make sure that the local media are carrying positive stories about them. They have money in their budgets to promote themselves to their constituents through mail campaigns. Most attend all important community meetings to make themselves known. Sitting councillors have such a huge advantage over their opponents that they have to do something that angers a very large number of people to be defeated.

For example, seven new councillors were elected to Toronto's forty-four member city council in 2014, but only one, Jon Burnside in Ward 26, defeated an incumbent. The other six were elected in wards where the incumbent did not run. In Ontario, once a councillor is elected, they have a near sinecure for life. That helps to create conservative councils averse to taking risks or change.

At the level of mayor there is much more interest, but incumbents are still re-elected over and over again. In the GTHA, the only incumbent defeated was Linda Jeffrey in Brampton, and that was due to accusations of corruption and possible criminal behaviour.[7]

WHO IS ON TORONTO'S COUNCIL?

At every level of politics in Canada our elected politicians are unrepresentative of their constituents. Our politics are dominated by people with professional and business interests. Fully 88.8 percent of the seventy-two Toronto mayors from William Lyon Mackenzie to John Tory were either lawyers, other professionals, or from business. It is no different today than it was in the nineteenth century. Of the ten Toronto mayors from David Crombie to John Tory, only one, June Rowlands, was not a professional or a business person. The three from business, Mel Lastman, Rob Ford, and John Tory, are multi-millionaires.

Few working people get elected to council anywhere in the GTHA, and despite the fact that almost 50 percent of Torontonians are visible minorities, only five were elected to the current council. One member is African-American, and four of east Asian origin. There are councillors from the Jewish and Italian communities, but most of the rest are Anglo-Saxon. The last council (2010–14) had fifteen women or 33.3 percent. On this council (2014–18) the number dropped by one to fourteen, or 31.8 percent.

Age, of course, is another way that Toronto City Council and municipal councils across the province are unrepresentative of the population. On Toronto's new council, only three members are younger than thirty-nine.[8] Very few people under the age of thirty get elected to public office at any level in Canada. This is one of the reasons why the issues of young people are ignored, and why so many of the young develop a distain for politics and refuse to vote or participate.

The most important split on the 2014–18 council is between councillors elected from the pre-amalgamation Toronto and those from the inner suburbs. Of the forty-four councillors, sixteen are from the old city. Fourteen of the sixteen are either very or somewhat progressive, while only two are conservative. Nine of the sixteen are women. Among the other twenty-eight councillors from the inner suburbs just four can be considered progressive or somewhat progressive and only five are women.[9]

Toronto city councillors tend to be old, white, male, and conservative, and their votes on issues reflect their conservative political views. This does not signal a healthy democracy.

CAMPAIGN DONATIONS

"Follow the money" is the first rule of politics.[10] Money is the "grease" of politics because it is needed to win campaigns. Where politicians get their campaign donations tells us a great deal about their allegiances and how they will vote on issues.

In the GTHA the major donors to municipal campaigns traditionally have been companies involved in the land development business. That includes the developers, real estate companies, sewer and road paving contractors, real estate lawyers, and the complex of interests that circle the developer's world. The reason they make campaign donations is that municipal councils make decisions that control developing approvals. They want to influence those decisions.

The Old Guard in Toronto before the rise of the Reform Group in the early 1970s got their campaigns paid for by the developers,[11] and we have seen how the overheated real estate market in York Region led to political problems in the late 1980s. At the core of that scandal was campaign donations from developers and how they shaped the way politicians voted on development approvals.

Not all politicians take campaign donations from the development industry. Those on the left accept money from unions but rarely from developers, either because they are not offered the money or because they want to be independent. The late Allan Sparrow, a Toronto city councillor from 1974 to 1980, would only take donations from individuals. He felt raising money from voters was part of the role of a politician. "If you can't raise money for your campaign from individual voters then that is telling you something. Maybe you shouldn't run for office," he once told me.

In 2003 the Liberal government of Jean Chrétien in Ottawa passed legislation that banned corporate and union donations for federal election campaigns. Some political insiders that I know claim that ban led to the decline of the federal Liberal Party, because in the past their campaign donations came almost exclusively from corporations. The Conservatives and NDP, on the other hand, benefitted because they had always raised the money they needed for campaigns from individual donations.

It was assumed that the rule of no corporate and union donations would spread across Canada, but the Ontario legislation has not been amended. Because there has been no change in the provincial legislation, there are no restrictions on who municipal politicians can raise money from in Ontario. Toronto is the exception, as we will see.

In recent years there has been interest in campaign donations. In the GTHA one of the leading researchers on donations is Robert MacDermid, a political scientist from York University who I interviewed about politics in small towns. Bob and I were both volunteers for VoteToronto, a group of researchers and writers who published material on municipal politics online.[12] MacDermid did an analysis of campaign funding of ten GTA municipalities in the 2006 municipal election and found that well over 50 percent of the donations in the outer suburbs came from corporations. These are his figures for ten of the municipalities (Hamilton was not included in this study):[13]

Table 10: Source of 2006 campaign donations in 10 GTA municipalities

	Corporations	Individuals	Unions	Candidates	Contributions
Ajax	22.4%	28.1%	0.0%	49.5%	$121,409
Brampton	57.5%	18.5%	0.0%	24.0%	$885,088
Markham	35.7%	53.9%	0.2%	10.2%	$1,081,356
Mississauga	49.6%	21.5%	0.3%	28.6%	$737,624
Oshawa	51.6%	9.2%	4.0%	35.2%	$351,006
Pickering	76.7%	18.1%	0.5%	4.6%	$236,383
Richmond Hill	62.2%	19.1%	1.2%	17.5%	$356,478
Toronto	12.0%	66.3%	2.2%	19.6%	$5,440,269
Vaughan	62.8%	20.9%	0.2%	16.1%	$1,517,988
Whitby	50.0%	13.2%	1.8%	35.1%	$223,043

The figures illustrate a number of interesting things. Candidates in the big suburban municipalities rely on corporate donations. MacDermid also looked to see what corporations were making the donations, and almost all were part of the development industry. It is also interesting how little unions gave to the campaigns. Many believe that "big labour" has huge political influence, but judged from the point of view of campaign donations, that is hardly the case. Individual donations are still important for most candidates.

What also stands out is how different Toronto is from the other municipalities. Only 12 percent of the city's donations came from corporations in 2006. This is even a marked change from previous elections. Six years before, in the 2000 election, MacDermid found that 57.5 percent of campaign donations in Toronto came from corporations. It is not clear why this happened. Certainly developers continue to be very active in Toronto. Perhaps they have come to understand that they cannot buy influence on Toronto council with campaign donations.

Armed with this and other data showing the influence of developers on municipal politics, VoteToronto and Fair Vote Canada mounted a campaign to ban corporate and union donations in municipal campaigns. We argued that the development industry should not be making campaign contributions to politicians who would be voting to approve their projects. This was a conflict of interest. We also said that voters are citizens with rights and obligations.

Corporations and unions are organizations, not citizens, and should not be allowed to influence campaigns with money.

These arguments prevailed in Toronto City Council with the support of Mayor David Miller and his allies on council. A bylaw was passed and corporate and union donations were banned in the 2010 municipal election. But this fell on deaf ears outside Toronto. Not one of the GTHA municipalities adopted this rule. In the 2014 election campaign donations from corporations and unions was not even a major issue.

In Toronto it would be wrong to say that the city is free of corporate and union influence. When David Miller was mayor he led the effort to stop the control of issues by those with vested interests, and established a lobbyist register. Shortly after Rob Ford took office in 2010 he declared that Toronto was "open for business." Lobbyists have been flocking to city hall ever since. The lobbyists register shows there were three times as many lobbyists in 2012 as in 2010.[14]

POLITICS IN THE OUTER SUBURBS

Robert MacDermid is convinced that campaign donations shape politics, and nowhere is this more obvious than in the outer suburbs. This domination of councils by real estate interests has led, in his words, to "unsustainable urban sprawl, high transportation costs, environmental degradation, and a weak sense of community that undermines political organization and representation."[15]

There are indications that the relationships between developers and politicians are changing. In the 1980s the developers needed political influence to get priority for their projects. Today, the "Places to Grow" policy statement calls for greater housing densities. Citizens' groups are challenging any development on farmland. The old generation of developers have passed from the scene and their children have taken control of their development companies. The new generation is more corporate and less confrontational than their fathers, but that does not mean to say that they are above wielding influence to get their projects approved.

Don Cousens, the mayor of Markham from 1994 to 2006, tells a story that illustrates how the changes in the industry have changed the relations between politicians and developers. Cousens and others on Markam Council became convinced that a 243-acre parcel of land owned by Rudy Bratty, one of the old-time developers of York Region, was the best place to build a high-density community of townhouses, condo towers, and offices. Cousens went to Bratty with the concept, but the developer didn't agree. He wanted to build houses. That's what he knew how to build, and he also knew he could sell the houses and make a good profit. It took time but ultimately Cousens persuaded Bratty, and the 243 acres are now being transformed into a high-density community.[16]

To say that developers operating in the outer suburbs work co-operatively with politicians to build high-density, efficient communities is a leap of the imagination that I am not willing to make. Developers are still driven by the desire to make profit, and lobbying by vested interests is still going on in every municipal council in the GTHA, but there seems to be much less influence peddling than in the past. The province has set down rules for development that are widely accepted. But there remain many problems with development in the outer suburbs. Who is defending the public interest? Who is the Adam Vaughan in the suburbs, examining the plans in detail to see if they meet community needs, and who is defending the vulnerable in these communities?

The main problem of municipal politics in the outer suburbs is the lack of public interest. The expense account scandal surrounding the former mayor of Brampton is an example. Brampton politicians on the 2010–14 council had been in office for an average of twenty-two years. Councillors operated like a type of cozy club. Expense claims were treated on an honour system, where members of council approved their own expenses.

Then, unexpectedly, it got out of hand. The mayor, Susan Fennell, racked up expenses totalling $172,608, and the rest of council turned in expenses for $46,000. Citizens became aware that there were abuses, but they had to pay $250 to launch a complaint — an obvious disincentive — and for seven years there were no complaints. Finally, an integrity commissioner filed a report on the mayor's expenses. For his efforts, council fired the commissioner. The media finally took notice and the city politicians had a major scandal on their hands.[17]

To conclude that this is how all councils in the outer suburbs operate would be wrong, but there are elements of this in many municipalities. When there is little interest in politics, and politicians are elected over and over again, they come to see themselves as invulnerable, and that can lead to a disregard for the public. Toronto and Hamilton both have an active culture of civic engagement, but that is not the case in many of the municipalities in the outer suburbs.

The reasons are complicated. In many cases these are new communities and residents have not put down roots. People in the suburbs are very mobile. They live in one municipality, work in another, shop in a third, and have friends and family scattered across the entire region. As a result they have little identity with their home community and no interest in its politics. In Brampton a large number of the new residents are from South Asia, and there is little tradition of local government in those countries. Many of the immigrants don't understand the complicated system of local, provincial, and federal government that we have in Canada.

I did a rough survey to see who is on the (2010–14) councils of ten municipalities in the outer suburbs, from Burlington in the west to Oshawa in the east and as far north as Newmarket, including all of the big municipalities in the region.[18] Out of 101 councillors and mayors in these ten municipalities, there were 29 women, a little less than 30 percent. Mississauga, with 7 women out of 12 members of council, was clearly the leader on this score, but Ajax has 4 women out of 7 council members. Markham with 2 women out of 13, and Pickering and Burlington, both of which have only 1 woman member out of 7, are doing much worse on the issue of gender equality.

What is even more striking is the lack of representation of minorities. Markham, a city of 301,709 in 2011, has a large East Asian population, but only 2 councillors out of 13 are of East Asian origin on the council elected in 2014. Brampton, a city of 523,911 people in 2011, has a population of 67 percent visible minorities, but of the 23 councillors, only 1 is from a visible minority community. This did not change in the 2014 election. Mississauga, with a population of 713,443 in 2011, and with 54 percent of its population visible minority, has an entirely white council. This pattern is common throughout the municipal councils in the outer suburbs.

There is no doubt that this will change in the future. There was a time when Jews and Italians rarely got elected on councils, and now they are well represented. But in surveying the councils the impression is that politics in the GTHA is overwhelmingly controlled by middle-aged, Anglo-Saxon men, most of them with real estate, or legal backgrounds.

HAMILTON POLITICS

Is my old hometown of Hamilton any different? Not really. There are sixteen members of council, including the mayor, and only four are women. There are no members of visible minorities in sight. But the city is different from municipalities in the outer suburbs in some unique ways. Virtually all of those municipalities are new cities. Hamilton, by contrast, has a long history, and people feel rooted in the city — with all of its problems and advantages.

Hamilton has had a highly developed political culture for decades, built around competing interest groups like the trade union movement and business. There have been many intensely fought issues over the years: the Civic Square development in the 1960s and 1970s, the battle against amalgamation, and the Red Hill Expressway controversy (discussed in the next chapter).

The issue of campaign donations was important in the 2010 campaign. A former mayor had been convicted of accepting illegal campaign donations after a high-profile court case. All of the major candidates vowed they would not accept corporate donations, even though it was not banned by law. But in the 2014 election the issue of corporate and union donations was ignored.

Another element that has shaped Hamilton's political life has been the city's newspaper, the *Spectator*. It has followed local politics for decades. When I was living in Hamilton, I was so impressed by the impact the newspaper was having on local politics I wrote an article about it.[19] I am still convinced that local media, particularly daily newspapers,[20] have a greater impact on local politics than any other media. A serious problem for cities in the GTHA like Mississauga, Brampton, Vaughan, and Markham is they do not have daily newspapers with reporters digging up the news. A city without a good newspaper, in my view, is in trouble because there is no consistent coverage and criticism of local issues.

For me the most interesting recent development in Hamilton politics is the emergence of an active group of citizens who follow local issues and publish their findings online. Hamilton *CATCH* (Citizens at City Hall) newsletter is their online publication. They summarize issues before council and report on how the local councillors vote on issues, but they do much more than that. CATCH News gathers information about the city, analyzes it, and reports its findings. Recently, for example, it reported on the failure of the Hamilton Street Railway, showing how all other GTHA systems were growing and Hamilton's ridership remained relatively static.

We should be concerned with the decline of newspapers. The hope is that online publications will fill this gap and provide even greater coverage and opinion. Hamilton's *CATCH* is a model that citizens in other GTHA cities should follow. We need many more like it.

REFORMING LOCAL POLITICS

The complaints about the practice of local politics in the GTHA are legion. This is particularly true in Toronto. People complain that the politicians just don't get along. "It's a hornet's nest," someone recently told me, and so it is. The politicians argue endlessly and consensus is difficult. Personally, I don't see this as a problem. Politicians should hold strong beliefs, and be willing to fight for them, but there are serious structural problems with local politics.

Toronto is different than other municipalities in the GTHA because the city is bigger and the council is larger. Over the years there have been a number of suggestions about how to improve the functioning of Toronto council and some have been implemented. Not all of these proposals apply to other municipalities but they all are interesting. Let's review five of them.

The "Strong Mayor System"

When David Miller was mayor of Toronto he developed a relationship with Premier Dalton McGuinty. Miller convinced the premier to revise the City of Toronto Act to give the mayor additional powers. The argument was that the mayor is elected by all of the people, and has responsibility for city-wide issues and problems, but still had only one vote on council, the same as any other councillor.

The changes that were legislated to create the strong mayor system were limited. The most important was that the city was to establish an Executive Committee made up of the chairs of the standing committees. The mayor was given the right to appoint the members of the Executive Committee.

In practice what this meant was that the mayor has been given a way to control the votes of the thirteen members of the Executive Committee, plus the chair of the Toronto Transit Commission who is also appointed by the mayor but does not sit on the Executive Committee. As a result, the mayor can count on fifteen votes when an issue comes before council. This is not quite the majority of twenty-three votes needed to carry a motion on the forty-five-member Toronto council, but it strengthens the leadership of the mayor enormously.[21] That is why it is called the strong mayor system.

The political controversy around the land transfer tax in 2009 illustrates how the system works. When the tax was proposed the real estate and development industries mounted an intense lobbying effort opposing it. When the item came before council, the motion lost by one vote. Miller had been confident that it would narrowly pass, but one of the members of the Executive Committee, Brian Ashton, voted against the motion. The mayor acted with dispatch. Ashton was removed from the Executive Committee and a new member was appointed. The motion was redrafted and resubmitted to council. It passed by one vote.

Miller was able to use the additional powers of the strong mayor system by carefully choosing who he put on the Executive Committee and calculating the votes on every important issue. Rob Ford was not able to do the same. He lost vote after vote on his issues when they came to council. It remains to be seen whether John Tory can use the strong mayor system as effectively as Miller.

Cut the Number of Councillors in Half

This was Rob Ford's proposal to reform council, and it is absolutely the worst possible solution. Today, Toronto wards have an average population of 60,000. To double the number to 120,000 would make it simply impossible for local people to have a say in their municipal government. The consequence would be to strengthen the control of corporations, particularly those in the real estate industry.

We need to strengthen local control in order to deepen democracy. Rather than reducing the number of councillors, their numbers should be increased, but there is no support for that at the present time.

Political Parties

The most prominent reform proposal is one I have already mentioned, a political party system. Myer Siemiatycki, a professor of politics and public administration at Ryerson University, published an article in the *Toronto Star* in October 2010 called, "Is it party time for municipal elections?" in which he laid out ten reasons why he felt that now was the time for a political party system in the city. This is a summary of his points.[22]

- Elections would be focused on issues not personalities;

- Better informed voters would lead to higher voter turnout;

- Political parties would boost accountability of elected politicians;

- A party system would bring more diverse candidates, particularly women, minorities, and youth;

- Parties would make fundraising for party candidates easier;

- Party politics already exists in the political factions of councillors, and it is more honest to have those divisions out in the open;

- Parties at city hall would be independent and would not mirror the parties at the federal and provincial levels;

- This system would produce more stable and cohesive government;

- Fresh and new ideas would be injected into local politics; and finally,

- Party discipline would not be as rigid at a municipal level because there are regularly scheduled elections, and no such thing as the parliamentary tradition that the government must maintain the confidence of the House.

I agree with all of this. In fact, I would go further. Political parties could organize fundraising, allowing the candidates to meet the electorate and focus on the issues of the campaign. A party system would help to create discussions in ward elections that focus on city-wide issues, not just ward issues. Once elected, members would caucus and develop unified positions and strategies. They could collectively support the issues that are on their platform and work to get them adopted. All of this would help to end the wild freelancing for attention that is often seen in council meetings.

There is one other key reason to have political parties that we should have learned since the 2010 election. In a system dominated by party politics, it would almost be impossible for a politician like Rob Ford to get elected mayor because it is unlikely that he would have the support of other members of his or her party. Political parties promote their stars who have demonstrated leadership, not mavericks.

The only problem is that political parties at a municipal level are not going to happen in Ontario in the foreseeable future. The people don't want parties. They see them as controlled by the "back-room boys." Most of the existing municipal politicians also don't want parties, for a number of reasons. The primary one is that they like the freedom the present system gives them.

Even provincial legislation conspires against political parties at a municipal level because it does not allow groups of politicians to raise money collectively and disperse it to those in need. That is one of the fundamental functions of party politics.

RaBIT

Another proposal for reform of the system, and one that just might make it into practise, is called the Ranked Ballot Initiative or RaBIT. It has been promoted by Dave Meslin, a remarkable political activist, and a core of supporters. You can find a description of the proposal on their website.[23]

The current system is called "first past the post." Candidates with the most votes win the election, regardless of whether they get over 50 percent of the votes or not. With the ranked ballot system, voters would rank the top three candidates they support in order of preference. If no candidate received 50 percent of the first choice votes, the candidate with the least votes is eliminated and the second choices of those voters are distributed to the remaining candidates. This goes on until one candidate receives 50 percent of the votes cast.

When this proposal came before council in early 2013 it was adopted, but the provincial government has to change the City of Toronto Act to permit the change in the voting system. Premier Katherine Wynne has indicated that she likes this proposal, and it may happen by the 2018 election.

RaBIT could have some limited impact on municipal politics, making it more difficult for incumbent politicians to get re-elected, but it is unlikely to affect the outcome of many ward elections.

Term Limits for Councillors

Councillor Mary Margaret McMahon, Ward 32, has proposed that there be a three term limit on all councillors. Municipal elections are every four years so this would limit the length of time that councillors could serve on council to twelve years and eliminate the practice of councillors winning over and over again for no other reason than their name is recognized.

This is not an unusual electoral rule in the United States — the American president is limited to two terms — but it is not part of the British political tradition that we follow. This change would be strongly opposed by most members of council because it would threaten to limit their career. Again, it would require provincial legislation, and I expect Queen's Park politicians would oppose it because they would fear that this limitation would be imposed on them.

Of all of the proposed reforms that we have discussed, term limits would have the greatest impact on council because it would open up council and bring fresh faces and new ideas.

DEMOCRATIC REFORM OF THE GTHA

All of these reforms are interesting, but they are not going to fundamentally change the way we practise local government in the GTHA. Reform has to be deeper if there is to be change.

What we need to keep in mind is that the GTHA region has become something very different than any other part of the province or the country. We now have a city of 7.3 million people, and yet our local government is divided, for historical reasons, into scores of independent municipalities. How do we coordinate services, infrastructure, transit, development, and all of those other things that government delivers, and yet still have local government that responds to issues at a neighbourhood level?

Effective government in the GTHA must become a joint responsibility of the province and municipalities. Technically, that is the case now. Municipalities are the creatures of the province and operate within provincial legislation, but at the same time municipalities are very independent and guard their independence jealously. The province plays a watchdog role but rarely interferes.

Part of the reason it is difficult for these political entities to co-operate is they operate in very different ways. At Queen's Park, party discipline, and control of the legislature by the governing party, has centralized decision-making in Cabinet and the premier's office. Decision-making in municipalities is chaotic. There is no party discipline, every politician clamours for attention, and the outcome of many issues is never certain until the votes are counted. Added to this, provincial leaders are very wary of municipal politicians because they have far better access to local media than those at Queen's Park.

If there is going to be greater coordination, it will have to be the province that takes the initiative. There have been attempts. The province of Ontario set up a secretariat called the Office of the Greater Toronto Area, but it was little more than a think tank of civil servants.[24] Metrolinx is another provincial agency; it has responsibilities for transit across the GTHA. This is a beginning, bringing provincial coordination in the all-important area of transit, but it has to go beyond this, and the only way to do that is by having the politicians, not just the bureaucrats, involved.

What is needed is a provincial Minister of the Greater Toronto and Hamilton Area who meets regularly with local politicians to work on problems and insures that there is coordination across municipalities, and to insure that provincial policy is followed. This would not be another level of government. Many, perhaps most, of the meetings could be private, but there should be some open meetings where there could be discussion and debate about the types of priorities the region should adopt. Provincial leaders are wary of this because it sets the province up as a target for criticism, but open debate and discussion is what politics should be all about.

The main problem with local politics in Ontario is not just with the politicians. It is with the lack of public oversight of local government. The recent spending scandal in Brampton would never have happened if local people were paying attention to what was going on at their city hall. Fiddling with the structure of local government will not bring good government. A vigilant press helps, but only active citizens watching and criticizing the operations of their council will ensure good government.

MEGACITY AND THE PROBLEMS OF TORONTO CITY COUNCIL

The City of Toronto is a special case. Megacity has thrown two very different types of communities together — the downtown and the inner suburbs.

This is not a minor issue. The fundamental differences between these groups are making it difficult for the councillors representing them to find compromises and, thus, making it hard for them to govern. Even a consensus builder like John Tory will find it hard to bridge this divide. The other serious problem is that the wards are so big they are hardly "local" at all; it is very difficult for councillors to represent the many interests within their wards.

One solution that some have advocated is to break up Toronto into four or six separate municipalities, shrink the size of the wards, and increase the number of politicians. Essentially, this would be going back to the pre-amalgamation structure of Metro Toronto. I have talked to people who follow city politics, and most think it is impractical. It took the city staff several years to adapt to the amalgamated city, and to unravel that would be too difficult. But there is another, simpler solution.

The greatest points of division on council are around things like planning approvals, cycling, traffic, and controlling the public domain. Already council has community councils that look at these issues: Toronto and East York, Scarborough, North York, Etobicoke, and York. But the problem is that these councils only have an advisory role. Neighbourhood issues first go to community council and then to city council for ratification.

If the City of Toronto Act was changed to give community councils full control over these types of issues, it would strengthen local control and remove the most contentious issues from city council. City council would still have responsibility for the budget and other city-wide issues.

The lesson that should be drawn from Megacity is that local government is very important. People want and need local control over their communities. The problem in a city like Toronto and a large region like the GTHA is how to give effective local control while at the same time providing region-wide coordination. That isn't easy, but it can be done.

DEEPENING DEMOCRACY

We have developed a conservative municipal political system in Ontario and the GTHA. There are progressive voices, particularly in Toronto and Hamilton and even on councils in the outer suburbs, but if we are going to develop an activist form of local government that will implement a New Urban Agenda, we have to use the tools of government to bring meaningful change and new programs to our communities.

Alan Broadbent, the author of *Urban Nation*, and the chair of Maytree, a foundation that has provided support to a number of progressive organizations and programs in Toronto, believes that the fundamental problem is that municipalities lack the funds to bring reforms and provide better services. He appeals to senior levels of government to provide the money and give municipalities greater taxing powers.[25] But money will not solve everything. The problems are much deeper than this.

We have to change our political culture at the local level. Federally and provincially, our politics are much more progressive. Canadians are forward-looking people, open to change. We want to build a more equal society with good public amenities and services, and we can do it.

Our task is to deepen our democracy, and the way to do it is by empowering communities, groups, and individuals in the political process. This does not mean that we should dismantle our political system. We need local politicians. Our councils should become forums where local people can bring forward ideas and programs, and then the political system is mobilized to bring change. That is the only way we will be able to create a New Urban Agenda.

That's what we will explore in the next chapter.

NINE

POLITICS, PEOPLE, AND PARTICIPATION

Municipal politicians will point out that there is ample opportunity for citizens to participate in the political process. By law, all meetings are open to the public.[1] There are various committees of council with community representatives and opportunities for citizens to make deputations and express their views. This is true, but participation rates are still very low, and that has serious consequences.

There are some parts of the GTHA where there is a high level of participation. Downtown Toronto is one. Hamilton has long had an engaged political citizenry. But the reality is that this is not the case in many parts of the region. In the inner and outer suburbs, people remain unengaged in the life of their communities.

It is controversies that stir the political blood and get citizens active in local politics. In Hamilton in the late 1960s a pedestrian walkway over King Street had the public up in arms and the politicians quickly withdrew the proposal. In Toronto in 2014 it was the proposal for jets at the Billy Bishop Airport that packed council chambers with outraged citizens.

When there is a lack of community involvement, our political life is impoverished. In my judgment, virtually every issue that engaged the public improved the final resolution of the controversy. Politicians need to hear from the public or they will be making decisions based largely on the views of those who are going to benefit, like businesses or vested interests. That is the worst kind of political decision-making. Participation is a central issue of democracy and essential for reform.

FOUR SUBWAY PROJECTS AND ONE EXPRESSWAY

Political participation by citizens is usually focused on very local issues, like a new housing development that does not fit into the existing neighbourhood or the need for speed bumps in a community. Some big issues, like subways, transit, and expressways, have had difficulty to engage the public because they are city-wide and so enormous. We pay a price for the lack of participation with some serious mistakes. Here are five examples.

Mistake 1

In the late 1960s and early 1970s the biggest controversy in Toronto was the Spadina Expressway. It pitted the suburban Metro councillors, who were in favour of the expressway, against the downtown councillors, who were opposed. When Premier Bill Davis cancelled the expressway in June 1971 the suburban councillors were furious.

Not long afterward, a debate came up at Metro Council about the route of the University Subway Line north of St. Clair West station. One proposal, supported by TTC staff and downtown councillors, was for the route to continue north along Bathurst Street through medium-density neighbourhoods. The alternative was to swing the line west from the St. Clair West Station and then go north in the centre lane of the Allan Expressway. The argument against this route was that no one lived in the immediate area — the neighbourhoods that flanked the expressway were low density. That would mean there would be low ridership.

In the vote on the route, the suburban councillors supported the Allan Expressway route because they saw it as vindication of their support for the Spadina Expressway. They had the votes on council, and they prevailed in the debate. Subsequently, the University subway line has been plagued by low ridership.

Mistakes 2 and 3

The next set of blunders involved not one but two subway lines: the Eglinton West subway and the Sheppard subway line.

The Bob Rae provincial government (1990–95) was hampered by a very sharp recession, but toward the end of its mandate the economy was picking up and more money became available. The government promised to fund two new subway lines for Toronto. One would go west from the Eglinton West Station following the street underground to the far western reaches of Metro.

The other was the Sheppard line that was to go from the Sheppard Station on the Yonge line to Don Mills, five-and-a-half kilometres to the east.

In the discussion after the announcement, there was support for the Eglinton West line. It went through fairly high density, moderate income communities and would have high ridership. The Sheppard line, on the other hand, went through low density, higher income communities, and it would have low ridership. The difference was that the Sheppard line had the strong support of the North York mayor, Mel Lastman, a Conservative and an ally of the provincial Conservatives.

After the Rae government was defeated in 1995, the Conservatives cancelled the Eglinton West line. The premier, Mike Harris, went so far as to order that the tunnels be filled in. At the same time, Harris confirmed his government's support of the Sheppard line. When the issue came to Metro Council, the TTC CEO recommended against the Sheppard Line because it would be a drain on TTC resources and have low ridership, but Metro Council, dominated by the suburbs, voted in favour.

Since its opening, the Sheppard line has never come close to covering its operating costs. Both the Queen and King streetcars carry more people. The popular name for it is "the subway to nowhere."

Mistake 4

The Scarborough subway promises to be the biggest and most expensive mistake of all. The controversy reveals a great deal about the chaotic way that decisions on transit are made in Toronto. It all boils down to politics.

Scarborough is a vote-rich part of Toronto's inner suburbs with a population of 600,000 people. Many of those people depend on transit and yet the service they receive is not very good. Bus rides are long and tedious and the nearest subway station is Kennedy, a distance away from much of the population.

It is understandable that people in Scarborough are envious of the transit facilities of those who live in the central part of the city. Not only does downtown have good transit, but residents have much higher incomes that those in the inner suburbs. An added element to the debate is that people in Scarborough realize that they will be paying for the new transit across the GTHA with their tax dollars, the same as everyone else, but feel they are getting very little benefit.

A major part of the proposal for new transit for Scarborough was the replacement of the Scarborough Rapid Transit with a new LRT. This is how Glenn de Baeremaeker, the Ward 38, Scarborough Centre councillor, described it to me:

> Everybody who gets on the Rapid Transit line says it's a piece of crap.... When it snows the rail line shorts out and it stops.... So when you offer people an LRT in Scarborough no one wants it because the one they know is such a piece of crap. People are sick of them. They call them cattle cars. They are squeaky. They are noisy. They rattle back and forth.

Attitudes like this have prevailed in Scarborough for a long time, and although the LRT is a different technology from the aging Rapid Transit, people still felt it was inferior. They wanted subway lines.

David Miller's Transit City proposal was to build an LRT line that would cost $1.48 billion. It would replace the Scarborough RT, go about ten kilometres from Kennedy Station, making seven stops, including the Scarborough Town Centre, and then continue on to a station on Sheppard East at the campus of Centennial College. As the debate around transit heated up, many people in Scarborough demanded a subway, not an LRT.

As it happened, there was a provincial by-election in the riding of Scarborough–Guildwood, and suddenly, in the summer of 2013, it seemed like everyone was demanding a subway for Scarborough. Then-Mayor Rob Ford said the LRT plans should be scrapped and a subway built in its place. The Liberals were in a minority government, and they desperately needed to win the Scarborough seat. They saw how the wind was blowing, and so said they were in favour of a subway, reversing what they had said about transit in Scarborough up until that time. Even the federal government got into the act.

There was a serious financial shortfall between the costs of the LRT and the cost of a subway. Conservative finance minister Jim Flaherty, a close family friend of Rob Ford, offered $660 million out of infrastructure money. A new consensus seemed to have emerged in favour of a subway over the LRT because that was where the Scarborough votes were going. But when the issue got to Toronto City Council, the deal did not look so good, because some politicians and the media dug down and revealed facts that made supporters of subways very uncomfortable.

The route of the LRT line would have provided good transit to "priority neighbourhoods." (That is political talk meaning low-income neighbourhoods.) The seven stops on the line would mean a short walk for most of the riders. The LRT would have terminated at the Centennial Campus with 10,000 students, most of whom rely on transit. The route also went through land that provided opportunities for redevelopment into higher density housing that would provide more transit users in the future.

By contrast, the proposed subway line will go through more affluent neighbourhoods with lower densities. It will only have three stops and most subway riders will have a long walk to a station. The terminus will be two kilometres from the Centennial Campus. This will reduce transit use. The subway route also does not go through areas that can be easily redeveloped into higher-density housing.

The real problem is the financing. The cost of the Scarborough LRT would be $1.48 billion. This would have been paid for entirely by the provincial government. The cost of the Scarborough subway is $2.5 billion, over $1 billion more than the cost of the LRT. With both the provincial and federal money, there was still a shortfall of $745 million, which will be borrowed by the city. This will result in an increase on average of $41 a year on property taxes across the city for the next twenty years.

The upshot of the controversy was to make many people very nervous. Here we were in 2013, almost ten years into the process of creating a new transit strategy for the GTHA and with some projects already in the construction phases, and yet the politicians are still flip-flopping on one of the central Toronto projects.

Ken Greenberg, the planner, says it is a ludicrous decision to spend nearly $3 billion on a subway that will provide service to fewer people than the LRT. "It's a trophy subway.... I don't know another city that is rich enough to do this kind of thing. We should be spending our money on appropriate technology that gives the best service at the most reasonable cost."[2]

This became an issue in the 2014 mayoral election. John Tory and Doug Ford supported the Scarborough subway plan, while Olivia Chow opposed it. Tory won the election, in part, with support by Scarborough voters and the subway will go ahead.

Mistake 5

The Gardiner Expressway was built between 1955 and 1966. Now, fifty years later, it is in bad repair, with chunks of concrete falling off and the rebar showing in several places. It will cost hundreds of millions of dollars to make the expressway safe and maintain it into the future.

City staff and Waterfront Toronto are recommending that the portion of the Gardiner between Sherbourne Street and the Don River be taken down, and a new road at grade be constructed. The reasons are not only that the Gardiner will be very expensive to repair and maintain, but if it is taken down it will open a parcel of land that Waterfront Toronto can redevelop. It will also help to connect the city to its waterfront.

Around the world about one hundred cities have taken down their inner city expressways like the Gardiner. Different reasons are given in different cities for these decisions, but the common one is that expressways encourage cars to come into the downtown, bringing with them pollution and health hazards. They also create barriers in communities.

But not in Toronto. City council is dominated by suburban councillors who are pro-car. They argue that taking down the Gardiner will increase gridlock and increase the length of commutes, but the real reason is these politicians are opposed to any proposal that would threaten the use of cars in the city. Despite the planning advantages and the high costs of maintenance, they oppose the demolition of the expressway.

CITY-WIDE ISSUES AND CITIZENS

These mistakes on subway projects and the Gardiner are instructive. The politicians made their decisions on political considerations alone. On the surface it is difficult to understand why citizens groups have not become involved in these decisions. After all, transit and highways, particularly subways, cost a lot of money, and affect the lives of hundreds of thousands of people.

The boards of these organizations claim there is citizen involvement, but it is politicians who make all of the important decisions. Metrolinx claims that they formed their Big Move plans with citizen consultations and focus groups, but in reality there was very little citizen input into these plans.

The problem is that it is difficult for groups to mobilize around the process. Citizens groups are almost always organized around local neighbourhood issues, while TTC, Metrolinx, and highway projects are vast systems that affects the entire City of Toronto and beyond. Local groups find it hard to understand how the decisions impact on their community and so they don't get involved. Even experts have a difficult time being heard. In the case of the Big Move, the Neptis Foundation hired an international transit expert to comment, but its critique was simply ignored.

There are few able citizen transit critics. Steve Munro is one, but he is a single voice, not a citizens' movement. What are needed are vibrant community groups that bore into city-wide transit and expressway decisions and uncover their flaws.

The Stop Spadina movement fought, and ultimately defeated, the expressway. The organization of the opposition was at a neighbourhood level. What mobilized people was learning that the expressway would tear the heart out of their communities. Gradually a huge coalition against the expressway was built, neighbourhood by neighbourhood, and that show of community power ultimately led the provincial government to cancel the expressway.

In my experience, whenever the public becomes engaged in political decision-making, it improves the decisions, and perhaps more important, the public is more committed to the project. Fortunately, citizen engagement in local issues in the region is on the rise.

CITIZEN GROUPS

Across the GTHA there has been a remarkable growth in the number and effectiveness of citizen groups. Neighbourhood associations, rate payer groups, and community organizations operate virtually everywhere in the GTHA. Many of these groups have the ability to mobilize large numbers of people around controversial issues that affect their community. Their members are volunteers, and are independent of political parties. Their work is not done for political gain. What mobilizes people is their desire to protect the quality of life and stop environmental damage to the communities where they live.

These groups are engaged in a variety of different issues, but virtually all of them involve government in some way. The community groups use the political process to their advantage and almost always work within the system. A development application that is opposed by a significant number of people will have public hearings by local politicians. This gives citizens' groups the opportunity to make representations before a committee or committees of council. They present briefs, make deputations, write letters, issue press releases, and use every means to make their position known.

Careful, detailed research is at the core of the efforts of citizen groups. Evidence is gathered that supports their cause. Research is done on the impact of the project on the community, and experts are recruited. For example, the Clean Train Coalition, who demanded improvements to the rail link to Pearson Airport, effectively used the testimony of experts to make their point that diesel train engines would bring pollution to all of the communities along the rail line. Electric engines, they argued, are much more environmentally and economically sustainable, and more efficient.

All of the citizens' groups are very conscious that they are waging two campaigns. One is to get a favourable final decision from the local council or regulating agency, and the other to convince the public of the justice of their cause. That is why community groups are very careful about how they present themselves. Usually they will appoint a spokesperson for the group to control the message. Most often this is the chair or president of the association, but sometimes it is a member who is particularly good at handling the media. Spokespersons are key members of the group because they are the public face of the organization.

Because the issues are public controversies, and the decisions that determine the ultimate outcome will be made by public bodies, how the media treats the issue is of special concern. The assumption is that the media will be neutral and report in a factual way, and it is a shock to some community members when the media take sides and use their editorial pages to push their point of view. The *Toronto Star*, for example, a newspaper with a progressive reputation, has supported the expansion of Billy Bishop Airport in the past, and their editorial pages reflect that point of view. Even many of the *Star's* news articles on airport expansion reflected that bias.

In an effort to get their message out, community groups have adopted the Internet and social media with enthusiasm. Research is widely available online. Twitter, Facebook, blogs, and other websites are easy to master and are being used more and more to inform the public. This is a direct form of communication, without interference from reporters and editors. Videos distributed via YouTube are another technique that some groups have adopted.

Corporate leaders are often uneasy in a public forum because it soon becomes obvious that they are motivated by profit. Their strength is they have deep pockets and can buy lobbyists, experts, and lawyers. By contrast, the strength of a citizen's group is the public nature of the way that they operate. They claim their objective is the broader public good, not private gain. That gives them credibility with the public.

ISSUES AND CITIZENS' GROUPS

There are many different citizen groups in the GTHA, and all of them are organized around issues. Some have been very successful and others less so. Here are a few examples:

Hamilton Urban Renewal

A citizens' group emerged in Hamilton to protest the destruction of the city core by urban renewal in the late 1960s. That project went ahead, transforming the city centre and leaving problems in its wake. Ultimately, the federal government cancelled the urban renewal program because of citizen protests. Some in that group went on to found "Save Our Bay," a group trying to stop the pollution of Burlington Bay. Citizens' groups in Hamilton played a leading role in transforming the city's waterfront and improving water quality in the bay.

People or Planes

In the early 1970s the federal government announced they were going to build a huge international airport in Pickering. The reaction was swift. Local groups established People or Planes (POP), and set about organizing opposition to the proposal. The federal plans continued unabated. In 1972 the government expropriated farm land and all of the property in the town of Altona. In total, 3,051 hectares were acquired. POP reacted with a series of actions that became more creative as time went on.

There were leaflets, petitions, and advertisements. On one occasion members of POP dressed up in priest-like robes and marched up University Avenue to Queen's Park carrying fake coffins marked, "Mother Nature." Another had a symbolic public hanging of Premier Bill Davis and Prime Minister Pierre Trudeau. A home guard called Claremont Fusiliers was formed. Militia members would dress up in fake nineteenth-century military uniforms and parade about at public events denouncing the airport and calling for the need to protect the community against interlopers. The most dramatic protest was when one of the members flew a hang-glider with POP signs over Parliament Hill in Ottawa.

By 1975 the group had grown to 8,500 members dedicated to stopping the airport. Candidates were run in the provincial election that year on a platform of opposition to the airport. One of the candidates won and the others polled strong numbers. It was this political action that became the turning point. Bill Davis, the premier, announced soon after the election that the province would no longer support the airport, and the federal government quickly followed.

But as it turned out the struggle was not over. The federal government refused to sell the land they had expropriated. In 2010 a new study was ordered, and on June 13, 2013, the then-finance minister, Jim Flaherty, announced that the government would be going ahead with an airport in the future, albeit one considerably smaller than the original one announced in 1972.

Immediately citizens in Pickering began to organize opposition. Soon a new group was announced called "Land over Landings" (LOL); many of the activists were veterans of POP. This will be a long struggle judging from the efforts of citizen groups against other airports.

Landfill Sites

In the late 1980s the Adam's Mine controversy in Toronto increased the awareness of garbage and waste in the region. When the Bob Rae government announced a search for a landfill site in the GTA to handle Toronto's garbage, targeting forty-four possible sites, citizen groups sprung up around virtually every one of them. In time it became clear that it was impossible to create a mega-landfill site anywhere in the GTA without intense citizen protest. For over a decade Toronto's garbage was hauled by truck to a site in Michigan. The issue was finally solved when Mayor David Miller negotiated a deal for Toronto's garbage to be taken to a landfill site near London, Ontario.

Citizens for Local Democracy

There was a huge citizens' movement called "Citizens for Local Democracy" set up to fight the Mike Harris Megacity proposal. It failed despite the widespread opposition. Megacity was imposed and has caused political problems in the City of Toronto ever since.

The Red Hill Creek Expressway

The Red Hill Creek Expressway in Hamilton was a proposal to build a four lane highway from the Queen Elizabeth Highway to the Lincoln Alexander Parkway on the Mountain. It was to go through the Red Hill Creek Valley and over the Niagara Escarpment. The project was first proposed in the 1950s but it took until the 1980s before it was finally approved.

A citizen's group called "Save Our Valley" was formed to oppose the highway. It advocated turning the valley into a park. By the early 1990s the provincial NDP government cancelled funding for the expressway. Support for the highway continued, and David Crombie was appointed to resolve the issue, but to no avail. The Mike Harris Conservatives were elected in 1995, and they restored funding. The Liberals in Ottawa countered this by demanding a full environmental assessment.

In 2003 a pro-highway mayor was elected in Hamilton, and the project was ready to go ahead. It was then that the protests began in earnest. They were led by a group called "Friends of the Red Hill Valley" and a First Nations group from the Six Nations reserve. Access roads were blocked, injunctions were filed, police were called to open the roads, young protesters climbed trees slated to be cut for the road and refused to come down. Finally, in 2004 construction began in earnest, and the highway was finished in 2007. Today there are still unresolved legal proceedings between the City of Hamilton and the federal government.

The saga is remarkable for the tenacity of people on both sides. A solution was imposed by those with political power, but environmentalists remain deeply dissatisfied with the outcome. The Red Hill Creek Expressway fight motivated more people in Hamilton to fight to improve the environment.

Protecting Greenfields

Several groups continue to fight greenfields developments in Vaughan, Markham, and Pickering. These controversies are described in more detail in Chapter 7.

It will be important to watch what happens in these issues because they pit environmentalists against developers and their political supporters on councils in the outer suburbs. Different citizens' groups have emerged to fight the issues, but all of the issues are similar. Developers own land and want the right to build. The groups and their members challenge that right, saying that it will create unsustainable suburban sprawl.

The provincial government has already intervened in Pickering to rule that those lands are on the Oak Ridges Moraine and cannot be developed because development would violate the greenbelt policy. In the other cases the legalities are less clear. The province does have the power to intervene if they deem it to be in the provincial interest. It is not clear what will happen.

Concerned Citizens of King Township

"Concerned Citizens of King Township" are committed to maintaining the rural nature of the township. This group has been active for years in protecting the Oak Ridges Moraine and maintaining the rural nature of King Township.

They are led by conservationists and environmentalists that have broad support from the community. In the past they have challenged developers who wanted to build on the moraine, but they have not always been successful. In one case the province allowed a developer to build housing on the moraine because the company had been granted approval by the local council. That decision angered local people and mobilized more support for concerned Citizens of King Township.

Unlike others, this citizens' group has been actively engaged in local politics and has endorsed candidates during elections.

Durham CLEAR

Durham CLEAR (Citizens Lobby for Environmental Awareness and Responsibility) engaged in an intense six-year campaign to stop an incinerator being built in the municipality of Clarendon in Durham that would burn garbage from Durham and York Regions.

This was a sophisticated citizens' group that mounted a major campaign. They raised funds, did extensive research on the health hazards of incinerators, and organized protests of local people. The province responded by conducting an environmental assessment, and after the report was released the incinerator was approved. Finally, in 2011, Durham Regional Council approved the incinerator by a vote of sixteen to seven. Legal action was taken to stop construction, but that also failed. In the end, the incinerator was built and is operating.

Citizens for Clean Air

No community group has had as much impact on provincial politics in recent years as Citizens for Clean Air. The controversy that they created led to the cancellation of two gas-fired power plants, and contributed to the resignation of Premier Dalton McGuinty and the Energy Minister Chris Bentley.

The Ontario government closed the coal-fired Lakeview Generating Station, in Mississauga, in 2005. In 2008 the government decided that two gas-fired stations were needed to meet the electric power needs for the GTA, one in Mississauga and the other in Oakville. It was not long before local residents began to organize and formed Citizens for Clean Air. In 2009 the group began mounting protests to try and force cancellation of the two power plants. Pressure was put on local Liberal members of the legislature. A rally to generate publicity was held at Queen's Park in October 2010 featuring the American environmentalist Erin Brockovich.

The government responded first by cancelling the Oakville plant in October 2010, but the controversy continued because the group demanded that the Mississauga plant be cancelled as well. In September 2011 a provincial general election was being held and the Liberals were in trouble. Both opposition parties had promised to either cancel the plant or to undertake an independent environmental assessment. The pressure was so great that a week before the election the Liberals announced the cancellation of the Mississauga plant.

This announcement helped the Liberals and they were able to hold onto government, but only as a minority. It still did not end the controversy. The cost of the cancellation was the most difficult issue. For some time the minister claimed it would cost $230 million. Later, in October 2013, the auditor general put the cost of cancellation at least $930 million. Another element of the story is that it was learned that after Dalton McGuinty resigned, the premier's staff or others had erased all emails and other files having to do with the controversy. To the opposition and the press this looked like an illegal cover-up.

The leaders and members of Citizens for Clean Air had nothing to do with the subsequent political troubles for the Liberal, but they played a major role in the cancellation of the gas-fired power plants. After the resignation of the premier and the minister, the Liberals were re-elected with a majority government led by Kathleen Wynne. Still the controversy rages.

Clean Train Coalition

The "Clean Train Coalition" involved thousands of people living in Toronto's west end. The group failed to win their objective of turning the rail service from Union Station to Pearson Airport into a public transit line, but Metrolinx has promised to convert all of the GO train service from diesel to electric, one of the group's objectives.

Code Blue

"Code Blue" was a community group that opposed a proposal by Councillor Doug Ford to turn property controlled by Waterfront Toronto into a mega-mall. The proposal was withdrawn because it had no support from the public or city council.

No Casino Toronto

"No Casino Toronto" opposed the proposal to bring a major casino to the city. The pro-casino group was well financed and sophisticated. By contrast, No Casino Toronto raised money from individual donations and challenged each proposal with well-researched arguments. The casino proposal failed at council.

Billy Bishop Airport

The Island Airport, now called the Billy Bishop Toronto City Airport, has been the longest and most intense citizen struggle since Stop Spadina. Opposition began in 1929, when the proposal of an airport on the Island was first made. Today the opposition is stronger than ever.

The bridge to the Island Airport became the defining issue of the 2003 Toronto municipal election. All of the leading candidates for mayor, with the exception of David Miller, supported the bridge. Miller's opposition distinguished him from the others. It became the wedge issue in the campaign, and Miller used it to win the election. The bridge was cancelled. The first victory went to the citizens. But that has hardly been the end of the controversy.

In 2006 Porter Airlines began commercial airline service out of the Island Airport with Bombardier Q400 turboprops, but in 2013 Porter announced it wanted to fly jets out of the airport. To make this happen the runways will have to be lengthened by two hundred metres at both ends. Suddenly the struggle against Porter became a struggle to try to save Toronto's waterfront from jets and all the noise, pollution, traffic, and the filling in of the harbour and lake that that jets would create.

As of this writing, there is no sign that the issue is about to be resolved.

» «

Citizens groups like these are essentially opposition groups. They are most effective when they oppose the imposition or expansion of a project like an airport, a highway, or a new development on an existing community. These types of groups can rally opposition because they are fighting to preserve the community, and protect its quality of life, but this is also their weakness. They are defensive groups and rarely propose changes that are needed to improve their communities, but there are others who have caught the need for change.

GRASSROOTS VISIONARIES

There has been an explosion of interest in the cities across the GTHA, and scores of new groups with ideas of how we can enhance the urban environment have come into existence. There are talks, books, and films about cities and neighbourhoods. All of these different projects, groups, and interests promote what Jan Gehl calls "lively, safe, sustainable, healthy cities." These are some examples.

The Toronto Environmental Alliance has been very successful in advocating for environmental programs. The Co-operative Housing Federation of Toronto for years has supported the funding of affordable housing. Even older organizations like the United Way of Toronto now advocate innovative social projects and fund programs like this.

In Toronto a group called Jane's Walks was formed to honour Jane Jacobs while at the same time giving people an opportunity to explore the city. The organization sponsors walks in neighbourhoods led by knowledgeable volunteers. The intent is not only to explore the city and local communities, it is to promote and build vibrant neighbourhoods. In 2014 the organization sponsored 150 walks in Toronto that showcased the city's neighbourhoods, parks, ravines, and its diverse cultural mix. Today, over one hundred cities around the world participate in Jane's Walks and more are joining every month.[3]

Cycle Toronto is a grassroots organization that promotes cycling in the city. There has been a frustrating struggle to establish good bike lanes in Toronto because of the stubborn opposition from councillors who see them as taking away access to the city streets by cars. The movement began as a militant group called the Toronto Cyclists Union, but gradually changed to become an advocate for the promotion of healthy, safe cycling for everyone. They work closely with inner-city politicians who support the movement and city planners, but they remain passionate in their commitment that cycling will help to ease our transportation problems and promote a healthy way of life.[4]

Another group that recently emerged in Toronto calls itself Laneway Renaissance. They see the vast network of laneways, alleys, and other underused spaces as "an enormous untapped resource for the development and intensification of community, culture, business, and housing in Toronto."[5]

The group frames its arguments like the humanistic planners. They are concerned about housing costs, they support the quality of life of neighbourhoods, advocate the end of sprawl, and promote homes for families in the downtown.

This is a quote that comes from their website that reflects not only their aims, but shows the passion they have for creating a new type of city:

> When people are able to imagine laneways as something more than drab, rundown, and forgettable service lanes, and when they begin to see compact, efficient houses, businesses, streets, gardens, and hubs of culture, they may begin to uncover solutions for the creation of a more resilient and diverse city.

It is not politicians who will lead the new urban movement. It is grassroots activists like this who understand the need for a new type of city and have the passion, drive, and political stamina to make it happen.

WOODGREEN COMMUNITY SERVICES

Most groups focus on single issues but there are a number that have a much broader focus, and look at all community needs. The mandate of WoodGreen Community Services seeks to provide services for everyone living within their community. It works in the East End of Toronto and the former municipality of East York. The organization provides different services needed by the community, rather than just one. Its mandate is to strengthen the community and promote grassroots control of neighbourhoods by the people who live there.

WoodGreen has over 400 employees and runs 72 programs operating out of 32 locations. The programs range from housing and social centres for seniors and the homeless, to seven daycare centres serving 700 children. WoodGreen runs services for the mentally ill, education programs for parents living in poverty, tax clinics, and after-school programs. These programs are not run along ethnic or religious lines. They are open to everyone who lives in the community, regardless of their backgrounds.

Brian Smith is the recently retired president and CEO of the organization. For the past forty years, he built WoodGreen into a multi-service, community-based agency that that provides services to thousands of people. Brian presents himself as an easy-going, relaxed person at the end of his career, but that is just the public front of an astute program innovator and an effective administrator.

I went to talk to him about how organizations rooted in neighbourhoods can be the building blocks to meet the social needs of people and help them regain political control of their communities. I was not disappointed. These are some of the ideas he expressed:

> A city is like an orchestra. To have a great community, a great city, a great place to live, everyone has an instrument to play, a role to play.... People need to have the opportunity to be engaged in building their city and make whatever contribution, large or small, that suits their abilities....
>
> I have lived in the East End most of my life and I always found it a really great place to live. There was always sense of community. I knew everybody. The streets were safe. Things were good. But there were a lot of people who were marginalized.... We saw people in crisis and we were in many ways helpless. We didn't have any resources and were constrained by lots of rules and regulation. We had to break that if we were to help....
>
> I try and break it down to the human level. On the street whether your neighbour is Italian or Filipino you all are trying to create a community where everyone will feel safe and significant. You may not particularly like your neighbour, but you have to live beside him, and you have to find a way to live in some sort of peaceful coexistence. The fact is, that what is happening on the street, from cleaning the snow away, to picking up garbage, to the schools in your community. All those are your common interest and when you work to find solutions it helps to build a sense of neighbourhood and community....
>
> You need a solid base to work from. WoodGreen was an organization before I came and gradually we built it so we have been able to deliver more services. At the same time, we did more community development. We have been able to do both. But you need a bottom-up organization involving people, making representation to the government. That's how you get heard....
>
> The problem with the community centres the city provides is that they are about sports and other things like that. They don't really care if you show up or not. It is not something that reaches out. We need to engage the community....

I think creating neighbourhood centres that would serve an area is the way to go. You don't need a lot of staff for those things, somewhere between three and six. You create a place where people can come, feel safe, exchange ideas, and work on common issues that face the community.

People know how to do these things themselves. They just need a little help or direction.

COMMUNITY CONTROL

What Brian Smith was telling me was that ordinary people are the ones who have the skills and knowledge to manage their own communities. They need help and organizational support, but they can do it themselves, and in doing this their connection to their community deepens and becomes more meaningful. These are also the very people who know the needs of their community. They know how to solve problems and help others.

What has happened in big cities is that the power that people once had over their communities has been taken away from them by government and politicians. This wasn't done in a malicious way; it was thought to be the best way to deliver services, but it is time to return power back to the people.

All public servants, whether politicians or staff, need to think carefully about the role they are playing. Governments who only deliver services are turning people into clients, not effective, full-blown citizens who control the communities where they live. We need facilitators helping to empower people. That is what WoodGreen does so well.

And promoting community control does not mean that we can do away with the politicians or civil servants. We need them because they have to deal with budgets, making sure that services are delivered in an equitable way, and dealing with any number of other things that governments must attend to.

As I reflected on this I came to understand that community empowerment has long been the case in my own community, Toronto Island. Islanders don't have to get political permission to have an art show, or a meeting to discuss community problems. We do it ourselves. If a neighbour needs help, others pitch in to offer aid. It is the way that things have always been done on the Island. Local control is so complete that a couple of decades ago the police pulled their detachment off the Island. "There's no crime. It's not a good use of our resources," we were told. Islanders like it that way.

It is easier to have local control in a small community like the Island and much harder in the city with a large, diverse population, but it happens there as well. WoodGreen is one example and there are many others. Self-help and collective decision-making is the ethos in the housing co-ops in the city. Active condo associations look after more than their building. They play a role in their surrounding community and they go out of their way to help those in need.

Other groups do the same. The East Scarborough Storefront project has played a remarkable role in building community and organizing new initiatives.[6] They have developed a unique program to welcome immigrants and help them integrate into their community.

Friends of Dufferin Grove Park have transformed an ordinary city park into a community facility with bake ovens, a fire pit, arts festivals, sporting events, and a farmers' market. They manage park maintenance, with the help of the city parks department, and try and deal with community issues before they develop into problems.[7]

There are dozens of examples like this across the GTHA of groups of people acting on their own to take control of their communities. In the process they strengthen grassroots control. They connect people, help them identify with where they live, and give them control over their own street, shopping district, their own environment, and their own lives.

PARTICIPATORY BUDGETING

One of the most interesting examples of empowering communities is participatory budgeting. This is a practice that originated in Latin America. The city of Porto Alegre, in Brazil, began participatory budgeting as early as 1989. Neighbourhood meetings and assemblies are held to discuss how the city should spend its budget for a variety of city-wide and neighbourhood projects. The mayor, councillors, and other officials attend these meetings to give information and participate in the discussions, but it is the people who make decisions on things like transportation, recreation, health, education, and economic development. In recent years there have been up to 50,000 people involved in this process in Porto Alegre, a city of 1.5 million.

There have been experiments with participatory budgeting in New York City and Chicago. In Canada, the leader has been the city of Guelph, in Ontario. Again, it reflects the progressive politics of that city. Guelph was the fourth city in North America to practise direct citizen involvement in the budgeting process. Now Hamilton has become the fifth city, and the first GTHA municipality to introduce the process.[8]

To understand how participatory budgeting works it is best to see it at a local level. Hamilton's Ward 1 councillor, Brian McHattie, formed an advisory committee of twenty-one community members to decide how $1.6 million of the ward's budget would be spent.

The committee met several times to discuss different projects with the help of city staff. They had to develop a compromise budget on the spending proposals, ensuring that the cost of the projects did not go over the money allocated. Once the projects were identified, then the final decisions on which projects would be funded was decided by an online poll. A committee was set up to see that the projects were implemented.

It is interesting to see what projects the citizens finally agreed on. They included sidewalk repair, public art, historical signs, a pedestrian signal, a free lunch program, a speed bump, a school nutrition program, fixing public gardens, and an outdoor gym in a city park — hardly outrageous or radical projects. The decisions of the citizens were binding on the politicians. None of these projects would have been funded by city council, but they were completed as result of this process.

Now a Toronto councillor has begun to experiment with participatory budgeting. Shelley Carroll, councillor for Ward 33, Don Valley East, used $500,000 of section 37 money for local projects. She set up a committee of local people, and ultimately seven projects in the ward were chosen. Again, the projects were local. They included landscaping and beautification of public property, a computer hub in a local library, outside fitness equipment, a dog park, a skateboarding park, and basketball courts. Every one of these projects improved the public domain or public services.[9]

There are many benefits to participatory budgeting. Perhaps the most important is that it involves citizens in real decision-making about projects in their neighbourhood. It is local people who know how to make decisions that improve their community, because they know its needs. This is far better than city politicians or bureaucrats making funding decisions about communities they don't live in or understand. It is "bottom-up" rather than "top-down" decision-making.

There are criticisms. Only a small number of the people of Ward 1 in Hamilton or Ward 33 in Toronto, were involved in the process. But these are only experiments — a trial run at participatory decision making around budgets. With more experience, and greater confidence, participatory budgeting can be expanded until people have real control over how local governments spend their money in their communities.

BUILDING GRASSROOTS CONTROL

Ford Nation emerged as a political movement to support Rob and Doug Ford, but it is also an expression of the frustration that many people feel about their government. In my view, their grievances are legitimate. There are problems with the way we practise government in Toronto, the GTHA, and this country. The people of Ford Nation are following a strategy of electing right wing politicians, but unfortunately those politicians have no idea how to reform the political system and satisfy the grievances of their followers.

The only strategy that will work is finding ways to encourage people to become involved at the grassroots to improve their communities, using the tools and funds of government. There are a host of ways that this can be done, but they are being frustrated at every turn.

Let me describe one more community organization that I learned about from Michael Shapcott, the housing expert. He explained that in the old City of Toronto, before Megacity was imposed, many of the city planners were assigned to work in communities. Their job was to help local people study and understand the characteristics of their neighbourhood. The planners created an inventory of what existed in the community, and helped people to identify what was needed to improve the quality of life. Gradually, solutions emerged, and when funds were available from the city, they were allocated to solve the problems.

Amalgamation killed that experiment. Planning today has become an approvals system of new development. It's time to get planners and other city staff back into the communities, working with local people to help them enhance public spaces and bring facilities that are needed.

Our cities have grown into enormous conglomerations of millions of people, but our political structures have not been adapted to meet the needs of the new urban environment. What has emerged is a top-down political system, efficient for the bureaucrats and politicians, but alienating for local people. We have to reconnect people to politics by decentralizing political decision-making so that the needs of local neighbourhoods can be met. This is the promise and challenge of democracy.

In my dreams of local democracy, the city councillor is not only a decision-maker, but his or her primary role is as a facilitator. Politicians should not just sit back and vote, "yes," or "no," on issues brought forward by bureaucrats. They should work with community members developing proposals, and consult with staff to see if the city has the resources and finances to undertake projects. City council meetings, then, can be the place where the councillors discuss and debate, make compromises and concessions, in order to determine what projects will be supported.

Community organizations like WoodGreen can play an invaluable role in helping people formulate the needs of neighbourhoods. Citizens' groups set up to oppose projects will still be a part of the political process. They are essential vehicles to express the needs of the community. Citizens working directly with city staff should be encouraged. Participatory budgeting needs to be instituted and expanded everywhere. All of this is part of a strategy — a program — to involve citizens in their communities, and their city, because that will give us the best possible government. In the process it will deliver real democracy.

This I know. We will never develop a New Urban Agenda capable of truly transforming our city unless we develop grassroots democracy. In the next chapter we detail the elements of that agenda.

TEN

THE NEW URBAN AGENDA

As I write this, the 2014 municipal election is just over. Candidates talked endlessly about what they thought would solve problems in their municipalities, but their promises were limited, and how they would keep them was sketchy, at best.

John Tory had four main promises: the SmartTrack transit plan, jobs, holding the line on taxes to the rate of inflation, and ending the chaos and divisions of the Rob Ford years. His is a pro-business approach to government that will rely on the private sector, but it doesn't begin to deal with the problems of climate change, affordable housing, poverty, or encouraging participation.

Across the GTHA politicians talked about transportation and holding down taxes. The incumbents took credit for new transit that will be paid for by the province. Planning and development were issues, but most politicians understood they have little ability to attract new projects or to control and shape them if one was proposed. Most did not to go beyond this because they knew they didn't have the money or resources to make much happen.

For all of the "sound and fury" at election time, the vast majority of politicians were elected because they were incumbents. "Better the devil you know than the one that you don't know," is the rule. The opportunity to discuss real issues that would benefit people and the cities was lost.

This lack of policy discussion at elections is particularly distressing because, with a clear understanding of the problems we are facing, it is not difficult to see what should be done. We need a comprehensive plan that will solve the problems of our cities, and an outline of how we can finance and implement that plan. That is what the New Urban Agenda is designed to do.

THE NEW URBAN AGENDA IN OUTLINE FORM

Deepening Democracy

The implementation of the agenda will not happen unless there is broad political and popular support led by people in the neighbourhoods. Provincial and municipal leadership is important, but support from grass-roots is essential.

The way to build this support is through extensive consultation with residents who will be affected by the changes. Only when people understand how these changes will enhance the quality of their lives, safeguard the life of their neighbourhoods, save money, improve the environment, provide thousands of new jobs, and lead to a more efficient, affordable city, will they support it and make the New Urban Agenda happen.

Empowering individuals and communities must become a top priority. Community organizations that engage in issues, participatory budgeting, city staff working in communities with residents, all of these things will help lead to progressive social change and lessen the sense of political alienation. Participation of local residents will also help them understand and accept the new programs that will be necessary to improve buildings, reduce traffic, and lessen pollution.

The key to citizen empowerment is reliable, timely information about what is happening on the local scene, and what community groups are accomplishing in other cities. Good local media helps, but in the future groups of community activists will use the Internet to build an information system with archives, accounts of what is happening in local government and politics, and information about other cities.

Accurate, reliable information, the strengthening of democratic practices, and mobilized, engaged citizens are all essential for meaningful change.

Transit and Transportation

Improved transit that will get people out of their cars and provide rapid, efficient transportation at an affordable cost is a high priority if the agenda is to be realized. The province has led the way with planning, and a remarkable level of funding for rapid transit across the GTHA. Municipalities also have to come to the table to provide local services that connects the neighbourhoods into the rapid transit system.

The downtown relief subway line is essential to solve transit problems in the densely populated Toronto core, but the suburbs cannot be ignored. High-speed bus service in dedicated lanes along the arterial roads leading to rapid transit lines is the most cost effective and efficient way to provide good service in both the Toronto and GTA suburbs.

This is just the beginning of an effective transportation system. Municipalities and the provincial government must implement the next logical stage of these plans — discouraging the use of cars in the city. Implementing disincentives to driving will be politically difficult, but it must be done or the enormous investments in transit could be wasted. Tolls on the expressways, increased parking fees, the reduction in the number of parking spaces, the elimination of free parking for employees, restriction of car access to some streets, speed bumps on residential streets: all of these disincentives are good ways to calm and reduce traffic. A reduction of the number of cars on the streets will make it much easier for the delivery of goods across the city and on the expressways.

Cycling is an essential element of the transportation network in the GTHA. Protected bicycle lanes must be built through all parts of the city to provide an efficient, safe network for commuters and recreational riders. The objective should be to have 50 percent of all commuter trips by bicycle in the near future. This will help to ease traffic and transit congestion. Other cities have achieved that goal and there is no way why it can't be done in the GTHA.

Reducing the use of vehicles that burn fossil fuels is essential if we are to eliminate the threat of climate change and improve the health and safety of the population. E-cars and other technologies should be encouraged in various ways, such as providing recharging stations, and tax incentives for vehicles that produce no greenhouse gas emissions.

As this new type of transportation plan for cities is developed, the Canadian government must implement a system of high-speed trains connecting cities in the GTHA, Canada, and North America.

When all this is accomplished, the country will have a transportation system worth bragging about. It will be an efficient, fast, non-polluting, low-cost way of moving people. Commuters, then, will make the logical choice to choose transit over driving cars. That, in turn, will significantly reduce pollution, and make a major contribution in the creation of affordable, safe, healthy, and economically competitive cities. It will also improve the quality of life in our neighbourhoods.

Redesigning the Public Domain

The next step in city building must be redesigning the public domain. This is particularly important in the city cores of Toronto, Hamilton, and the new downtowns being created in the outer suburbs. The public domain of residential neighbourhoods also need attention.

Pedestrians and cyclists must be given priority in all neighbourhoods, particularly in the densely populated retail districts of the city. Sidewalks must be widened and the use of cars discouraged. Art on the streets, benches for pedestrians, small parks, opening up the laneways to pedestrians and shops — all of these changes to the public sphere will help to enhance the look of our streets and improve how they function. This is how our downtowns can become lively social places where commerce coexists with people simply taking time to enjoy their city.

In residential neighbourhoods, the priority, again, must be on calming traffic. These streets need to be made safe for children and people of all ages. This can be done with speed bumps and even closing some streets to traffic. Perhaps at certain times of the day some streets could be reserved for kids to play street hockey, soccer, or baseball.

Special attention must be given to neighbourhood shopping districts. These centres, along with schools and other facilities, are the focus of residential communities, and it is important that they are successful. Business Improvement Associations have grown up, but they would benefit from the involvement of residents. Opportunities for craftspeople, farmers' markets, or those selling creative or even quirky products, help to enhance a shopping district.

There are other facilities in residential neighbourhoods that benefit from the involvement of residents. Dufferin Grove Park in Toronto has been virtually taken over by local people. Withrow Park offers "Dusk Dances" in the summer. Other communities have helped to create local skating rinks. Vacant public spaces can be turned over to neighbourhood gardeners to plant flowers and shrubs. Community vegetable gardens promoted in a number of municipalities are very successful programs that give enjoyment to a variety of people.

Local people investing time and energy in their community not only improves the quality of life, it promotes a type of identity and commitment to the neighbourhood that builds solidarity and lasting friendships. This gives strength to communities and bridges the divide between different cultures, religions, and age groups, and helps to involve young people.

Public/Private Partnerships

The public/private partnership model is the best way of implementing large projects, like affordable housing, that results in a mix of market and rent-geared-to-income units. It can also be appropriate for the retrofitting of aging apartment buildings and houses, district energy projects, and the installation of solar power. These types of projects are a marriage between private enterprise and the public.

Public/private partnerships will need start-up funding from governments and they must operate within terms of reference set by government, but it is important that they remain independent and able to make arrangements that are of advantage to both parties. The start-up money needed for the projects can come from grants or loans from government. Once established, the partnerships can raise the needed funds from financial institutions, pension funds, and by selling debentures or other instruments. In this way, the debt will not be an additional burden for government.[1]

All of those projects will be designed in such a way that they will cost money in the start-up phase to do the work, but those costs will be recovered when new units in housing developments are sold or costs recaptured from energy savings.

Planning

Ontario's planning system is broken and must be reformed if we are to build better cities. The approval of new private development is important, but planning priorities must also focus on how buildings relate to the public spaces, and the provision of housing needed by the public, not just profits for developers. There are a number of principles that can be followed.

Greenfields development must be disallowed or severely restricted, and new development should be integrated into existing communities. Increasing the densities of all communities in the suburbs must be a priority. This means building medium- to high-density affordable housing along the transit corridors and leaving the existing single-family housing intact.

Architects, designers, and developers should be encouraged to use interesting and unusual materials and designs in private and public buildings. Zoning must be changed to allow mixed-use buildings with residential, retail, and work spaces. The waterfront, ravines, creeks, and river banks should be opened for recreational use.

Reforming the planning system is essential if we are to have real planning rather than an approvals system for private developers. The OMB must be disbanded and the official plans of municipalities must show greater detail. The details of those plans should be followed in all but exceptional cases. That will give predictability and provide a type of consistency to neighbourhoods.

Heritage buildings need much better protection in Ontario. Victorian houses are rapidly disappearing, and many fine art deco buildings are under threat. This must become a priority or our cities will become overwhelmed by new buildings.

Affordable Housing

The building of affordable housing will be a high priority in the New Urban Agenda. Market housing will remain, but affordable housing has been neglected for far too long, and the need in the GTHA is pressing.

This is an opportunity to increase densities in the suburbs and rejuvenate and revitalize deteriorating parts of the city. Higher densities, in turn, will make those communities more efficient with improved services. The program will result in mixed developments with people of various ethnic groups, incomes, and ages. A high priority must be given to families. Affordable units must be large enough to meet their needs.

A good affordable housing program must provide a variety of options. In some cases private sector developers of large projects will be required to set aside 25 percent of new units for low-income housing. The development of co-ops and non-profit housing, with units reserved for low-income families, is a preferred option of many. Seniors housing must remain a priority, and special effort must be made to provide housing for those with special needs and the homeless.

No doubt developers will see an affordable housing program as a threat, and will use their considerable political influence to oppose it, but affordable housing is rental housing for individuals and families with middle or low incomes who cannot get the housing they need in the private market. Condos for high-income people will continue to be built by developers in downtown Toronto, and other choice locations in the GTHA. The strong economic incentives for private housing will not change.

Some of the costs of the affordable housing program must be borne by the federal and provincial governments. Municipalities cannot pay for this program with their limited revenue. Seed money from government will be needed to start projects. In mixed developments of market and subsidized housing, the buildings can be mortgaged and paid for over time out of the sale of condos and rents paid by tenants. The rents of low-income tenants will be supplemented with the rent-geared-to-income program.

Retrofitting Buildings

Retrofitting buildings for energy conservation will be essential in order to reduce greenhouse gas emissions, make the buildings more efficient and affordable, and provide better amenities and services needed by the residents. The retrofits will also increase the life of these buildings, providing good housing for years to come.

This will be a huge program, employing thousands of people. There are about one million buildings in the GTHA and virtually all of them are of an age that they need some remedial work. It will require new companies producing innovative products and thousands of new skilled and semi-skilled workers. This will be an enormous stimulus to the economy.

The best way to organize an extensive program such as this is through public/private partnerships. The City of Toronto building retrofit program is excellent, but it is very limited. Only a public/private partnership program dedicated to retrofitting buildings can mobilize the scale of work that is needed.

There will be resistance to this type of program by some building owners, and it will be challenging to get agreement. It would be possible for the province or municipalities to require the retrofitting of deteriorated buildings, but that should be avoided if possible.

Better to have this program managed by local people working through a public/private partnership. That will give residents confidence in the project and encourage whole neighbourhoods to be retrofitted at the same time, reducing costs. When homeowners understand that a reasonable financing plan is in place, and that the program will reduce energy costs, and save money, it will be welcomed.

This program will take several years to implement, but it will result in greater savings, reduce greenhouse gas emissions, and make our city more affordable. That, in turn, will make the GTHA more economically viable and encourage investment.

District Energy

The advantages of district heating and cooling systems are very compelling. This is another way that greenhouse gases and energy costs can be reduced significantly. Programs developed in Guelph, Ontario, and by Enwave in downtown Toronto, have demonstrated their worth. The problem is organizing these systems, financing them, and getting public approval. Again, a public private/ partnership will help make this possible.

The technology requires a central heating and cooling facility and insulated pipes buried underground to carry hot and cold water to the buildings. If the systems are run entirely electrically, they will eliminate the air pollution emissions for the heating and cooling of buildings. This will help us reach our commitments to reduce greenhouse gas emissions, and be a major Canadian contribution in the international effort to reduce climate change.

The Electric City

With investments in transit and the transportation system, renovation of buildings, district heating and cooling of buildings, and the generation of alternative energy by solar and wind, we will have created an electric city, where virtually all of our energy needs are produced in a non-polluting way.

The strategy is three-fold: energy conservation that will reduce our needs; increasing the production of alternative energy; and building energy storage capacity. At the moment cities are unable to produce all of the electricity they consume, and it is likely that will continue for a long time, but the province is encouraging the production of alternative energy.

Ontario is a North American leader in alternative energy. All of the coal-fired electric power stations have been closed in the province, reducing a major source of pollution and greenhouse gas emissions. The huge windmills and solar power systems that are being built in rural areas of the province are one part of this strategy.

Solar power is the promise of the future for cities. Many schools, public buildings, apartments, and factories have flat roofs where solar panels can be installed. Scores of private houses have been retrofitted with panels. In Ontario, individuals can sell power into the grid and receive payment from Ontario Hydro or a reduction in their hydro bill.

But alternative energy production involves not only solar power. There are now soundless wind turbines that are being developed that can be mounted on top of houses.[2] These generators, along with solar panels, can create much of the energy needed for houses. They can also be put on top of apartment buildings and even installed on hydro poles to generate power for streetlights. The potential to produce alternative power in the GTHA is huge.

Conservation measures and alternative energy projects are reducing the amount of electricity we consume. Our objective should be to produce all of the energy we need without burning fossil fuel. That is now a possibility. Buildings can be heated and cooled using district energy systems powered by electricity. Subways and streetcars now use electric power, and buses can be converted. Metrolinx has already made the decision to convert GO trains to electricity. Some industry, like those that smelt and refine steel or other minerals, will find it difficult to abandon fossil fuels, but government working with companies can help to find and finance alternatives.

The biggest difficulty will be in converting private cars and trucks, but even that is changing. Already the trucking industry of North America is discussing converting their fleets to natural gas. This is still a fossil fuel, but natural gas engines are more fuel efficient, less expensive to operate than diesel and gasoline, and produce less greenhouse gases.

Electric cars now exist. Their main limitation is their battery storage systems. Once the range of electric vehicles has increased to five hundred kilometres on a single charge, there will be no reason to keep our gasoline-powered vehicles. As an added benefit, there are significant long-term savings. Even with the drop in the price of oil, it is still less expensive to recharge an electric car than to refuel a gasoline car.

The Green Economy

In a letter to the editor of the *Globe and Mail*, Matt Burgess, a professor specializing in environmental studies, writes, "New evidence arrives almost every day that the clean technology revolution is coming.... Countries that get out in front of the pack will take home larger shares of this economic pie.... There will be enormous demand for clean knowledge and technology."[3] That "clean technology revolution" means jobs for the country or region that moves decisively to take advantage of this opportunity.

There has been much talk by provincial politicians of developing the green economy to replace the loss of manufacturing jobs. The New Urban Agenda opens a number of possibilities to replace the loss with well-paid jobs. The building retrofitting program, for example, will need thousands of workers with a variety of skills. The program will require many different types of jobs. An energy audit of buildings in the program will have to be completed, and a plan developed for each building. Materials will be selected, costs calculated, financing arranged, contracts signed, windows, doors, and insulation manufactured. All this will have to be done before the installation can begin. The same process will be necessary for the installation of alternative energy and new heating systems.

It will not only be the construction industry that will be stimulated by programs such as this; it will also result in a boost to manufacturing. Windows, doors, and new types of insulation will have to be fabricated. There will be home-heating systems designed and made, geothermal products, insulated pipes, solar panels, and battery storage systems. The impact of a program like this will go right through the economy.

Other green industries are possible. An urban gardening movement is catching on in some cities, where vegetables are grown on vacant plots of land. Greenhouses are being built in cities. In Japan high-rise towers have been constructed to grow vegetables. Urban gardening not only reduces the cost of food and provides work for local people, but it eliminates the cost of trucking, and the greenhouse gases that the trucks produce.

Green industries are not the entire answer for the ills of the GTHA and Ontario economy, but it will make a huge difference. Building a sustainable city will result in hundreds of thousands of jobs. A green economic strategy is the wave of the future. The GTHA can become a leader in these new technologies with the New Urban Agenda.

Social Support

The growing disparity between rich and poor is reshaping our cities in many negative ways. Slums, like those of the past, have disappeared, but there are high-rise developments in the GTHA that have all of the characteristics of slums, other than the dilapidated look of the buildings.

There are ways of dealing with income inequality through our tax system. This is beyond the scope of this book, but it is one of the burning issues of our age, and must be addressed or we will pay a price in social dissent, political protest, and personal hardship for the most vulnerable people in our society.

The key elements of an adequate social support program include a more equal distribution of income, and affordable housing. It also includes daycare, universal school nutrition programs, immigrant settlement help, and youth job programs. Increasing numbers of policy experts believe the way to do this is through a guaranteed annual income program.

AN URBAN POLICY STATEMENT

I have emphasized the key role of building grassroots support for the New Urban Agenda because I know from my community involvement how important it will be if a program like this is to be supported and implemented. Activists working through local organizations at a community level are the most important element for change because they can build support for programs.

But governments are still key components. They have money and policy tools that can make things happen very quickly. At Queen's Park the Liberal government has shown determination to fund and create effective transit in the GTHA. In Ottawa the Conservative government has no urban strategy, but both the Liberals and NDP opposition parties are committed to increasing federal funding to cities.

I have argued that what we need is a provincial Minister of the Greater Toronto and Hamilton Area supported by a good staff of civil servants. The GTHA has merged into one region, but it is divided by many different municipalities and agencies. There is a pressing need for coordination and co-operation. A minister would have the power to make this happen.[4]

The most sensible and simplest way to implement the New Urban Agenda is through a provincial policy statement that requires municipalities to establish policies and programs consistent with provincial priorities. What we need is an "Urban Policy Statement."

It is not difficult to imagine what a statement like this would say. It would direct municipalities to establish building retrofit programs, and set up public-private partnerships to fund and administer that program. It would improve the standards for new buildings and encourage or require district energy programs to heat and cool buildings. It would set up a program for mixed income housing and mandate how the affordable housing component of that program would be funded. A program to encourage, and help fund, new and emerging alternative technologies would be established.

Those are the most obvious elements of the policy statement, but if it is to be successful, it will have to move well beyond this. Stipulating traffic calming measures in densely populated parts of the city will be essential. The statement would set standards for the widening of sidewalks, require municipalities to provide protected bike lanes to encourage commuters to cycle to work, and encourage the restriction of cars on some streets.

There is little doubt that some municipal politicians will rail against an urban policy statement, complaining that the province has moved into their area of responsibility, but that day has passed. If we are going to develop the vibrant cities we need, we must have co-operation at all levels of government.

It is time for new programs that will revitalize our cities, make them more affordable, reduce the production of greenhouses gases, and improve the quality of life of our neighbourhoods. At the same time, the New Urban Agenda will help to make our cities efficient, where green industries can prosper and new jobs can be created.

CAN WE AFFORD IT?

The one question that inevitably comes up when new programs are proposed is, "Can we afford it?" It is a legitimate question. Nothing produces opposition to government programs faster than the suggestion that it might lead to higher taxes and debt. The beauty of the New Urban Agenda is that it will lead to a more efficient city with no appreciable tax increase. In the long run, it will reduce the costs of living in cities.

Of the issues listed in the New Urban Agenda, only two are expensive: transit and affordable housing. The province has already agreed to pay most of the costs of new rapid transit in the GTHA. The social need for affordable housing is so great we must make this public investment to meet our obligation to help those in need. Only the federal and provincial government have a tax base that can deliver affordable housing. Our tax system grants upper income homeowners great benefits. It is only fair that renters also receive help.

The other ideas that have been discussed, like building retrofitting, district heating and cooling, and alternative energy are self-financing. A program to reconfigure public space can be paid for out of the normal budgets of local governments.

Political changes are in the air. More and more citizens are engaged in local issues. The New Urban Agenda is common sense. Once communities become mobilized, change will be inevitable.

A NEW URBAN LIFESTYLE

There is a new lifestyle that is emerging in Toronto. Even in the outer reaches of the GTHA, people are influenced by it. There is a shift to high-density condo living. This is led by young people who want to live in high-density communities. As time changes, they will demand units big enough to raise children. People are talking about transit, cycling, the waterfront, the downtown, and all it offers.

The change in our lifestyle will not happen overnight. It took fifty years to create the suburbs in the GTHA, and Jen Gehn points out it took forty years to transform Copenhagen, but signs of a deep and lasting change to the way people live their lives are everywhere. Even people living in the GTHA have changed. The white, Anglo-Saxon world that I grew up in after the Second World War is disappearing, and in its place is an incredibly diverse city that is dynamic and exciting.

There is an energy about Toronto and the GTHA that engages me. The look of the streets and the buildings; the young strutting their stuff; seniors coming to live in the downtown neighbourhoods because they enjoy the intensity and buzz of the city; and the ease of transit. There is always something going on: a new restaurant, a jazz session in a local bar, a basketball game, theatre, art shows, or the screening of foreign movies portraying lives much different than our own.

Almost without noticing it, people are adapting to this new environment. Everywhere you look in the GTHA there are new creative ideas bubbling forth. The latest I have come across is the transformation of back alleys into usable spaces for any number of things, from housing to play areas. Those are ideas I would never have thought of. The old city of suburbs and car dependency has not disappeared, but it is in retreat, not only here but across North America. Let me exit this book by describing how some people are attempting to create neighbourhoods that are radically different from suburban life, and yet still part of the fabric of the city. It is a movement called "car-free communities."

There are now over two thousand car-free neighbourhoods in the world. They vary in size from whole cities, like Venice, where nature has imposed limits on the car, to small groups of houses of a few hundred people. The Europeans are leading the way, as they are doing in so many urban things, but the car-free movement is taking hold around the world, even in car-dependent North America.

Vauban, a city of five thousand people in Germany, has created the largest car-free neighbourhood in Europe. Vehicles are allowed, but they must go at a walking pace and, in practice, there are rarely cars on the streets. Communities like this are in Amsterdam, Copenhagen, Vienna, Cologne, Hamburg, and Nuremberg.[5] All of them have strict rules for the use of cars, but exceptions are made for emergency vehicles and deliveries.

What is interesting about these experiments is that the physical changes in these communities help people relate to their surroundings in a different way. There is little concern about safety because cars are not hurtling down the streets. Children run free and the adults hang-out on the streets talking to their neighbours. This promotes a much different, more intimate, engaged lifestyle. Many of these communities have developed street festivals and markets. Neighbourhoods have become collective enterprises where people feel connected and at home.

Toronto Island and the Gooderham-Worts development are local examples of car-free neighbourhoods in the GTHA. Others could develop in the same way. Riverdale, parts of Bloor West Village, and the Annex would all be good candidates. There will be resistance from some Toronto city councillors who still believe in car culture, and opposition from some local residents, but the advantage of the car-free neighbourhood movement is that it can be tried as an experiment. Maybe one street could be closed to traffic and gradually the car-free zone could expand as the movement gains support.

The lifestyle of people will gradually change as the new city with a new agenda emerges. They may not live in car-free neighbourhoods, but if we work hard at transforming our urban environment, the quality of life of all of our communities will improve. People will know their neighbours and volunteer their time to make the place they live truly wonderful. That will be essential if we are to reinvent Toronto and the GTHA.

And all this brings me back to think about my own community and my own lifestyle. I changed when I moved to Toronto Island because the physical constraints of the community forced me to change. The Island was always a place rich in culture and sustained by a remarkable level of voluntarism, and I have become a part of it. Hardly a weekend goes by without an event run by Islanders in one of the club houses. It is a lifestyle that my family participates in and we have benefitted enormously.

My partner Paulette and I live in a modest house. Here we are surrounded by our friends and neighbours. Members of our extended family drift in and out on a regular basis. We all have different interests but together we live a type of collective life that we enjoy. My bicycle is parked out behind the house waiting for me to climb aboard to explore my city.

ACKNOWLEDGEMENTS

The approach, and the ideas in this book, have emerged after a lifetime of writing and political activism. It is not possible to thank everyone who influenced this work, but I should start by mentioning the teachers and students of the Social Science Graduate Program at McMaster University, the Hamilton steelworkers who taught me about the rough and tumble of union politics, and the politicians and political advisors I have worked with over the years. If there is one movement that shaped my ideas more than any other, it has been the citizen groups I have participated in.

This book draws heavily on the research done by social agencies, independent researchers, academics, and government departments. The writings of journalists covering the daily news have often been an inspiration.

I would like to thank Christopher Hume for his generous foreword. I have long admired his columns in the *Toronto Star* and was flattered when he agreed to contribute to this book.

I interviewed a number of people, and their names are mentioned in the text. I would like to thank them for their time and insights. Others who have been an influence include, Brian Iler, Bob Kotyk, Barry Lipton, Mary Brock, Allan Sparrow, Sue Sparrow, Marc Brien, Pam Mazza, Ulla Colgrass, Paul Farrelly, Jen Chan, Glenn Gustafson, Michael Adair, and Dick Nielsen. My partner, Paulette Pelletier-Kelly, deserves special praise for tolerating my obsessive habits as a writer.

Thanks as well to Michael Melgaard and Kirk Howard at Dundurn Press. Without their support this book would not have happened.

NOTES

Introduction

1. The Conference Board of Canada publishes comparable statistics on their website: www.conferenceboard.ca.
2. Intergovernmental Report on Climate Change, "Climate Change, 2013."
3. Jane Jacobs, *The Death and Life of Great American Cities* (New York: Random House, 1993). Originally published in 1961.
4. Jan Gehl, *Cities for People* (Vancouver: The University of British Columbia Press, 2010).

1: The New City

1. Neil Smith, *The New Urban Frontier* (London and New York: Routledge, 1996), xv.
2. John Sewell, *The Shape of the City: Toronto Struggles with Modern Planning* (Toronto: University of Toronto Press, 1993).
3. Timothy J. Colton, *Big Daddy: Frederick G. Gardiner and the Building of Metropolitan Toronto* (Toronto: University of Toronto Press, 1980), vii.
4. Ibid., 61.
5. Antonia Zerbisias, "Toronto's date with density," *Toronto Star*, March 22, 2013.
6. Bill Freeman, "Downtown redevelopment: The Civic Square Project," in *Their Town: The Mafia, the Media and the Party Machine,* ed. by Bill Freeman and Marsha Hewitt (Toronto: James Lorimer and Company, Publishers, 1979).
7. "Comprehensive to the Core: Planning Toronto's Downtown," City of

Toronto Planning Department Report to the Toronto and East York Community Council, May 13, 2014.

8. TD Economics, "Toronto, a return to the core," January 22, 2013.

9. *Toronto Star*, October 5, 2011.

10. Ben Rabidoux, "Five reasons not to buy a Toronto condo," *Globe and Mail*, February 13, 2013.

11. *Toronto Star*, December 16, 2012.

12. "Need spurs shift in housing market," *Toronto Star*, June 7, 2014.

13. Tara Perkins, "A corporate commute to the core," *Globe and Mail*, November 10, 2012.

14. Martin C. Pedersen, "Q & A: Ken Greenberg on the future of urban planning," Metropolis Mag.com, January 22, 2010.

15. Ken Greenberg, "Extreme makeover: Toronto's density challenges," *Globe and Mail*, October 2, 2012.

16. Rachel Mendleson, "York Region's poverty rises along with wealth," *Toronto Star*, June 29, 2013. The work of David Hulchanski is the most detailed study of income inequality in the region. This *Toronto Star* article discusses poverty in York Region.

17. Leigh Gallagher, *The End of the Suburbs: Where the American Dream is Moving* (New York: Portfolio/Penguin, 2013). This is the title of a popular book. It also became an important documentary film.

18. Edward Glaeser, *Triumph of the City* (New York: Penguin Books, 2012), 42.

19. "Transportation Tomorrow, 2011 Survey Area Summary," prepared by Datamanagement Group, Department of Civil Engineering, University of Toronto. This study is available online.

20. I have edited Bob MacDermid's comments somewhat, but the text is almost a verbatim rendering of what he told me. I followed a similar practice with all of the interviews reported in this book.

2: The Social and Economic Costs of Inequality

1. Jack Mintz, "No Dutch disease here," *Financial Post*, February 3, 2012.

2. Bruce Campion-Smith, "Unbalanced economy fueling Ontario job losses, Thomas Mulcair says," *Toronto Star*, September 13, 2012.

3. Premier Dalton McGuinty held out the promise of a new Ontario economy based on green industries. It is now clear that there are not

enough jobs in that industry to compensate for the job loss in manu-facturing that Ontario has suffered.

4. Tavia Grant, "The 15-hour workweek, Canada's part-time problem," Report on Business, *Globe and Mail*, October 4, 2014.

5. Alan Walks, "Income Inequality and Polarization in Canada'sCities: An Examination and New Form of Measurement," Cities Centre, University of Toronto, August 2013. The polarization of income in Toronto and the GTA is also confirmed by the work of David Hulchanski.

6. Sean Gepbey, "The Young and the Jobless," Canadian Centre for Policy Alternatives, 2013.

7. The figures for the outer suburbs in this table are calculated from the Toronto CMA, with the City of Toronto excluded. Unfortunately, the Toronto CMA does not include all of the GTA municipalities but it does include the big ones: Mississauga, Brampton, Vaughan, Markham, and Pickering.

8. J. David Hulchanski, "Three Cities within Toronto," Centre for Urban and Community Studies, Research Bulletin 41, 1.

9. Anna Mehler Paperny, "Super wealthy enclaves endanger diversity," *Globe and Mail*, December 21, 2010.

10. City of Toronto, "Toronto Facts," www1.toronto.ca. The City of Toronto website has this and much more information about the origins of people in the city. Other regions in the GTHA do not have information at this level of detail.

11. "Toronto's Vital Signs," *Toronto Star*, October 6, 2009.

12. Xuelin Zhang, "Low income measurement in Canada: What do different lines and indexes tell us?" Statistics Canada, May 26, 2010.

13. Laurel Rothman, "Child Care and Poverty Reduction: Where's the Best Fit," Canadian Centre for Policy Alternatives.

14. "Toronto's Vital Signs: Toronto Foundation's Annual report on the state of the city," *Toronto Star*, October 7, 2014.

15. Tavia Grant, "Food bank use continues to rise," *Globe and Mail*, November 4, 2014.

16. "Wage Gap Between Women and Men," Library of Parliament Research Publications, Parliament of Canada, 2012.

17. "Toronto's Vital Signs," *Toronto Star*, October 6, 2009.

18. Nancy F. Johnson, "Tackling Poverty in Hamilton," 2006.

19. Shelley White and Janet Menard, "Peel Poverty Reduction Strategy: Awareness, Access, Opportunity," Region of Peel.

20. Rachel Mendleson, "Immigrants still struggling in Peel," *Toronto Star*, April 8, 2013.

21. Aurora Banner, "12.7% of York residents live in poverty: study," www.yorkregion.com, November 14, 2012.

22. United Way, Toronto, "Vertical Poverty: Poverty by Postal Code 2," January 2011.

23. Jennifer Pagliaro, "Poverty reduction efforts floundering," *Toronto Star*, November 24, 2014.

24. Laurie Monsebraaten, "Poor health result of poor pay in Ontario," *Toronto Star*, July 30, 2013.

25. Pagliaro, "Poverty reduction efforts floundering."

26. United Way of Greater Toronto and Canadian Council on Social Development, "Poverty by postal code," April 2004. This was the original study of poverty in high-rise apartment buildings. They did a follow-up study, called "Vertical Poverty," published in January 2011.

27. Social Planning Toronto, "New Data Shows Epidemic Levels in Toronto," August 27, 2014. See also, Laurie Monsebraaten, "Child poverty rates at 'epidemic' proportions," *Toronto Star*, August 28, 2014.

28. "Poverty report raises red flags for Durham Groups," www.durhamregion.com, September 10, 2012.

29. Frances Lankin and Munir A. Sheikh, "Brighter Prospects: Transforming Social Assistance in Ontario," Report of the Commission for the Review of Social Assistance, October 2012.

30. Carol Goar, "Ontario takes a pass on real welfare reform," *Toronto Star*, May 5, 2013.

31. Region of Peel, "We Heard Report: Peel's Housing and Homelessness Plan."

32. City of Hamilton, "Examining the Housing and Homelessness Environment in Hamilton," October 2011.

33. CERIS — The Ontario Metropolis Centre, "Working Paper Series," December 2011.

34. Stephen Gaetz, Jessie Donaldson, Tim Richter, and Tanya Gullivar, "The State of Homelessness in Canada, 2013," Toronto: Canadian Homelessness Research Network Press.

35. Canadian Alliance to End Homelessness, "The State of Homelessness in Canada, 2013."

36. Monto Paulsen, "Homelessness cost BC Taxpayers up to $1 billion a year," *The Tyee*, October 16, 2009.

37. Andre Picard,"Housing is most cost-effective treatment for mental illness, study," *Globe and Mail*, April 8, 2014.

38. Murray Dobin, "Who needs $80 billion: starve us some more," *The Tyee*, June 2, 2014.

3: The Environmental Report Card

1. Office of the Auditor General of Canada, "2014 Fall Report of the Commissioner of the Environment and Sustainable Development," October 7, 2014.

2. As a side note, I have to add that I am often distressed when I hear environmentalists condemning politicians and the public for not doing enough to save our environment. That only discourages people. A much better approach would be to say, "Look at what we have accomplished over the past fifty years to clean up our environment. With a little effort we can do so much more to reduce pollution and save the wilderness." It is easy for me to say that today, but once I was a young and impatient myself.

3. Pamela Fayerman, "Air pollution nine times deadlier than car crashes, UBC researchers say," *Vancouver Sun*, October 21, 2013.

4. Toronto Public Health, "Path to Healthier Air: Toronto Air Pollution Burden of Illness Update," Technical Report, April 2014.

5. City of Toronto Staff Report, "Summary of Toronto's 2011 Greenhouse Gas and Air Pollution Emissions Inventory," March 27, 2013.

6. "Markham's Greenprint Sustainability Plan, 2011," City of Markham.

7. City of Mississauga, Planning and Building Department, "Green Development Standards: Going Green in Mississauga," December 2010.

8. City of Toronto, "Change is in the air," March 2007.

9. For more information look at the website for the Energy Services Association of Canada.

10. Envida Community Energy, "District Energy: Strategic plan for the City of Guelph," 2013. There are a number of reports produced by Envida and Guelph Hydro about the project that can be found online. This is a good place to begin.

11. If the electricity is generated using fossil fuel, however, the system will still be creating greenhouse gas emissions, but a system like this produces much less pollution than home heating and cooling.

4: The Promise of Transit

1. Metrolinx, "The Big Move," 2008. A draft report was released in September 2008. There were consultations and amendments to the report. The final report was approved and published by Metrolinx on November 28, 2008. There are several reports and documents available online from Metrolinx that describe their transit plan in detail, but the key document is "The Big Move."

2. Tess Kalinowski, "Transit plan to cost families $477 a year," *Toronto Star*, May 27, 2013.

3. Liam Casey, "Car quicker for transit for commuters," *Toronto Star*, August 25, 2011.

4. Ibid.

5. Toronto Public Health Backgrounder, "Air Pollution Burden of Illness from Traffic," November 2007.

6. Deborah White, "The Causes of Global Warming," About News, http:/ usliberals.about.com.

7. Benjamin Dachis, "Beating the traffic jam blues: The hot option for reducing road congestion and raising revenues," C.D. Howe Institute, August 31, 2011.

8. The $16 billion figure comes from a *Toronto Star* article published on May 27, 2013. "The Big Move" figure is $13.5 billion.

9. Michael Schabas, "Review of Metrolinx's Big Move," Neptis Foundation, December 2013.

10. During the election, Olivia Chow attacked John Tory's SmartTrack plan on the same grounds. The point she made was that transit is very important and expensive. It cannot be designed by an amateur with a plan made on a napkin, and that is how SmartTrack was created.

11. Some of this table comes from CATCH News, November 24, 2014. The figures for Toronto come from the TTC. I calculated "Ridership by Population, 2013" by dividing ridership by the population by municipality.

12. *Toronto Star*, May 11, 2013.

13. My interview with Bob Bratina was held while he was still mayor. He did not run in the 2014 municipal election and plans to run for the Liberal Party in Hamilton Centre during the 2015 federal election.

14. Mark Ferguson and Christopher Higgins, "The North American Light Rail Experience: Insights for Hamilton," McMaster Institute for Transportation and Logistics, April 2012.

15. Gary Mason, "Stockholm a key to unclogging Vancouver roads," *Globe and Mail*, June 22, 2013. When the congestion tax was proposed in Stockholm, 70 percent of the population opposed it. During a trial period rush hour, traffic dropped by 20 percent and support for the tax increased to 70 percent.

16. Edward Keenan, "Mayoral candidates steer away from gridlock fix," *Toronto Star*, October 11, 2014.

17. Richard Warnica, "John Tory lays out 'reasonable' cycling platform, countering Olivia Chow's plan for 200 km of bike lanes," *National Post*, September 16, 2014.

18. Jared Kolb, "Life in a faster, better, stronger bike lane," *NOW Magazine*, March 20-26, 2014.

19. Quoted in, Christopher Hume, "Jen Gehl on making Toronto liveable," *Toronto Star*, November 12, 2014.

20. Oliver Moore, *Toronto Star*, March 4, 2013.

21. Toronto Public Health, "The Walkable City," April 2012. This study found that 40 percent of people walked at least part way to work. Seventy-four percent of Torontonians strongly value walkable communities.

22. Zack Furness, *One Less Car* (Philadelphia: Temple University Press, 2010).

5: The Problems with Planning

1. www.tridel.com/communities/tenyork. Virtually all new developments have handsome websites with statements like this that are used to help sell condos.

2. Christopher Hume, "Chief planner skeptical of Mirvish/Gehry project," *Toronto Star*, October 7, 2013.

3. Christopher Hume, "Toronto gives definite maybe to Gehry-Mirvish tower project," *Toronto Star*, December 19, 2013.

4. Adam Vaughan, interview, January 17, 2013.

5. www.adamvaughan.liberal.ca. When he was a Toronto city councillor, Vaughan had a map of Ward 20, which he represented, that showed all of development projects that were either under consideration or under

construction. Notes described the stage that each project was at in the development process. This is an example of how the Internet can be used to keep constituents up to date on the development projects in their neighbourhood.

6. *Toronto Star*, February 7, 2012.

7. This is the reference to Toronto's Official Plan. www1.toronto.ca/wps/portal/contentonly?vgnextoid=03eda07443f36410VgnVCM10000071d-60f89RCRD.

8. Ibid., 1-1.

9. Ibid., 1-5. I suspect "re-urbanization" in this sentence means redevelopment, but we can't be sure.

10. Ibid., 1-1.

11. City of Toronto website, www1.toronto.ca/wps/portal/contentonly?vgnextoid=ae9352cc66061410VgnVCM10000071d60f89RCRD.

12. My thanks to Paul Farrelly, who brought the St. Nicolas Street example to my attention and did the research on the benefits that the city accrued from section 37 amendments in Ward 27.

13. "The Greenbelt Plan (2005)," Ontario Ministry of Municipal Affairs and Housing.

14. "Places to Grow," Ontario Ministry of Infrastructure. See also: "Places to Grow: A Guide to the Growth Plan for the Greater Golden Horseshoe, 2006."

15. John Sewell, interview, January 28, 2013.

6: Development and the GTHA Cities

1. Jock Ferguson and Dawn King, "Behind the Boom," *Globe and Mail*, October 26, 1988 to November 3, 1988. This was an eight-part series running every day.

2. Ibid., October 28, 1988.

3. Ibid., October 28, 1988.

4. Alex Bozikovic, "The man who built Toronto," *Globe and Mail*, December 16, 2008.

5. Ferguson and King, "Behind the Boom," November 1, 1988.

6. Rosario Marchese, the NDP provincial member for Trinity-Spadina from 1990 to 2014, tried on several occasions to introduce amendments to the Condominium Act to strengthen the position of buyers, but they were never accepted by the government in power.

7. Amanda Kwan, "Seeking a village feel for a high-rise cluster in North Toronto," *Globe and Mail*, December 14, 2012.

8. Andres Duany, Elizabeth Plater-Zyberk and Jeff Speck, *Suburban Nation* (New York: North Point Press, 2000).

9. Rachel Mendleson, "York Region's poverty rises along with wealth," *Toronto Star*, June 29, 2013.

10. Actually, the Markham plan pre-dates the announcement of "Places to Grow," but there has been little effort to try and implement this plan.

11. Vaughan Metropolitan Centre," www.vaughan.ca.

12. Adrian Morrow, "How Toronto's suburbs are trying to switch from sub-divisions to density," *Globe and Mail*, August 18, 2012.

13. "Places to Grow," Ontario Ministry of Infrastructure.

14. *Toronto Star*, October 28, 2010.

15. See: "Markham Vacant Land," www.markham.ca.

16. Phinjo Gombu, "Vaughan urged to slow down," *Toronto Star*, May 17, 2010.

17. John Barber, "Where will the wild things go?" *Toronto Star*, October 11, 2014.

18. These prices were calculated from MLS statistics.

7: Affordable Housing and Rebuilding the City

1. The agency was originally called Central Mortgage and Housing Corporation but changed to Canada Mortgage and Housing Corporation in 1979.

2. For a summary, see the City of Toronto report "Tied in knots: Unlocking the potential of social housing communities in Toronto." See also: Stephanie Findlay, "Toronto social housing wait lists growing," *Toronto Star*, August 20, 2012.

3. Ibid.

4. CMHC, "Rental Market Report, Greater Toronto Area," Fall 2013.

5. Ontario Non-Profit Housing Association "Where's Home," www.onpha.on.ca/AM/Template.cfm?Section=Where_s_Home.

6. United Way, Toronto, "Vertical Poverty," January 2011, 8.

7. Ibid. All of these quotes come from the United Way report, "Vertical Poverty." www.unitedwaytoronto.com/downloads/whatWeDo/reports/ExecSummary-PovertybyPostalCode2-VerticalPoverty-Final.pdf.

8. Canadian Press, *Toronto Star*, July 26, 2013.

9. I have followed Waterfront redevelopment since its inception because it is

literally across Toronto Harbour from where I live on the Island. Over the years I have had many friends who have participated in the project and have described the level of public involvement at different stages. Ken Greenberg worked as a consultant on different aspects of the project, and he spoke about it during my interview with him. The information in this summary was taken from Waterfront Toronto's extensive website, www.waterfronto-ronto.ca, and anyone wanting more detailed information should refer to it. Better still, visit the waterfront and see the transformation that is going on.

10. Laurie Monsebraaten, "City to buy lakefront condos to use as affordable housing," *Toronto Star*, October 29, 2013.

11. www.torontohousing.ca/investing_buildings/regent_park. This is a Toronto Community Housing site that describes all twelve of these types of projects that are currently underway in this program.

12. http://urbantoronto.ca/news/2013/05/lawrence-heights-revitaliza-tion-moves-forward .

13. The best known of these studies is the Vertical Poverty Report done by the United Way. www.unitedwaytoronto.com/downloads/whatWeDo/reports/ExecSummary-PovertybyPostalCode2-VerticalPoverty-Final.pdf.

14. "Tower Renewal Guidelines," 2009, Daniels Faculty of Architecture, Landscape and Design.

8: Local Government

1. John Sewell, "Sewell: After Toronto heads to the polls in October three huge decisions await new council," *Post City*, Toronto, September 2014.

2. Marcus Gee, *Globe and Mail*, September 29, 2014. Thanks to Marcus Gee for pointing this out.

3. In theory, taxes are supposed to be "progressive," taxing those with higher incomes at a higher rate than those with lower income. In reality, the Canadian tax system is not progressive because upper-income people can shelter their income in various ways.

4. City of Toronto, "Blueprint for fiscal stability and economic prosperity, a call to action," Fiscal Report, February 21, 2008, 37.

5. This was Ari Goldkind.

6. Myer Siemiatycki, "Is it party time for municipal elections?" *Toronto Star*, October 25, 2010.

7. The Toronto situation was unique. Councillor Doug Ford ran in place of his brother Rob, but he defended the mayor's actions and politics, and, therefore, took responsibility for his behavior.

8. John Sewell, "Unlike our city, our city council is male, white, old," *The Bulletin*, November 2014.

9. Ibid. Thanks to John Sewell who pointed out this striking difference.

10. This saying comes out of the movie *All the President's Men*, a film about the Watergate scandal.

11. Jock Ferguson and Paul Taylor, "Developers frequent guests at councillors' fund-raisers," *Globe and Mail*, December 14, 1987.

12. VoteToronto is now inactive, but Robert MacDermid's data is still available on the VoteToronto website, www.votetoronto.ca.

13. Published with permission from Robert MacDermid.

14. Marc Ellison, "The monitors the sales pitches at city hall," *Toronto Star*, July 31, 2013.

15. Robert MacDermid, "Funding City Politics: Municipal campaign funding and property development in the Greater Toronto Area."

16. Alex Bozidovic, "The man who built Toronto," *Globe and Mail*, December 16, 2008.

17. There have been a number of news accounts describing the expense spending scandal in Brampton. This *Globe* article is a good summary: Dakshana Bascaramurty, "Brampton spending scandal: How accountability fell by the wayside," *Globe and Mail*, August 16, 2014.

18. The councils included the following: Oakville, Burlington, Mississauga, Brampton, Vaughan, Markham, Newmarket, Pickering, Ajax, and Oshawa.

19. Bill Freeman and Marsha Hewitt, "Ten years at The Spectator," in *Their Town: The Mafia, the Media and the Party Machine* (Toronto: James Lorimer and Company Publishers, 1979).

20. The *Toronto Star* and the *Spectator* are both owned by Torstar.

21. The City of Toronto Act also stipulates that all administrative officers are appointed by the mayor. This means that the mayor has the power to become a CEO that controls the bureaucracy. David Miller was able to use this power very effectively, but Rob Ford's administrative ability was so minimal that the city manager, Joe Pennachetti, ran the administration. John Tory has had extensive experience running large organizations, and I expect he will take control of the city bureaucracy.

22. Siemiatycki, "Is it party time for municipal elections?"

23. You can find a full description of the reforms advocated by RaBIT on their website: www.123toronto.ca.

24. I was a policy adviser to the minister of municipal affairs during the NDP government (1990–95). The Office of the Greater Toronto Area was one of my responsibilities.

25. Alan Broadbent, *Urban Nation: Why We Need to Give Power Back to the Cities to Make Canada Strong* (Toronto: Harper Collins Canada, 2008).

9: Politics, People, and Participation

1. There are some meetings, like discussions of personnel or contracts, where the meetings are held *in camera*.

2. Greenberg is quoted in John Sewell, "After Toronto heads to the polls in October, three huge decisions await new council," *Post City* [Toronto], September 2014.

3. The best way to follow groups like this is to visit their websites. This is the site for Jane's Walks: www.janeswalk.org.

4. See Cycle Toronto's website: www.cycleto.ca.

5. These quotes are taken from the Laneway Renaissance website: http://lanewayrenaissance.com/.

6. David Hulchanski brought the East Scarborough Storefront to my attention. It is a model of a community group that brings together local people from a wide variety of ethnic and racial groups to work on local issues. Deborah Cowen and Vanessa Parlette, "Toronto's Inner Suburbs, Investing in Social Infrastructure in Scarborough," University of Toronto, June 2011.

7. The struggle to control Dufferin Grove Park has been a see-saw battle between the local residents and the city bureaucracy that is not over. This is a link to the website of the Friends of Dufferin Grove Park. http://dufferinpark.ca.

8. Samantha Craggs, CBC News. Posted September 19, 2012.

9. Shelley Carroll, "Ward 33, Participatory Budgeting Pilot Program," www.shelleycarroll.ca/wp-content/uploads/2014/06/PBprojectFlyer.pdf. This flyer describes all of the projects funded in the Ward 33 program.

10: The New Urban Agenda

1. If loan guarantees from government are required, it will add to the debt of the government, but once a public/private partnership is established it should be able to raise money without a guarantee.

2. Megan Treacy, "Silent rooftop wind turbines could generate half of a household's energy needs," *Treehugger*, June 2, 2014.

3. Matt Burgess, letter to the editor, *Globe and Mail*, September 27, 2014.

4. The *Toronto Star* has editorialized on the need for greater coordination on several occasions. The most recent item was an editorial on November 15, 2014, "It's time to act like one region."

5. Steve Melia, "Car-free cities: an idea with legs," *The Guardian*, October 29, 2009. Wikipedia has an item that lists car-free communities around the world that is pages long.

INDEX